Strong-Willed
Child *or*
Dreamer?

Strong-Willed Child *or* Dreamer?

Dr. Dana Scott Spears
Dr. Ron L. Braund

OLIVER
NELSON

THOMAS NELSON PUBLISHERS
Nashville • Atlanta • London • Vancouver

Published in Nashville, Tennessee, by Thomas Nelson, Inc., Publishers, and distributed in Canada by Word Communications, Ltd., Richmond, British Columbia.

The Bible version used in this publication is THE NEW KING JAMES VERSION. Copyright © 1979, 1980, 1982 Thomas Nelson, Inc., Publishers.

Lyrics to Harry Chapin's "FLOWERS ARE RED," on pages 60–62 © 1978 FIVE J's SONGS. Used with permission. All rights reserved.

Library of Congress Cataloging-in-Publication Data

Spears, Dana Scott, 1957-
    Strong-willed child or dreamer? / Dana Scott Spears, Ron L. Braund
    p. cm
    Includes bibliographical references (p.   )
    ISBN 0-7852-7700-5 (pbk.)
    1. Child rearing.   2. Child psychology.   3. Parenting.
  4. Cognitive styles in children.   I. Braund, Ron.   II. Title.
HQ772.5.S67   1996
649'.1—dc20   95-42121
                                                        CIP

Printed in the United States of America.
1 2 3 4 5 6 — 01 00 99 98 97 96

To Phillip M. Spears, Anna Kate Spears, and Marshall S. Scott—dreamers all.

D.S.S.

To Adam L. Braund, my son and fellow dreamer.

R.L.B.

Contents

Part 3: Parenting the Dreamer Child

Acknowledgments

Our special thanks to:

All the dreamers who shared their stories and their dreams.

Our faithful proofreaders, especially Melanie Wofford and Laurel Justice, for their comments and encouragement.

Our colleague at AlphaCare, Pat Zier, for her excellence in the nitty-gritty details and her ever-encouraging spirit.

Our families: The Spearses and the Scotts for their patience with this project and their loving attention to Anna Kate. Ginger, Rich, Don, and June Braund for their understanding and support of the often perplexing dreamers in the family.

Freelance writer Amy Colgan Eytchison who through her research and editorial comments, like the child in *The Velveteen Rabbit,* loved this book and made it real.

A Note for Our Readers

We have interviewed many dreamers and their parents for this book. Only a few real names will be used with permission. Some stories may involve the combined experiences of more than one dreamer. Minor details have been changed at times to protect the identities of the persons involved.

Because dreamers can be male or female, we have used *he* and *she, him* and *her* interchangeably throughout this text.

Part 1

Defining the
Dreamer
Worldview

I WAS BORN A DREAMER

David C. Page

It was a secret, of course, even to me.
To my parents, I was "frustrating."
To my teachers, I was "not working up to potential."
To my peers, I was "a loner."
To me, I was an alien.

It has been a me and them world.
They did it their way, I did it mine.

They watched the surface of things.
I looked into them.

I saw relationships between things.
They saw things.

They learned to use equations and formulas.
I estimated answers.

They played baseball.
I sat in tree tops.

They rode their bicycles someplace.
I just rode my bicycle.

They slept at night.
I swam in darkness.

They lived according to rules.
I found order in chaos.

They lived today.
I lived yesterday, today and tomorrow.

They needed a reason to do anything.
I cried over nothing at all.

They survived on facts.
I survived their facts.

They know because they have learned.
I know because I know.

I was born a dreamer,
when pulled from the womb,
the drum beat I heard was set to rhythm by poets
and artists who had preceded me.
I found their parental guidance on gallery
walls and in music.
I was born a dreamer, I will die a dreamer,
and in between,
I will have seen a glimpse of eternity.

Chapter 1

Parenting in the Third Dimension: Defining Cognitive Style in Children

O body swayed to music, O brightening glance,
How can we know the dancer from the dance?

William Butler Yeats

When Augusta's mother arrived to pick up her daugher from dance class, she found her ten-year-old in the corner of the ballet class, weeping.

"Mrs. Bell HATES me!" Augusta sobbed. And that was *all* she would say about it. For the ninetieth time that week, Augusta's mother was baffled. Augusta's friends, Jenny and Lila, didn't know what to make of it either. In their minds, nothing much unusual had happened that day. But in Augusta's mind, the class had been devastating. It took her two days to calm down enough to tell her mother about that dance class.

"Now, girls," Mrs. Bell said for the third time in a month, "you three can't dance well if you stand that close together." But this time, she backed up her instruction by taking each one by the shoulder and moving the girls farther apart.

Jenny bristled. *As soon as she's not looking,* she thought, *I'm moving right back. I can dance just fine by Lila and Augusta. In fact, I was dancing beautifully!* And she did dance beautifully.

For a moment, Lila fought to hold back the tears. *She'll be mad at me*, thought Lila, *if I don't do exactly what she says. If Mrs. Bell is mad at me, Mom is sure to find out. I'm standing right here for the rest of the class.* Lila continued dancing, but was much stiffer. She made sure she kept a proper distance from the other girls.

Augusta, who normally danced with such abandon that Mrs. Bell said she was in "her own little world," wasn't moving at all. *She HATES me!* thought Augusta. *Well, if she hates me, I hate her! She wants me here. Fine! I'm never moving.* And Augusta didn't move.

Mrs. Bell told Augusta to "participate or leave the floor." Augusta stood resolutely.

Jenny moved closer to Augusta. She whispered, "What's the matter with you?"

Why is everyone blaming me? thought Augusta. Then she broke into tears and ran into the hall. In previous classes, Mrs. Bell had tried talking to Augusta when stubbornness set in, but she was not successful. This time, the teacher decided to ignore her. *She's just being stubborn as usual,* Mrs. Bell thought. *She'll get over it.*

But Augusta won't get over it so easily because she is a dreamer. She is a paradox of a child. Stubborn, yet sensitive. Wanting to please, yet not a pleaser. Augusta leaps from joy to despair in a heartbeat. Soaring and crashing, dreamers improvise their steps to the beat of a different drummer.

Much of the dance going on within Augusta is unseen, as it is with most dreamers. Her behavior seems contradictory because she does not clearly communicate her thoughts and feelings. In the book *Little Women* by Louisa May Alcott, the main character, Jo, is a dreamer. In Alcott's largely autobiographical story, she introduces us to an intriguing concept about how to learn what is going on inside a dreamer's head that she calls "the law of contraries."

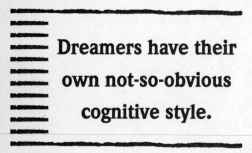

Dreamers have their own not-so-obvious cognitive style.

Jo's sister Meg knew that Jo had a secret: "Jo's face was a study the next day . . . she found it hard not to look mysterious and important. Meg . . . did not trouble herself to make inquiries, for she had learned that the best way to manage Jo was by the law of contraries, so she felt sure of being told everything if she did not ask."[1]

Like Meg, Augusta's mother waited to learn what her daughter was thinking. Patience pays off with the Augustas of the world because dreamers have their own not-so-obvious cognitive style.

Three Ballerinas, Three Cognitive Styles

Our three ballerinas—Jenny, Lila, and Augusta—are the best of friends. Yet they are as different as any three ten-year-olds could be. Jenny tends to dominate the others without really meaning to by the sheer force of her personality. Lila is bubbly and easygoing, a real charmer. And no one knows what Augusta will do, but it is sure to be inventive and heartfelt.

Jenny, Lila, and Augusta represent three cognitive styles or ways of looking at the world. When a child faces situations of potential conflict with parents or teachers, the child's cognitive style is a key to understanding the meaning of his behavior. Many child guidance models have focused on observing a child's behavior, which is important. But we have found that two children can exhibit the same behavior for very different reasons. Or like our three girls in ballet, they can exhibit very different behavior in response to the same event. Understanding a child's feelings and behavior begins with understanding the child's mind.

For practical children such as Jenny and Lila, you can watch what the child does and have a pretty good idea what she's thinking. That's why personality models with an emphasis on observable behavior such as the DISC tendencies (dominant, influencing, steady, and cautious) illuminated by Voges and Braund,[2] Smalley and Trent's personality strengths (lion, otter, golden retriever, and beaver),[3] or Dobson's strong-willed versus compliant child model[4] have been so helpful to many parents. But for children like Augusta, the meaning behind the behavior is not always apparent from observation.

To understand Augusta's personality, we have to look beyond her behavior to her thoughts. But getting Augusta to express her thoughts wasn't easy, even for her mother. And when she did express what she was thinking, it wasn't clear how she could have drawn the conclusion that Mrs. Bell hated her from the sequence of events. Jenny and Lila didn't think Mrs. Bell hated them. Why did Augusta?

Different children can have fundamentally different ways of looking at the world. Jenny, in our example, is a goal-oriented, strong-willed child. Her concern is with personal control or power over her situation. Lila, by contrast, is a compliant child. She wants everyone to be happy and do the right thing. But Augusta is one of the millions of dreamers who are neither pleasers nor power seekers and who often feel misunderstood.

This book is written specifically for parents because they are "in the trenches" with dreamers through the daily events of life. But our hope is that a few nonparents will want to learn more about dreamers, too. All of the adults involved in the lives of dreamers, whether teachers, pastors, coaches, extended family members, or friends, can benefit enormously from exploring how dreamers think, feel, act, and react. Once you understand the unique and often paradoxical thinking of dreamers, you can begin to provide the emotional sustenance they need to become the next Thomas Edison, Sarah Bernhardt, Margaret Mitchell, or Martin Luther. Many dreamers of the world, though misunderstood, have persevered and have flourished. But how many more never reached one-tenth of their potential because they were crushed just as they began to blossom?

> **Dreamers are the most imaginative, sensitive, and idealistic of all children.**

Welcome to the Dreamer's World

Dreamers are the most imaginative, sensitive, and idealistic of all children. They can be described as compassionate, moody, original, and stubborn. Because their logic may not be like parents' logic, dreamers can be among the most difficult children to parent. To many parents, dreamers are enigmas.

In this book we hope you will learn

- what many personality models overlook in describing dreamers.
- what dreamers need most from their parents but don't know how to tell you.
- why dreamers often struggle against the realist's view of the world.
- how to tell the difference between a strong-willed driver and a stubborn dreamer.
- why dreamers aren't compliant, although they care about pleasing people.
- how to read the many moods of your dreamer child.
- how to reduce emotional volatility in a dreamer child.
- how dreamers learn and how it differs from the way most schools teach.
- how to motivate dreamers in school and why pushing them rarely works.
- what dreamers need from a career and how to help them find their calling.
- what dreamers need to flourish instead of flounder at each stage of childhood development.
- how to tell the difference between a dreamer and a child with attention deficit disorder (ADD), as well as how to recognize a dreamer with ADD.
- how to respond to and raise a responsible dreamer teen.

Dreamers We Have Known

Dreamers are born, not made. We have known many dreamers. You have, too. Our pursuit of dreamers began several years ago in a counseling office at AlphaCare in Atlanta, Georgia. Dr. Dana Spears, who is quite different from dreamers, decided that she wanted to know more about these children:

"My brother Marshall is a dreamer, as are my husband, Phillip, other family members, and dear friends. I suppose I have been attracted to dreamers and their wonderful, whimsical personalities for most of my life. But it wasn't until I became a child development specialist that I began to see how tenuous life can be for a dreamer child. In my counseling practice, I have had many days in which *most* of my clients were dreamers or the parents of dreamers.

"Despite my personal experiences with dreamers, I began to see that I had a lot to learn. The parents I was working with had a lot to learn, too. When families delight in their gifts for vision, compassion, and creativity, dreamers thrive. When they are encouraged to be themselves, dreamers can be wonderfully loving children. But without that nurturing and unconditional support, no personality is more vulnerable to disappointment, despair, or even rage than the dreamer.

"When I began to talk with my colleague, Dr. Ron Braund, about the dreamer children I was seeing, and how perplexing they were, he said he could 'really identify'—not with me, but with them. Ron is a true visionary. He always seems to be going in about ten directions at once, but in the end, somehow he arrives where he was planning to go. Ron's son, Adam, is also a dreamer."

Ron describes his experience as a dreamer and with dreamers this way:

"What I know about dreamers from an insider's perspective makes it all the more painful to stand by and watch families when they misunderstand a dreamer child. Through the years in my counseling practice, I have seen how the lack of communication between dreamers and doers results in personal pain and conflict, especially within the parent-child relationship. This tension and struggle between the dreamer and nondreamer can have significant long-term implications for everyone involved. But somehow, the dreamer seems to be the most dramatically affected by conflict and misunderstandings. If these things are left unresolved, a gulf may develop in family relationships that can take many painful years to bridge.

"In contrast, when parents make a commitment to enter the world of a dreamer child, there can be many rewards. When a dreamer is cultivated properly and pruned responsibly, a balanced environment is created to equip him to respond to the challenges he will face.

"Reflecting on how my parents responded to my dreamer world as a child and teenager, I have tremendous appreciation for how they guided me during my years of personality development. They encouraged me to be myself and pursue my dreams. I had freedom to make choices within defined limits. When I experienced setbacks, there was support to get back up and go at it again. I was blessed to have parents who allowed this dreamer to blossom rather than become stifled.

"Whereas compliant children respond well to a nurturing parent, and strong-willed children respond favorably to an assertive, task-oriented parent, dreamers require a more inventive approach. This style of parenting can be difficult to implement consistently. However, it can open the door to exciting adventures and enriching opportunities for you and your child. We call it parenting in the third dimension."

We call it parenting in the third dimension.

Is There a Dreamer in the House?

Most parents don't realize that they have a dreamer child. Oh, they see the child as "having his head in the clouds," but they think any obstinacy is due to a strong will. Although stubborn, dreamers are sensitive, emotional, and compassionate: traits not usually seen in true strong-willed children. Dreamers aren't primarily concerned with power. So why do they often act power hungry?

In the mind of a dreamer, his behavior is rarely defiant; it has a meaningful and logical root. When your child does not respond to the discipline recommended by experts for willfully defiant behavior, and becomes even more resistant, you can become confused and unsure of how to respond.

You may be tempted to read a little about dreamers and then jump ahead to the specific how-tos. Okay, doers, slow down a minute. Before you can effectively apply the parenting principles that work with dreamers, you need to know the characteristics of the dreamer cognitive style. Gaining control of your child is probably not the primary goal to have as the parent of a dreamer. A better goal is for your child to develop self-control. But you'll never really understand how to get to that point until you take the time to read through the chapters that take you inside a dreamer's head.

There are no shortcuts or quick reference lists when you are talking about these complex children. Even Ron, as an adult dreamer, occasionally misunderstands his dreamer son because he has forgotten how a dreamer *child* thinks. We want to share more about our journey to understand the dreamer child. But first, just a hint about how you can know whether or not you have a dreamer or a doer child.

Those Practical Doers

Dr. James Dobson, in his classic book *The Strong-Willed Child,* developed a doer model of general personality styles in children. In his dyadic model, Dobson has eloquently described the differences in "compliant" children and "strong-willed" children, with focus on the needs of the strong-willed child. Dobson describes the differences this way:

> When there are two children in the family, it is likely that one youngster will be compliant and the other defiant. The easygoing child is often a genuine charmer. He smiles at least sixteen hours a day and spends most of his time trying to figure out what parents want and how he can make them happy. . . . The second child is approaching life from the opposite vantage point. He is sliding on all four brakes and trying to gain control of the family steering mechanism.[5]

Dobson sees these differences as being inborn; the strong-willed child is difficult from birth, while the compliant child is a pleasant, happy baby. We have found this dyadic model to be helpful for the parents of doer children who are practical in their interests and ways of functioning. Because doers make up the majority of the population, Dobson's dyadic model has received wide recognition as a valuable tool for parents.

DOBSON'S DYADIC MODEL

COMPLIANT ◄───────────────► STRONG-WILLED

We believe, however, that you can't fit dreamers into either the compliant or the strong-willed mold. They don't fall somewhere between compliant and stong-willed children. They are from another category entirely—almost from another planet. It is ironic that dreamers, being so different, desire to be understood more than other children. We hope that this book will bridge the gap of understanding between you and your child.

A New Model

Ever since Hippocrates, people have tried to understand the differences in the ways each of us thinks and acts. In our search for information on dreamers, we looked at the available personality models and related resources but couldn't find anything that spoke in detail to the enigmatic dreamer child who may be perceived as anything from just different to eccentric to downright weird. So we developed our own model as a means to communicate this distinction more effectively. Two-type and four-type models have seemed to be the most popular descriptors. Since dreamers hate following the crowd, in their honor, we have developed a triadic model:

THE SPEARS-BRAUND TRIADIC MODEL

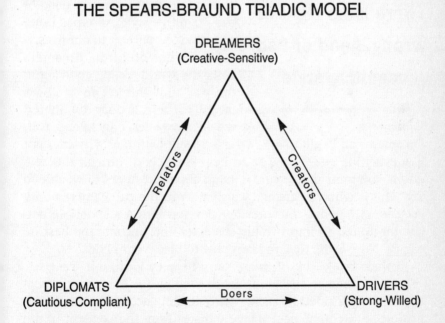

Some children fit clearly in one corner of the triangle. They are diplomats, drivers, or dreamers. Others have a combination of cognitive traits and are identified as doers, relators, or creators. You already know about doers. But let's talk about relators and creators.

Relators are sensitive children who fall somewhere between dreamers and diplomats and are the most nurturing of the imaginative types. Relators are especially attracted to hobbies and professions that involve caring for people and animals.

Creators fall somewhere between dreamers and drivers and are the most productive of the imaginative types. Many college professors are creators, as are many entrepreneurs. As a child, a creator might be an artist, musician, athlete, or president of the student body. Catalysts for change, creators tend to be involved in improving things wherever they are.

You may be thinking, *How do I know whether or not my child has stepped over the line from relator or creator to dreamer?* On a questionnaire we've provided, we will try to quantify this for you a bit, but there is no absolute line. There is no right or wrong, good or bad cognitive style. All types bring something important to our lives.

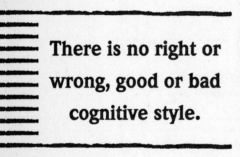

There is no right or wrong, good or bad cognitive style.

Like other children, dreamers enter the world feeling good about the way they think. The struggles of daily life in a doer-dominated world, however, can take a toll. Dreamers can begin to ask, "What's wrong with me? Why am I not like everyone else?" For you to help your child through this self-doubt, you must understand enough about dreamers to be able to say, "This is who you are and it's great!" You, the parent, play a critical part in helping your dreamer develop into a responsible person motivated to improve his character and become the best he can be. Now is the time to learn how to bless your child.

In their book *The Blessing,* Gary Smalley and John Trent say, "The best defense against a child's longing for imaginary acceptance is to provide him or her with genuine acceptance and affirmation. . . . Genuine acceptance radiates from the concept of the blessing."[6] Smalley and Trent tell us that one key element of a blessing is a loving message spoken to your child. Dreamers have a special need for this blessing

On a daily basis, you can affirm character qualities such as honesty, integrity, and loyalty. When your child shows consideration or compassion to another, compliment it. If she makes an extra effort on a project, point out her determination. When she admits failure, emphasize how truthfulness breeds trust. Even when she makes a careless mistake, use it as an opportunity to affirm character.

> **On a daily basis, you can affirm character qualities such as honesty, integrity, and loyalty.**

Ron recalls an incident on a trip with his dreamer son: "While Adam was eating his meal on the plane, he spilled gravy on a new shirt he had purchased. He blurted out loud, 'I'm so stupid!' I could have agreed with him. Instead I chose to focus on his internal criticism and said, 'Son, you're not stupid. We all make some careless mistakes and that's okay.' It wasn't five minutes later when I reached over without looking and knocked over a can of Coke, spilling it on my sweater. Adam immediately said, 'Dad, you're not stupid. You just make some careless mistakes and that's okay.' The returned blessing I received from Adam was worth the stain on my sweater."

You need to make a conscious commitment to look for opportunities to bless your child. The payoff will be worth it for you and your dreamer. In the coming chapters, we will first describe in detail how dreamers think and feel and then explore ways you can bless them by being an active listener and an advocate for positive change.

Chapter 2

Doers and Dreamers on the Plains of Life: Why Cognitive Style Makes a Difference

Those who dream by day are cognizant of many things that escape those who dream by night.

from *Eleanora* by Edgar Allan Poe

You may be familiar with the buffalo and birds analogy. Buffalo are strong and thunderous as they move across the plains. Their power is evident; their resolve, clear. But they aren't built to see the big picture. For all their power, they are powerless to see into the distance as they thunder along because their eyes look to the sides and their necks bend groundward, not skyward. Buffalo see things in a practical down-to-earth way.

Birds, on the other hand, are not in the least thunderous. They swoop and soar. As birds fly above the earth, they can see the big picture. Although they may appear harmless, birds will fight if they are pulled from their flight down to earth. For self-preservation, birds must fly.

Dreamers are like those birds. When they feel threatened, their fighting can appear thunderous. If you try to help an eagle caught in a wire fence, he will think you are trying to hurt him and react viciously.

While buffalo act on the world, birds react to it. Buffalo are like strong-willed children, moving toward the goal, headstrong and mighty, often ignoring potential danger. But buffalo get their security from the protection provided by the fences they try to trample down.

Dreamers (birds) don't get their security from specific limits like drivers (buffalo) do. They can feel as if they risk being destroyed when the limits are too rigid. Dreamers feel a desperate need to survive with emotions and imagination undefiled by the earth.

That desperation can appear completely illogical to drivers who are in positions to make the rules. Dreamers do not resist absolutes. Dreamers love grand absolutes such as justice, mercy, and obedience to spiritual ideals. But the "tedious," ungrand, uninteresting ideals such as clean rooms and completed homework feel too confining to them.

In this plains analogy, diplomatic (compliant) children are neither buffalo nor birds. Deeply grounded in practicality, diplomats tend to be pleasers and take great pains to be pleasant. On the plains, prairie dogs are such likable creatures. They make every effort to stay out of the way of buffalo and large birds, avoiding conflict.

The human counterparts of prairie dogs, the likable diplomats, may achieve popularity in the peer group that is envied by attention-loving dreamers. Diplomats are naturally endowed with the practical skills to get along socially. They are the pleaser children.

Power, Peace, and Purpose

Each cognitive style has extremes. The driver can fall into "power at all costs" thinking, and the diplomat is likely to choose "peace at all costs." For the dreamer, the thinking is likely to be "purpose at all costs," a much more abstract concept than power or peace. In the dreamer's pursuit of purpose, he can find few concrete signs that he has achieved his goals. This leaves plenty of room for self-doubt. Only the dreamer can decide if an activity has purpose.

Many parents confuse a dreamer's desire for purpose with a desire for power. For example, the peace-seeking diplomat will comply with a parental instruction to do a chore, whether or not the task has any meaning or value for her. The diplomat has reached the goal of peace in the family. In contrast, the power-seeking driver will resist the instruction to do a chore, even if the child sees the purpose in it. And the purpose seeking dreamer will resist the chore not because she seeks power, but because she feels the chore is purposeless. To the parent, the dreamer's behavior looks like the driver's. Only when the cognitive processes are understood do the differences become clear. Again, the behavior of children as different as buffalo and birds can look remarkably similar.

> **Many parents confuse a dreamer's desire for purpose with a desire for power.**

Our View of the Plain

The coauthors of this book, Dana and Ron, tend toward different corners of the triadic model. Ron is a true dreamer. Dana was the classic driver child. When we were first discussing this book with our editor, Ron described Dana as a "bulldog." He knew that she would drive hard to get this book done on time.

Ron, on the other hand, didn't plunge into the project so quickly. To Ron, Dana seemed ready to forge ahead without having a good idea of the big picture. Ron would think for days about what he wanted to say and how to say it. He struggled to meet deadlines. These differences in the approach to writing were due to different cognitive styles.

Dana's Dreamers

Ron and I have learned to appreciate the benefits of cognitive style diversity. As a child, though, I thought everyone should see the world in my driver way. In my family, I saw the world somewhat like each of my parents, but very differently from my dreamer brother Marshall. Throughout our younger years, my brother showed me great mercy. But he also had a strong stubborn streak about things he believed. Our intolerance of each other flared most during our teen years. He probably enjoyed some of the debating, but a dreamer tends to define for himself which discussions are debates, and therefore stimulating, and which are arguments, and therefore painful. My feelings rarely got hurt, so everything was just a debate to me, no matter how Marshall felt.

When he hears these stories, my dreamer husband says he is sure he would not have liked me as child, perhaps not even in high school or college! Yet Phillip and I have been blessed with a wonderful marriage. Because he can't be dominated or held too tightly in my more narrow view of daily life, I don't even try. I am free to release the earth just a bit. Phillip is able to help this buffalo get off the ground, not so much because he values freedom but because he values *vision.*

The happiness of our marriage has been a surprise to many of our acquaintances who believed I might trample over such a sensitive soul. They didn't know how gifted Phillip would be at inspiring his strong-willed wife to stop and smell the roses.

There's one other person in our household at the moment, our daughter Anna Kate. Although barely talking, she already shows some dreamer tendencies. Her sensitivity is evident. She can tumble down a hill and hit her head on the sidewalk without shedding a tear, but if you hurt her feelings, she is almost inconsolable. Anna Kate also shows a lack of awareness of concrete details. Her eyesight is fine. So when she cried for the pillow that goes in her doll bed, unable to see it though it was right in front of her, I thought, *Dreamer!*

Ron the Dreamer

As a dreamer, I am enthusiastic to play a part in explaining the dreamer cognitive style. However, my understanding of this third dimension of thinking in children did not begin to unfold until I became a parent.

During my childhood, like many other dreamers I felt that people often misunderstood my thoughts and actions. I had a great relationship with my parents who instilled confidence and strong values. As a teenager, I sensed I was different from my peers. I resisted following the crowd. After training to become a mental health professional, I focused on defining differences in personality. I coauthored a book on behavioral styles entitled *Understanding How Others Misunderstand You* because I believe that having a better understanding of ourselves and others and accepting our differences will help to resolve conflicts in relationships.[1]

Yet even after explaining to others what I had learned about myself from interpreting available personality inventories, I was frustrated by their perception of my actions. My family and friends viewed me more as a strong-willed person driven by multiple activities and a desire for achievement than as a caring dreamer. I often felt compelled to point out that below the surface I was not so dispassionate and industrious.

On the inside, I felt strengthened by compassion for others and wanted to help with causes. But sometimes I also felt constrained by sensitivity to correction and struggles with self-criticism. I had an internal need to be appreciated by others but had a stubborn streak that resisted conforming. I felt I was a paradox. It seemed that I thought more like the compliant diplomat internally and externally acted in a manner more associated with the strong-willed driver.

It wasn't until I became a parent and observed the definite contrast in my two children that I began to understand differences in cognitive styles. My older son, Rich, is a classic doer who values order and is usually cooperative. My younger son, Adam, is a dreamer. In Adam I recognized an internal struggle similar to what I experienced as a child: sensitivity mixed with obvious stubbornness. He frequently became entangled in power struggles with his mother. Ginger and I decided that we needed a plan of action to meet Adam's unique needs.

Working with Dr. Spears, who conducted a battery of child developmental tests on Adam, my wife and I began to understand more. Mixed in with Adam's creative-sensitive dreamer tendencies was the challenge of attention deficit disorder (ADD). (Chapter 11 of this book will explain more about the dreamer with ADD.)

Over the next couple of years, Dana and I periodically addressed the struggles of parenting creative-sensitive children on my daily radio program, *Marriage and Family Today*. The more I learned about the dreamer cognitive style, the better I understood not only Adam but also myself.

Fun and Funny Dreamers

Most dreamers are tremendously fun to be around despite their ups and downs. Dreamer children do things that other children wouldn't think to do in a billion years! In doing research for this book we heard many delightful stories. Here are a few that give you a flavor of those to come.

When Karla was four, she wouldn't do anything without her Barbie dolls. They had to be dressed just so before she would leave the house. She even slept with them. They became especially important to her when she had trouble sleeping while on medicine for a cold. Her parents, who weren't getting any sleep either, allowed her to play in her room quietly after they went to bed. When they heard her shuffling down the hall, her parents

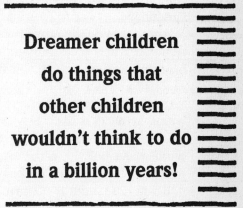

Dreamer children do things that other children wouldn't think to do in a billion years!

lay very still, pretending to be asleep. She peeked into their room and crept toward the bed. Her mother thought, *Oh, dear, she's going to climb in with us.* Instead, Karla placed one Barbie on the pillow by her mom and one by her dad. She knew how much they needed to sleep and thought that the dolls would help.

Another dreamer, Harris, is an accomplished artist and the father of three. But if his illustrations have gained him fame, his pranks have made him infamous, at least among his friends and coworkers. When he was about twelve years old, Harris, his brother, and a friend took a big black purse and went out to a wooded area along a well-traveled dirt road. They caught a snake, put it in the purse, closed the purse, and placed it alongside the road, where it was sure to be seen. Then they retreated to the woods to watch and wait.

Sure enough, a big old car came "toolin' down the road, really moving," Harris said. "It passes that purse, and the next thing you know, all four wheels lock up, and it slides to a stop in a cloud of dust. A skinny little kid hops out of the backseat, runs back down the road, grabs the purse, takes a good look around, hops back in the car, and it takes off again.

"We could just imagine that kid, back in the car, saying, 'Hey look, Mom, I wonder what's in it?'

"'Well, why don't you open it up and find out?' About twenty yards down the road, the wheels lock up again, and the car slides to a stop. All four doors fly open and everybody bails out of the car, jumping and shouting. I don't know what happened after that, 'cause we took off running." Harris still keeps everyone laughing.

Another endearing quality of dreamers is their genuine sense of remorse when they unintentionally hurt someone. When Dana's brother Marshall was two, just before Dana was born, her father, Jim, had a rather hair-raising experience with his son. Jim was sitting in a swivel chair that also rocked. He was leaning back when young Marshall walked over and lifted the chair slightly. This little lift caused the chair to go crashing backward through a picture window. As Jim lay in the window with a jagged piece of glass overhead, he screamed for his wife, "Jane! Jane!"

Being nine months pregnant and having gotten herself into the bathtub, Marshall's mother was not anxious to get up. *Jim always does this,* she thought to herself. *He probably wants something that's in the bathroom. I'll go all the way in there, only to find out I have to go back to find what he wants. Well, not this time.* She didn't move.

"Jane! Jane!" he continued.

"What do you want?" she responded.

Jim was too frightened to think. All he could say was, "Jane! Jane!"

This exchange continued for several minutes before she finally maneuvered herself out of the tub and into the den. There was her husband, about to be impaled.

Little Marshall looked up at his mother and cried, "Spank me, Mommy! Spank me!"

Looking Below the Surface

As you can see, dreamers are spunky, compassionate, and perplexing. To help you peek inside the dreamer's world, imagine that you are looking at a basket of brightly painted Easter eggs. On the surface, they seem the same. But some have been cooked and are solid on the inside. A few have tiny holes in the top and bottom; the white and yolk have been blown out. Others are raw.

You can pick up the cooked ones with a firm grip, and they won't break. You can crack the outside, and the egg inside will hold its shape. If you look closely before you grab, the hollow egg has tiny holes that will tell you it is delicate and must be handled with extreme care. But at first glance, there are no telltale signs differentiating the raw egg from the one that's firm inside.

Like these beautiful eggs sitting side by side, dreamers may look like drivers or diplomats to the untrained eye. But the driver's self-esteem is impervious to rough handling; like the inside of that hard-boiled egg, it remains intact and can endure a lot of "cracking." With the same treatment, the diplomatic child, like the hollow egg, breaks into a thousand pieces right away. People know how to handle them both. The dreamer may seem tough on the outside, just as the shell of the raw egg resembles that of the cooked egg. But he is deceptively fragile.

You need to take a closer look underneath the surface of your child's behavior so you can deal with her according to her internal makeup and not the mask she may wear. By the way, we're not saying drivers are hard-boiled and diplomats, hollow. They're all "good eggs," so to speak. But they need to be handled differently, with an eye to the complex cognitive style.

Perhaps that's why dreamers intuitively understand the meaning behind the Mother Goose rhyme about Humpty Dumpty. We believe that it's easier to teach you how to keep Humpty from falling than how to put him back together again. The next chapter is devoted to helping you understand dreamer idealism so you can relate to your child in a way that will help her to thrive instead of take a nosedive.

Chapter 3

The Key to My Child's Heart: Characteristics of Idealistic Dreamers

But maddest of all is to see the world as it is and not as it could be.

from *Man of La Mancha* by Dale Wasserman, based on the work of Cervantes

"Dr. Spears, I just had to call you," the conversation began. "You probably don't hear from most of the people you've helped, but I have been so amazed by the changes in Kim that I had to call. She is a different child. I can't believe that one visit and the short paper on dreamers you gave us to read could make such a difference. You warned us that it might take time to see a change, and that she might get worse before she got better. But in less than one week, there were no more tantrums. She is a happier child. I had been praying for a year for the key to my child's heart, and God has answered that prayer dramatically."

What an encouragement! Dana thought as she hung up the phone. And what a great way to describe the problems that so many parents face in trying to understand a child. Parents need a key that unlocks what is in the dreamer child's heart. That key can be found in understanding the dreamer's idealistic thinking. But more about that later.

After the phone call, Dana made a note to herself for this book and then turned to her next client. She was not at all surprised to find that this family also had a dreamer child.

"I don't understand Sarah," began Mrs. Brown. "She lives in a dream world. I asked her if she wanted to go for a walk, and she informed me, 'I can't. My feet aren't getting along.' Another time she was cranky for days, and she couldn't tell me why. Finally in the car she burst into tears, saying, 'I'm not little and I'm not big!' What am I supposed to say to a five-year-old having an identity crisis? I thought that stuff started in adolescence.

"Everything she experiences is so dramatic! And she makes up wild tales and defends them as true, even when she knows she'll be punished for lying. Sometimes I think she believes the stories. Punishing her hasn't made one bit of difference. And she needs constant reassurance, but it never seems to be enough. Sometimes her self-esteem is so low. Other times she seems overconfident.

"Sarah's moods change so fast, it makes my head spin. As children go, she's definitely high maintenance. I could describe her forever, but I wouldn't come any closer to figuring her out. Please tell me that this is just a stage! I would hate to think what she'll be like as a teenager if it's not!"

> **Everything she experiences is so dramatic!**

Does this sound more like an emotionally disturbed child than one of the delightful dreamers we described in chapter 2? Despite all their wonderful qualities, dreamers confuse others. It is as if their way of looking at the world, their cognitive style, is from another planet. And if the outside world is disapproving or uninteresting, dreamers retreat into their inner world of dreams and ideals, often focusing their thoughts on how to get back at the world or change it.

Dreamers Want to Change the World

Changing the world—that is what dreamers do best. As children, they have a disproportionate impact on families, schools, clubs, and churches. As adults, dreamers strongly influence culture through religion, the arts, literature, journalism, teaching, counseling, and a host of other professions and hobbies. Dreamers have broad interests and are endless founts of ideas. We think of dreamers as artists, but they can just as easily be athletes.

> **Changing the world—that is what dreamers do best.**

Did you see the movie classic *Chariots of Fire*? It is a true story about two runners who were at the top of their sport and their journey to the 1924 Olympics. Both had a reason for running that was far beyond personal glory. Harold Abrahams was a driver whose running was fueled by his rage over religious bigotry. Eric Liddell, a dreamer, ran joyfully to glorify God and feel "His pleasure," while being criticized for the role his faith played in his running. After the Olympics, Abrahams stayed with sports, eventually becoming the head of the British Olympic Committee. Liddell went to China as a missionary and died in a Japanese prison camp during World War II.

> **Many dreamers suffer deeply from feeling misunderstood.**

From an outside vantage point, switching from athletic star to missionary seems illogical. Liddell the athlete and Liddell the missionary: What did they have in common? Liddell's diverse interests were held together by one ideal: to serve God. Understanding idealism and how it affects thought and behavior is what Dana's client described as the "key to my child's heart."

Perhaps it was a nondreamer observing a dreamer who said, "There's a method to his madness."[1] Of course, it isn't madness; it's a cognitive style with its own method or logic. But because dreamers have idealistic logic that differs dramatically from the logic of the practical majority, many suffer deeply from feeling misunderstood. In turn, dreamers misunderstand the good intentions of their befuddled friends and family.

In this book, we hope to give doers some "dreamer glasses" through which to view the world, enabling them to understand dreamer children and love them more effectively. Likewise, we'll fit dreamers with some "doer glasses" so they can see how more practical people, diplomats and drivers, interpret and misinterpret the meaning of dreamer behavior.

The Perplexing Idealist

Brent loves his brother Jason, and both love baseball. During childhood, on most Saturdays they played baseball at separate ballparks. Consequently, the two boys rarely got to watch each other's game. On one Saturday, Jason had a game, but Brent didn't. The whole family was looking forward to being at Jason's game. Unexpectedly, the game was canceled when the other team forfeited due to an outbreak of the flu.

When Jason's father broke the news to Jason, he was pleasantly surprised to see how casually the boy took the news, heading outside, happy to have an unscheduled play day. He knew his older son, Brent, would not react that way.

"But we were all going to be together!" Brent said when he heard the news. "Jason must be so disappointed!" he added, bursting into tears.

Because Brent had been thinking about this special Saturday all week, he had a picture in his mind of the perfect day. When the ideal did not materialize, Brent was crushed. Jason, the realist, made an immediate adjustment and moved forward. Brent's adjustment took longer. Eventually, he enjoyed the unexpected free day but not without grieving over the loss of a perfect Saturday.

Dreamers can imagine all the possibilities, and they often imagine the ideal person, place, or event. This ideal becomes very real to young dreamers. Sometimes this belief in the ideal leads a dreamer to become involved in compassionate causes. Or it might lead her to hold an idealized view of someone she loves. This idealistic view of people and the world at large can motivate the dreamer to persist in helping others when a realist would have given up. But in contrast to the inspiration and determination that can come from idealism, there is tremendous potential for despair when the dreamer confronts hard realities she can't control.

> # Dreamers can imagine all the possibilities.

The dreamer child believes the veterinarian can bring his dead puppy back to life. The dreamer child believes a crayon drawing will bring her divorced parents back together even though Daddy is married to someone else. Dreamers weave colorful tapestries of what the world could be. Without that marvelous dreaming there would be no da Vinci and no Shakespeare. Yet when you try to visualize your dreamer child in a future full of such great successes, your hopes can become clouded by a frustrating present.

But your dreamer may surprise you! Things that seem like liabilities can become assets. For example, in an article on why it's hard to be both creative and neat, John Boe writes,

> Consider, for example, Alexander Fleming's discovery of penicillin. Fleming always meant to put his used culture plates in antiseptic, but often would let a huge pile grow, so that those on top were completely out of antiseptic. A colleague dropped by to visit one day . . . suddenly noticed that one of them had green mold on it, around which the staphylococcus colonies had disappeared. And so, because he was not tidy, Fleming discovered penicillin.[2]

Idealism and Sensitivity: Sensitive Dreamers, Insensitive Drivers

Perhaps you've already discovered that despite their moments of apparent obstinacy, dreamers are the most sensitive of all children. A dreamer sees *everything* that happens as if it is somehow related to the other person's intentions toward him. The dreamer may react insensitively toward that other person because he assumes that the peer or adult can read his feelings and is disregarding those feelings and purposely hurting him—not purposely setting a limit or stating a rule.

He looks at every behavior of another person as a clue as he seeks to answer the question, Does this person like me? If the answer is no in his mind, this child who wants so much to be liked will react by demonstrating dislike for the other person who has offended him. The "offending party" may actually like the dreamer and wonder why the dreamer child is acting so strangely.

When dreamer Tyler was five, he had a crush on a driver girl in his kindergarten class, Hunter, but she didn't know it. One day Tyler fell on the playground at exactly the same time that Hunter was laughing at another child's joke. Although she didn't notice Tyler fall, he was convinced that she laughed at him, a sure sign of rejection.

For the rest of the school year, Tyler tried to sabotage her. The teacher noticed his vengeful behavior, but the less-sensitive driver, Hunter, did not. She never noticed that Tyler had swung from intense liking to loathing. Later that year Hunter developed a crush on Tyler. As would any driver, Hunter used a more direct approach in expressing her feelings. Her compliments quickly dissolved Tyler's animosity.

In the dreamer's idealistic world, everyone should treat everyone else kindly. If a parent or teacher is stern, the dreamer will feel that the adult is angry with her. When you make a request or give a command, the dreamer's response is often, "Why are you yelling at me?" even though you haven't raised your voice. Your dreamer child can be disappointed by family and friends just because he wrongly assumes that everyone knows how he is feeling from minute to minute.

Idealism and Imagination: Intuitive Problem Solvers

We have already noted the dreamer's gift for imagining all the possibilities. Dreamers imagine not only the ideal but also the disaster. As they picture themselves in a friend's situation, the natural outgrowth of imagination is empathy. Dreamers also imagine themselves in fantasy situations that are neither good nor bad. They have original thoughts that they can visualize, hear, taste, touch, and smell mentally.

> **Original thoughts may come to a dreamer like the proverbial light bulb going on.**

Original thoughts may come to a dreamer like the proverbial light bulb going on. These ideas do not have to be completely original in the sense that no one has ever thought them before. They are original because the dreamer has not heard them from someone else.

In her junior year, Marie took a philosophy class. As always, her mind was tuning out and tuning in. Then one day, the teacher asked, "Can anyone think of a way to prove the existence of God?"

Marie, who wasn't particularly religious, had been turning this question over in her mind for months. She had come up with a theory, which she blurted out that day in class. Her philosophy teacher was taken aback. Apparently, her answer was the basis of a famous philosophical thesis—one that Marie had never heard, one that didn't appear in their textbook, and one that they had never discussed in class.

From the perspective of a doer observer, such original ideas may not appear to have a logical basis. In making decisions, doers must gather facts. Because dreamers can make decisions based on hunches, ideals, or original solutions that have no clear linear relationship to observable facts, dreamer thinking may appear illogical to the doer.

Using such intuition in decision making can lead to wrong assumptions about others, as in our opening story when Augusta incorrectly concluded, "The teacher hates me." However, it leads to enough correct assumptions to keep the dreamer relying on her hunches. As a parent, try to respect your dreamer's intuition. If you convince her to go against intuition and it backfires, because in that case her intuition was correct, she'll have less faith in your judgment in the future.

Success of intuition over fact-based decision making can lead dreamers to ignore obvious facts. Many parents of dreamers have said to us, "How can such a bright child ignore something that is right in front of his face?" Indeed, even when not depending on intuition alone, dreamers tend to focus on the big picture and may miss concrete details. With their rapidly changing ideas and imagination, they can be forgetful, even when forgetfulness repeatedly brings significant negative consequences.

> **Success of intuition over fact-based decision making can lead dreamers to ignore obvious facts.**

By observation, we might be tempted to think of dreamers as lacking attention to detail. But dreamers are very detailed about some things. Sensitive to every nuance of human interaction, dreamers notice abstract details such as implied meaning in a comment or facial expression. In some ways, we could say that dreamers are overly attuned to abstract detail. Their intuition makes them sensitive but also makes them too preoccupied to notice "less meaningful" details of life, such as clutter and dirty dishes.

When dreamers become bored, they can move on to a new idea before following through with previous ideas and commitments. As one friend put it, "I can't keep up with all the details because I have such an active inner life." The inner life creeps up and pulls dreamers away from mundane tasks, taking them into a much more interesting imaginary and ideal world. Dreamer Michelangelo prayed this prayer: "Lord, grant that I may always desire to do more than I can accomplish."

Idealism and Emotions: Mood Swings in Dreamers

When idealism and sensitivity come together, as they do in a dreamer, dragons can be fought, imagination can soar, and yet there can be pain and disillusionment. This tension between joy and sorrow results in mood swings that range from ecstasy and grandiose thinking to depression and despair. Some children move from one extreme emotional reaction to the other almost instanta- neously. Dreamers want you to be understanding of their moods; however, they are sometimes intolerant of other people's moods. A grouchy dreamer expects sympathy but is upset if you are short-tempered.

> **Some dreamers move from one extreme emotional reaction to the other almost instantaneously.**

With all of their ability to put themselves into the place of others through imagination and sensitivity, and all of their tolerance of their own moodiness, dreamers may be out of touch with the influence of their emotions on their decision making and treatment of others. Your dreamer daughter, who just compassionately comforted a friend, can suddenly yell at the same friend and not be able to explain why.

There is a reason. Usually, the dreamer feels rejected in some way. But feeling it in the heart and being able to get that feeling into words are not always the same thing. As with Augusta in dance class, a dreamer may need time to calm down and get enough perspective on events to explain her behavior.

One adult dreamer put it this way: Her volatile emotions make her a lot like a teakettle that's worked up to a rolling boil. She has to get off the burner for a while—away from the heat source— before she can stop the boiling inside.

Idealism and Determination: Those Stubborn Dreamers

A perplexing facet of the dreamer cognitive style is the tendency toward extreme stubbornness. It seems incongruous that a sensitive child should be so tough-minded about certain things. Yes, we know that an idealist can hold stubbornly to ideals, but why should he hold so stubbornly to the denial of taking a cookie when cookie crumbs are all over his face? And if a dreamer thinks so differently from a driver, as we have indicated, how do you know if he is being willful or if something is upsetting him that you need to know about?

For example, due to her sensitivity, a dreamer can react with stubbornness when she feels disliked or misunderstood. Your task as a parent is to distinguish driver stubbornness from dreamer stubbornness.

Imagine a science fiction movie in which alien robots suddenly appear among primitive people. The natives hurl arrows at the robots while the robots move ever nearer their goal. Driver children are like the robots, repelling the arrows of correction and criticism. A bazooka is needed to stop the driven robots. The bazooka won't destroy them, just stop them in their tracks.

In contrast, dreamers are flesh and blood with no metal plating around their inner workings. They are akin to the natives who face the robots. As the lasers come at the natives, they leave deep wounds. Yet the natives keep moving ahead, slinging spears and shooting arrows. Finally, the natives slip behind a log and continue shooting at their adversaries, fighting valiantly to the last breath.

Like the natives, dreamers can put up quite a fight, but they are scarred by criticism and sometimes by correction. The lasers of criticism and constant correction make dreamers fighting mad, but in the end they'll be deeply wounded. For drivers, correction is an annoying necessity. For dreamers, correction may lead to a deep sense of personal failure.

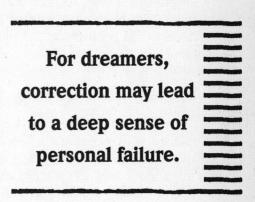

For dreamers, correction may lead to a deep sense of personal failure.

Are you trying to use a bazooka against your dreamer child? In coming chapters, we'll equip you with methods of discipline that teach dreamer children self-control without leaving scars.

Idealism and Fear of Failure: Internal Perfectionists

For dreamers, a fear of failure can accompany the process of learning, whether or not correction is involved. Because dreamers are idealistic, they may set such high standards that no one, let alone a child, could meet the standards. After they examine the task mentally, dreamers will not attempt it if they perceive that they cannot do the task well enough to meet their personal standard. Their internal perfectionism interferes with the ability to motivate themselves to work at a task until perfected—they want to do it perfectly, believe that they cannot, and so refuse to do it at all.

"Just do your best," the mother of a dreamer urges as she heaps on extra helpings of praise when her son makes an effort. But she doesn't understand that his best won't be good enough. If the product doesn't meet his internal standards, no amount of reassurance can convince him that the product is not a failure.

For example, if a dreamer doesn't like a picture he draws, he'll rip it up and throw it across the room in frustration. You'd see a far different response from an external perfectionist, the child we generally think of when we talk about a perfectionist. He works toward a desired goal until he can achieve it perfectly.

When they draw, external perfectionists work slowly and carefully, erasing whatever does not meet the precise standard they have set. Dreamers have difficulty with this slow and steady approach. If tasks or goals are extremely important to dreamers, they may become frozen and seek a lesser, more certain goal rather than persist toward something they believe to be unattainable.

Idealism and Caring: The Need to Be Needed

Perhaps in part because dreamers struggle to feel successful at achieving objective goals, they often focus on more subjective pursuits such as helping others. Dreamers have a tremendous need to be needed and, as children, are often drawn to troubled peers. Unfortunately, the dreamer is as likely to be pulled down into the despair of the friend as he is to pull the friend up out of despair. Gaining satisfaction from believing that he is making a positive impact on someone's life, he may disregard outside opinion, which he perceives as criticism of his compassionate nature. The same dreamer who is such a good listener to those in need can refuse to hear sound advice because he is so emotionally involved with needy friends.

Another motivation for dreamers to become deeply involved in the lives of others is an early awareness of spiritual reality and the need for life to have meaning. Dreamer Christine remembers how, as a third grader, she asked her father, "What happens when we die?"

He looked at her and said, "Nothing. Nothing happens."

"Even at that age, his answer sent me into despair," she recalls, "because I knew that if what he said was true, life had no meaning." With that conversation, Christine's search for true meaning began.

Despite their spiritual sensitivity, dreamers may reject organized religion if they perceive church or synagogue to be insincere or irrelevant. Even if they devoutly participate in church life, dreamers can appear to be full of doubts because they particularly enjoy playing devil's advocate during discussions about meaning and truth. The ideals of faith often form the foundation upon which dreamers build their identity and philosophy of compassion. If they do not find authentic and caring people in the church, however, dreamers can turn to cults in their search for the meaning of life. Or they can make causes the philosophical foundations upon which they build their lives.

From an early age, dreamers are people of passion. Dreamers long for meaningful involvement but sometimes lack follow-through. They may drop out of a cause-related organization because they are disappointed with others in the group.

In high school, Sally volunteered at a local political office, only to find that the major party leaders in her town were concerned less with helping the community than with getting political appointments for themselves. Other dreamers drop a cause when it becomes too routine and boring. Still others move away from an issue when they become overwhelmed by the length of time necessary to bring about real change.

> **Another motivation for dreamers is an early awareness of spiritual reality and the need for life to have meaning.**

Whether or not a dreamer persists in action toward an ideal, the ideal is likely to remain strong or to be replaced by an equally idealistic viewpoint. Dreamer children are never too busy to complain about how things should be.

Is Your Child a Dreamer?

You probably have already begun to discern whether your child exhibits the dreamer cognitive style. You can use the following checklist as a tool in determining whether or not a child has dreamer tendencies.

DREAMER/DOER DESCRIPTIVE CHECKLIST

(Although this checklist is helpful for rating young children, it is most accurate when used for rating children age six and older.)

Which term is *more* descriptive of the child? (Select one per line.)

A		or	B	
1. sensitive	___		logical	___
2. moody	___		even-keeled	___
3. compassionate	___		detached	___
4. dramatic	___		level	___
5. imaginative	___		productive	___
6. creative	___		practical	___
7. thin-skinned	___		thick-skinned	___
8. defensive	___		obedient	___
9. affectionate	___		somewhat stiff with everyone	___
10. scattered	___		focused on details	___
11. imagined fears	___		realistic fears only	___
12. disheveled	___		tidy	___
13. careless	___		precise	___
14. forgetful	___		dependable	___
15. clever	___		sensible	___
16. daydreamer	___		on-task	___
17. emotional	___		dispassionate	___
18. unusual	___		typical for age	___
19. original	___		imitator	___
20. playful	___		industrious	___

21. deep	____	realistic	____
22. intriguing	____	predictable	____
23. considerate	____	blunt	____
24. easily hurt	____	oblivious to teasing	____
25. feels rejected	____	feels confident	____
26. know-it-all	____	humble	____
27. blames others	____	accepts blame	____
28. self-critical	____	easygoing	____
29. relational	____	independent	____
30. articulate	____	inexpressive	____
Total This Column	____	**Do Not Count X's In This Column**	

A score of 24 or more indicates a definite dreamer; 20–23 likely a dreamer; 0–19 more likely a doer. (Note: If your child is an introverted dreamer, some of these characteristics may not be overtly expressed. Scores may underestimate the "dreamerness" of an introvert.)

Even if your child is not a classic dreamer, we believe that if your child is either sensitive or imaginative, having half of the dreamer characteristics, there is something in this book for you. Suggestions based on the specific traits that your child shares with dreamers can be helpful to you as you try to nurture compassion or imagination in your child. Conversely, because each child is a unique creation, there will be areas of this book that won't apply to your child even if the child appears to be an almost stereotypical dreamer. Those of us who have studied them long and hard still see surprising actions in the dreamers we know because dreamers are paradoxical children.

The Paradoxes of Dreamer Life

According to the *Oxford American Dictionary,* a *paradox* is "a statement etc. that seems to contradict itself or conflict with common sense but which contains a truth." By that definition, the behavior of dreamer children is paradoxical. Lacking "common sense" or doer logic, dreamers have intentions and needs that contradict their overt behavior. But guess what? Young dreamer children don't know that their cognitive style isn't the same as everyone else's. They think that you should be able to see their logic plainly. They expect you to see the "truth" or larger meaning of their actions.

When Jack was eight, he was in the Cub Scouts. His Scout leader, Mr. Fields, was a nice guy, but he had a tough demeanor. On a camping trip, Jack wandered off from the camp to see a waterfall close by. Imagining Jack to be lost, Mr. Fields became frantic. When Jack strolled back into camp, he was hit with a long lecture. Angry and hurt, Jack soon wandered off again to keep from crying in front of the other boys. Mr. Fields assumed that Jack was being willfully disobedient. When Jack returned the second time, Mr. Fields told him that he would be confined to his tent for the rest of the trip. Jack made the assumption that Mr. Fields knew his feelings and didn't care. He thought to himself, *Mr. Fields is trying to make me cry in front of everyone. He doesn't like kids; he just likes bossing them around.* At dusk, a tearful and angry Jack sneaked out of camp and walked the trail back to the cars in the dark. His actions only reinforced Mr. Field's view that Jack was rebellious. The two never understood each other. Jack quit the Scouts.

What Dreamers Need from Their Parents

Your idealistic child has special needs just because she's a dreamer; therefore, a lot of work is involved in meeting her needs during childhood and adolescence. In coming chapters, we will explain why dreamers need constant affirmation, gentle discipline, a listening ear, and understanding.

For the creativity, compassion, and vision of your dreamer to truly blossom, your child needs to feel that he has a purpose in life. Are you nurturing the spiritual sensitivity in your dreamer? In the spiritual realm, dreamer children have special needs to focus on the abstract, not a set of concrete do's and don'ts, to be allowed to doubt and debate, to know and learn from spiritually mature dreamers, and to be involved in serving others.

Your child needs your loving guidance to navigate life's adventures. Whether you are just beginning or need to make a midcourse correction, we hope to equip you for the journey.

Part 2

EXPLAINING DREAMER BEHAVIOR

Chapter 4

Strong-Headed and Softhearted: Why Dreamers Aren't Really Strong-Willed

Music has charms to soothe the savage breast,
To soften rocks, or bend a knotted oak.

from *The Morning Bride* by William Congreve

Never try to dominate a dreamer. If you come at a bird with a buffalo approach, don't be surprised if you get your eyes clawed at. Of course, guiding is very different from dominating. Like all children, dreamers need plenty of guidance. But if you use an aggressive parenting style, the dreamer will stubbornly stop all movement in the right direction. You may ask, "If this child is sensitive and wants my approval, why doesn't he just do what I ask?"

> **Never try to dominate a dreamer.**

One parent described it this way: "Sammy was always strong-willed—at least that's what we thought was going on at the time. We did everything the books said to do. We tried consistently punishing him for his angry, disrespectful behavior, but it only got worse. We got tired of the screaming matches. He always had to win. Sammy was only seven years old, and he was in complete control of all our time and energy.

"Then we talked to you about dreamers and everything made sense," Mrs. Smith continued. "So we tried a different approach and things dramatically improved. Now he's a delightful nine-year-old, but he's still stubborn about the funniest things. He has a toy airplane that he's had since he was three. He calls it 'Planey' and has very special feelings about it. When he was smaller, he gave it a personality and a life story. One day his younger brother decided to torment him by kidnapping Planey. My husband, Bob, was shocked at Sammy's extreme reaction to finding Planey in the freezer and made the mistake of saying, 'It's *only* a toy.'

"Well, that did not go over well at all! Sammy was never going to acknowledge that Planey was only a toy. 'You don't understand!' he said repeatedly. My husband and other son certainly did *not* understand the personal violation Sammy felt about his 'friend's' mistreatment. But if Bob had tried to get him to mouth the words, 'It's only a toy,' I believe they'd be standing nose to nose in that kitchen to this day. Those are words Sammy will *never* say."

Many events that tend to result in a round of dreamer stubbornness appear trivial to adults. "I innocently said _____, and she wouldn't speak to me for a week," the perplexed parent says. Such reactions are common from dreamer children. And the word *reaction* is key, for that is one way that dreamers are distinct from drivers. The strong-willed behavior of drivers can be reactive when someone comes between drivers and their goals, but it can be just as often a power move initiated by drivers—offensive rather than defensive behavior. In contrast, dreamers are motivated less by the desire for power than by the desire to be liked. When they feel disliked, dreamers are the most reactive of all children.

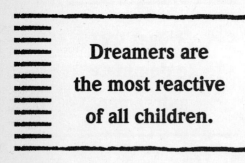

Dreamers are the most reactive of all children.

Reactivity is an outgrowth of the dreamer's sensitivity. A thin-skinned child cannot be a true strong-willed driver. More emotionally dependent than drivers, dreamers soak up the feelings of everyone around them and sometimes misinterpret the feelings. Dreamers are less able than more practical cognitive styles to separate the deed from the doer. They cannot believe that the disapproval of their behavior does not indicate a deeper level of disapproval from you or the teacher trying to enforce limits.

If you live with a dreamer, you are aware of the child's strong reactions to day-to-day events. But you may not think of your dreamer as emotionally dependent because dreamers can seem so independent. Dreamers are intellectually independent; they want to be different from the crowd and take the time to seriously analyze many issues. But that intellectual independence and apparent confidence can mask extreme emotional vulnerability.

Never assume that a stubborn dreamer has the high self-esteem more typical of a driver. Dreamers are emotionally dependent because their self-esteem directly coincides with their view of how others perceive them. Not that they care what others think in the classic sense that pleasers do. Dreamers are aware of the actions and attitudes of others but may react by doing the exact opposite of what others want. This attention to the opinions of others means that self-esteem can change radically from day to day or even moment to moment.

"Isn't that true of every child?" you may ask. Well, it is certainly true of diplomats and dreamers. But drivers seem to be born with self-esteem that is impervious to correction, perhaps because they are more goal oriented than people oriented. As one mother of a driver put it, "Holly wants me to center my life on her, but she couldn't care less how I feel about her behavior. My approval means very little to her except when my disapproval results in punishment that interferes with her plans."

You might believe that your dreamer is just as indifferent to approval if you look only at his stubborn behavior. But if you take time to discuss events with your child, you quickly realize how sensitive to criticism he is.

The Discipline Dreamers Need

The powerful parenting style that provides drivers with needed security is not as effective with dreamers because they perceive sternness as unfeeling and critical. Yet, the laissez-faire parent, who thinks whatever the dreamer does is wonderful, no matter how selfish or destructive, won't raise an emotionally healthy dreamer. Dreamers perceive passive parents as disinterested rather than approving.

At the core of their being, dreamers need to feel understood. Parents who vacillate between strict and lenient approaches find little success from either extreme. Dreamers respond best to parents who communicate understanding and acceptance.

To help your dreamer child or teen feel understood, you may need to change your approach to communication. Try praising your child's character. Our society values what a child *does* more than who a child *is*. A dreamer can feel undervalued in a doer world. Pointing out the dreamer's character traits, such as generosity or compassion, is more important for building bridges than praising his artwork because although a dreamer enjoys compliments on the externals, he craves recognition of the internals.

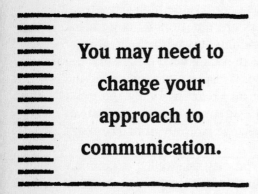

You may need to change your approach to communication.

In addition to character, affirm internals such as the dreamer's personality traits and intellectual interests. "You are so creative! How did you think of such a great solution to the problem? What have you been reading lately?" are examples of comments and questions that can open up dialogue with a dreamer; and opening up dialogue shows your child that you are genuinely interested and not just being polite. In the middle of a parent-child conflict, however, communication can falter.

If you take a powerful, no-nonsense, no-discussion approach with her, your dreamer's behavior may deteriorate. Your child may feel she has not only disappointed you but has also caused you to hate her. At least, that is how she tends to feel *at the moment.* While listening to your dreamer's feelings, try to take most extreme emotional statements with a grain of salt. (This does not include threats of suicide and other indications of severe depression that parents should always take seriously.)

If you are nurturing as well as strict, during a more positive interaction your child may decide that you don't hate him after all. However, his negative view may quickly return when he is punished again. A downward spiral can continue in your relationship until he is so angry with you that misbehavior is no longer childishness or selfishness but has become revenge.

Jeff's mother describes an encounter when he was twelve. Having recently taken a part-time job, she had asked Jeff to complete his chores before she came home from work. For several days, when she asked why his chores were not completed, he would always have an excuse such as, "There was a bird's nest up in the tree and I climbed up in the tree next to it to watch the eggs. I lost track of time." She was tired of coming home to her son's excuses day after day. She angrily told him she was *very* disappointed that he did not obey her.

Jeff's mother proceeded to cook dinner. Then when dinner was ready, she and her husband discovered their son was missing. Knowing his tendencies, they imagined he was hiding in the house someplace. They looked high and low but could not find him. They called out to him, but he did not answer.

They were frantic. His father drove all over the neighborhood calling out Jeff's name. Nothing. His mother called all his friends. No one had seen him. She was beside herself. If something happened to him, she would never forgive herself. When she discovered that the pillow from his bed was missing, Jeff's mother began to cry uncontrollably. She could imagine him walking down the road with his pillow and someone stopping to pick him up. Then just as she began to have a full-blown anxiety attack, Jeff walked calmly down the stairs and said, "Hi, Mom," as if nothing had happened.

He had climbed out of the upstairs bathroom window and onto the roof of the porch with his pillow so he would be comfortable. When questioned, he responded that he needed to get away and think for a while. Today, he admits that at the time, he wanted his mother to suffer, and he felt some satisfaction from seeing her cry.

Knowing How to Draw the Line

Jeff's mother was not wrong to draw the line with her son. But losing her temper didn't help. She set the limit but didn't follow through with a consequence. Too many parenting philosophies have stressed communicating with children while ignoring the equally important role of teaching children that behavior has consequences. Parents who treat their children like buddies and never set limits will have dreamers who blossom into full fledged brats, controlling others with their frequent temper tantrums. And because other people will not like them, dreamers will be miserable.

So, dreamers need limits, but if you are too stern, your efforts to discipline will backfire. How can you communicate a desire to understand without fostering self-centered behavior? Here are a few tips that will be discussed more later on. For starters, you need to hear the child's view *once*. A dreamer needs to be listened to. Clearly acknowledge your child's position and stay calm, no matter what your child says, but let her know that she has to face the consequences of her behavior. This tends to be the most effective method of teaching self-control without creating deep animosity.

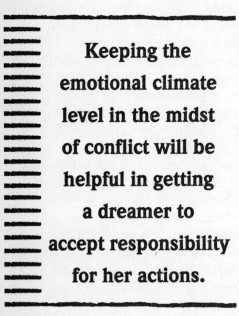

Keeping the emotional climate level in the midst of conflict will be helpful in getting a dreamer to accept responsibility for her actions.

And when the dreamer reiterates his view, tries emotional manipulation such as "You never listen to me!" or becomes disrespectful, what then? Don't stand there and listen to it. If you allow your dreamer to engage you in an argument, although you may be saying, "You can't talk to me that way!" your continued presence communicates, "You *can* talk to me that way."

Unlike driver children who use cause-and-effect, fact-based logic to make decisions, dreamers rely on subjective, feeling-based logic to guide their behavior. Keeping the emotional climate level in the midst of conflict will be helpful in getting a dreamer to accept responsibility for her actions. Internally aware that she is at fault, a dreamer may beat herself up over her failings, but she must feel safe before she will openly admit fault. She falsely believes that blaming someone else or blaming the circumstances will help her regain your approval, while an admission of error will be met with disdain.

We have found that for many parents and some teachers, the logic that we have just described is not considered logic at all. Some disregard the concept of a dreamer cognitive style and treat dreamers as if they are drivers, sometimes with tragic results.

A classic driver dad meets a dreamer son in the movie *Dead Poets Society*. On Neil's first day of the new academic year at Welton, a prestigious boarding school, the controlling Mr. Perry withdraws his son from some extracurricular activities without his consent and informs Neil of this fact in front of his friends. When his son protests, Mr. Perry hisses, "Never dispute me in public," and assures Neil it's the best course of action. Neil contains his frustration, stuffs his feelings of hurt, and fakes apathy to cover up his embarrassment in front of his friends.

Then a dreamer teacher awakens the dreamer in him. Mr. Keating urges his class to "seize the day" and "make their lives extraordinary."

Behind his father's back, Neil auditions for and secures the role of Puck in a community theater production of Shakespeare's *A Midsummer Night's Dream*. When Mr. Perry discovers it, he confronts Neil about his deceit, demanding he leave the play.

For perhaps the first time in his life, Neil rebels. He performs a superb Puck. Mr. Perry watches angrily from the back of the theater, feeling no joy in his son's fine performance. Rather than letting Neil have his moment of glory, Mr. Perry whisks him away in the car.

Once home, the grief-stricken son is informed he will be removed from Welton and enrolled in a military institute, with this explanation: "Son, I am trying very hard to understand why you insist on defying us, but whatever the reason, I am not going to let you ruin your life. . . . You *are* going to Harvard and you *are* going to be a doctor."

True to form, Mr. Perry will hear no arguments from his son. The despairing son retreats to his room. But while his parents sleep, Neil slips into his father's study, reaches into his desk for a key, and opens a locked drawer. Moments later, Mr. Perry awakens with a start. He runs through the house until he finds Neil, lying on the floor of the study, a smoking revolver beside him.

Though the father is a caricature of a controlling parent and is more extreme than almost any parent we have met, his blindness to his son and the resulting tragedy illustrate the pitfalls of using an authoritarian approach when parenting a dreamer. He believed the sensitive poetic side of Neil was just a phase. He casually dismissed his son's deepest longings and, in doing so, lost his son forever.

Selecting Consequences for Misbehavior

Hearing such stories could prompt you to overreact to potential danger. You may fear that setting *any* limits is being too controlling and therefore may fall into a pattern of passiveness that your child may perceive more as disinterest than as caring. Try setting the tone for discipline by saying repeatedly, "I really like who you are on the inside, even if you sometimes make mistakes or do things I don't immediately understand."

To teach this principle in a way that doesn't create prolonged anger, we suggest the use of natural and logical consequences. This approach works well with all children, whereas other methods work well only for one type of child. Your driver child won't be steamed that your dreamer is getting special treatment.

A natural consequence is one that would happen naturally if allowed, that is, a real-world consequence.[1] For example, you may be confident that if your son wears a certain outfit, his friends will laugh. But rather than ordering him to change clothes, making yourself into the bad guy, you might allow the natural consequence to occur by keeping your mouth shut and letting him find out for himself. Although this would not be the best solution if your dreamer is at odds with peers, it is a natural consequence that is not morally or physically threatening. Some natural consequences are never good options. We never let children be hit by cars to teach them not to run in the street, for example. When the natural consequence is unacceptable, try a logical consequence— one that is logically related to the misbehavior. "Let the punishment fit the crime," as William S. Gilbert of Gilbert and Sullivan fame wrote in *The Mikado*.[2]

Thinking of a logical consequence requires practice, but you can do it! If your child refuses to get ready for school, the consequence could be going to school in pajamas, staying home from school to rake the lawn all day, or no lunch at school because there wasn't time to make one. Although there can be several logical consequences for a situation, not all are equally appropriate for dreamers. In developing a plan of action, here are a few key questions you need to ask.

First, because dreamers are attention seekers rather than power seekers, ask yourself: Is the dreamer getting too much attention during the consequence? A long lecture or a spanking may reinforce the inappropriate behavior by making the child the center of attention.

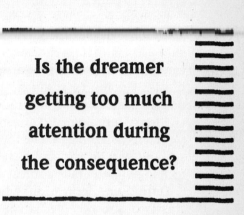

Is the dreamer getting too much attention during the consequence?

Dreamers need attention for positive behavior instead. Unfortunately, all of us can forget to praise cooperative behavior. Thankful to have a peaceful moment to get something done, we can forge ahead into activity without thanking the dreamer for cooperating. You may think children shouldn't be praised for doing their duty, but dreamers need recognition that their efforts to be self-controlled are noticed and appreciated.

In making sure that you are not giving attention to misbehavior, you can swing too far in the other direction. Therefore, your second question must be: Does this consequence give too great of an opportunity for self-pity as opposed to self-examination? Grounding for poor grades, for example, sometimes punishes you as much as

Does the consequence give too great of an opportunity for self-pity as opposed to self-examination?

your child because you have to stay home to monitor the grounding while providing your child with ample opportunity to be stubborn, inactive, and depressed. Don't assume that your child will use the time to study; if she is feeling hurt over the discipline, she is likely to pout or brood.

In these situations, parents often ask us, "Please help us with ideas for logical consequences. Whatever we do, she says, 'I don't care.'" In counseling dreamers, we have found that the child does care about the parent-child relationship and probably the grades but isn't going to admit it. "I don't care" is a popular dreamer defense mechanism and is used at much earlier ages than in other children. More dramatic dreamers may prefer self-blaming defense mechanisms, saying, "I hate myself! I wish I was dead!" When a six-year-old says he wishes he was dead, he is unlikely to act on that feeling but don't take a threat of suicide lightly at any age.

During the depression, when Dana's mother-in-law, Harriette, was two, she received a special treat. Her aunt brought her a brand-new bathing suit. Her aunt must have intended for the bathing suit to last a while, because it was very big. Her ten-year-old sister Kit was allowed to take Harriette and her sister Lou to the creek so that Harriette could swim in the wonderful new bathing suit. They were splashing and laughing when suddenly the suit was gone. Kit looked everywhere, but soon she knew that the bathing suit was on its way to the sea. Imagining the punishment if she returned with a naked Harriette, Kit despaired. She was going to "kill herself." In front of her younger siblings, she jumped off a low cliff into the creek. Had she gone headfirst, she might have really been hurt. Fortunately, the ten-foot plunge landed her on her bottom in about two feet of water. Needless to say, Kit survived. Today she has four grandchildren. But at that moment, she really wished she was dead.

Is the consequence free of humiliation?

Because dreamers are so sensitive and tend to self-doubt, in selecting a consequence you must ask: Is the consequence free of humiliation? There is no guarantee that any consequence won't *feel* humiliating to the dreamer, but it should not be *based on* humiliation. A recent effort at helping teachers gain control of their classrooms involves placing children's names on the board. While working well with drivers and scaring diplomats to death, this form of discipline starts a negative chain reaction for dreamers: from anger at the teacher, to an inability to concentrate on anything else, to a desire to cry, to emotional outbursts when slightly antagonized by a peer, to more punishment. You, too, can introduce humiliation into the consequences by making them too public.

Carol tells of her mother's failed attempt to get her to tidy her room more often than every couple of months. She kept the door closed, so Mom knew that even though Carol didn't clean it, she didn't want anyone to see it. Mom decided to humiliate this teenage dreamer by taking pictures of the room and slipping them into a slide show at a family reunion. Aware of Carol's sensitivity to embarrassment, her mother believed that her approach would be an effective motivator. She failed to realize that the result would be anger, not remorse. Carol dug in her heels and continued as before.

In selecting a consequence, ask yourself a fourth question: Does this consequence allow the dreamer to feel that restitution has been made to the offended or inconvenienced party? That is, does the consequence involve relationship restoration? Traditional punishment angers dreamers more than it changes their behavior because in their hurt and emotional turmoil, they don't see the adult's logic as much as the disapproval. Logical consequences that give your child or teen an opportunity to make things right with you, siblings, teachers, or neighbors are successful tools in teaching a dreamer about responsibility. Such consequences reduce the emotional upheaval through positive action and leave her feeling restored to the offended party, which decreases the potential for a downward spiral.

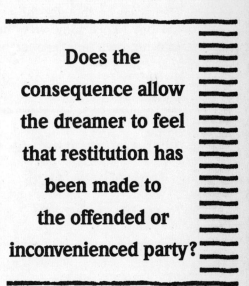

Does the consequence allow the dreamer to feel that restitution has been made to the offended or inconvenienced party?

One of Dan's high school teachers was stifling his creativity. She tried to make him fit into a mold that was out of character for him. Even though he was a bright individual, he rebelled by not doing his homework and by skipping class. This teacher assigned a project that each student had to complete that encompassed a large portion of the semester's grade. Dan had put off working on the report so long that he saw no way he would be able to complete it without skipping his classes to work all day on the project. Dan thought he had everything under control until a classmate called him after school to tell him that the teacher had said that he was going to fail the class if she found out he was skipping again. He immediately dropped into an extremely depressed mood. His parents found out what had happened and were very worried about him. When his mother called the principal to inform him of the circumstances, he asked to see Dan and his mother.

Instead of coming down hard on the boy, the principal focused on Dan's many wonderful qualities. He listed all the things Dan had accomplished in the past months and years. As he talked, the dreamer's attitude changed radically. The principal then asked Dan what he thought the consequences should be. He allowed the boy to see some ways he could regain his teacher's respect and his own self-respect by doing some extra work for the teacher.

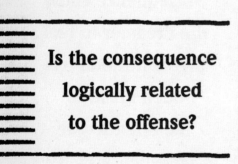

Is the consequence logically related to the offense?

A restorative consequence will generally meet one final test for appropriateness: Is the consequence logically related to the offense? As we have mentioned, natural and logical consequences teach dreamers what diplomats already know: Most rules aren't worth breaking. As idealists, dreamers will always ignore some rules in their efforts to rescue the innocent, improve an art form, or solve a problem that someone has said cannot be solved. But through appropriate parenting, they can learn that most rules are logical and just, and most rule breakers are acting out of selfishness, not conscience.

Preventing Power Struggles: Picking Your Battles

Most dreamers don't start out in life wanting to rebel. They just expect some flexibility. Emma, a generally cooperative teen, went several rounds with her mother over her 11:00 P.M. weekend curfew. Her mother meant, "In the house at 11:00." Angry that her previous good behavior had not been rewarded with flexibility, Emma bent the rule a bit. She arrived in the driveway by 11:00 but stayed outside in full public view talking with her boyfriend for another twenty minutes. Her mother grounded her. Emma became incensed. When she was free to date again, she came home ten minutes late—never later. In her mind, she was protesting the rule just as much as if she'd picketed her house. Her mother didn't realize this behavior was anything more than willful disobedience. No form of punishment changed the behavior.

Both Emma and her mother felt that a significant principle was involved. Her mother eventually gave up the punishment, and the stubborn dreamer felt that she had won. Actually, her mother decided that the issue was not worth the risk it posed to her relationship with her daughter. She decided to battle her own need to control rather than battle Emma. Both can laugh about this dispute now that they are older and wiser. However, Emma still stubbornly admits no wrongdoing: "After all, I was right!"

No matter what your parenting approach has been like in the past and no matter how stubborn your dreamer, it is not too late to change your game plan. Whatever consequences you select, your parenting must always communicate how much you love your child or teen. That means not only staying calm and handing out consequences carefully but also actively expressing love for your dreamer.

Turning Stubbornness into Determination

Many of our suggestions for addressing the problem of dreamer stubbornness are intended to help you reduce the amount of defensive behavior by your dreamer child. Because all behavior is rooted in thought patterns, we have focused on changing your child's external reactions by changing his internal responses. While discouraging stubborn responses to parental guidance, you can do things to encourage stubbornness in the face of peer pressure and other potentially negative influences. In other words, you want your child to be tenacious when it's in his best interest while reducing self-defeating stubborn responses.

Elizabeth Cochrane was a "spirited and occasionally stubborn" young girl, with a "flair for the dramatic." She read and dreamed of faraway places and composed stories inspired by what she read. When she came of age, unlike most of her female peers, she sought a career. But it was 1884, and few careers were available for a woman; every evening she returned home "dejected" after her search. Then Elizabeth read an editorial in the *Pittsburgh Dispatch* that mocked young women who sought careers; it made her fighting mad.

Fueled by righteous indignation, Elizabeth fired off a letter to the editor, signing it "Lonely Orphan Girl." Apparently, her writing needed improvement, particularly her grammar; but her impassioned rebuttal so impressed the editor that he ran an ad to the "Lonely Orphan Girl," invited her to his office, and offered her a job.

Under her pen name, Nellie Bly, she pioneered a bold new reporting style, that of disguising herself and trying to live the lives of her subjects, if only for a few hours. The "I was there" became her trademark, and using it, she exposed labor and housing problems, enraging "slumlords and unscrupulous business owners."[3] Whether or not you like the crusading reporter style she spawned, you can see how this stubborn dreamer changed the world of journalism.

When a child is stubborn in persisting toward a noble goal or in the face of adversity, we call that determination. Dreamers have tremendous potential for determination about their ideals. To understand how to encourage determination, we must first understand the obstacles that we can inadvertently place between dreamers and the development of this quality.

Parental behaviors that discourage determination and destroy confidence tend to be in one of three areas: harshness, passiveness, or overprotectiveness. Harshness leads to stubbornness. Passiveness leads to feelings of inadequacy and acting-out behaviors that are targeted at getting parental attention. And overprotection leads to general fearfulness and persistent fears such as phobias. Harsh and overprotective parents treat children as though they are incapable of making decisions independently and facing the consequences of their decisions. Conversely, passive parents allow children to make too many decisions and create insecurity.

But other parenting behaviors stimulate confidence in dreamers. When dreamers face the consequences of their stubbornness without lectures and power struggles, they respect parents and have more respect for themselves. Listening to your child and appreciating his unique abilities reduce emotional reactivity. When your child becomes less reactive, you set the stage for an increase in determination because, unlike stubbornness, determination is not simply a reactive behavior but grows out of ideals and the self-confidence to attain the ideals.

> **Determination is not simply a reactive behavior.**

Confident Dreamers

One source of self-confidence is living in a family where repentance is valued. Dreamers are acutely aware of their shortcomings, even if they don't openly admit them, and they need opportunities to feel that they have confessed. A family in which parents ask for the children's forgiveness when they lose their tempers or behave selfishly fosters repentance in the children.

One mother put it this way: "We have tried to be consistent with Louise, without being harsh, and have tried to model confession and repentance. When discipline must occur, she usually responds initially with rage. Fortunately, since she was about four years old, the rage has been short-lived. She then dissolves into tears—deep, sad tears—and often comes crying for forgiveness."

Children who can openly admit fault and learn that it does not result in parental disapproval, but instead gains parental respect, are well on their way to learning to turn stubbornness into determination. Confidence to admit when you're wrong breeds the confidence to be determined and stand against the crowd when you're right.

Much has been written recently about people who rescued Jews from the Nazi Holocaust. What made them different from those who went along with the German government and its genocidal policies? For the religious among them, it has been found that they held the common beliefs that God would be with them in the midst of great danger; that Scripture taught that some things were absolutes in life; that some things are always wrong no matter what the circumstances; and that God would honor their adherence to the ideal of rescuing the innocent.[4]

Like the Christian rescuers who were determined to protect their Jewish neighbors in the midst of adversity, dreamer children who hold to spiritual ideals can have a significant impact on their culture, whether the schoolroom, the playground, the ball field, or the family. And for the future, they can build on a foundation of spiritual maturity and idealism to confidently and powerfully face whatever challenges lie ahead.

Chapter 5

New Ideas at Every Turn: Imagination in Dreamers

When at home alone I sit
And am very tired of it,
I just have to shut my eyes
To go sailing through the skies ...

from "The Little Land"
by Robert Louis Stevenson

"Is she creative?" Mrs. Whitehead seemed to be unsure of the answer. "Well, she doesn't really like to color or things like that. And she's more interested in sports than music. No, I guess I'd have to say that she's not creative."

"Do you think of Emily as a practical child then?" Dana responded.

"Oh, no. Certainly not," answered Mrs. Whitehead. "That I am sure of. Why, just yesterday I asked her to put her new jacket away. Emily walked around with it for quite a long time not sure what to do. She said since it was a new jacket she wasn't sure 'where it lives.' I tried to explain to her that jackets don't 'live' anywhere. Then I took her through the steps of logically deciding where jackets go. She happily put the jacket in the hall closet and said, 'I hope my jacket won't be lonely in there or scared. It can be as dark as a troll's forest in a closet. Or maybe it won't be scared at all. Maybe all the coats have a silly party just as soon as we close the door." Then do you know what she did? She went over to the closet door and listened as if she expected a band to start playing as soon as the door closed. What an imagination she has!"

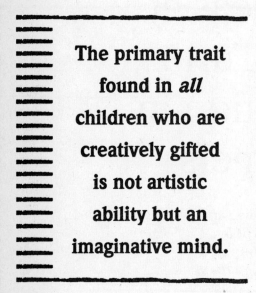

The primary trait found in *all* children who are creatively gifted is not artistic ability but an imaginative mind.

Emily isn't interested in coloring or music, so Mrs. Whitehead assumes that Emily is not creative. Yet clearly, Emily is not strongly grounded in the "real world," and she doesn't use logic that looks remotely familiar to her doer mother. As a child, Mrs. Whitehead would never have asked where a jacket "lives," even during the preschool fantasy stage of development. Indeed, Emily is imaginative, yet (so far) not artistic. Although our culture has defined *creativity* as if it is an ability limited to artists, the primary trait found in *all* children who are creatively gifted is not artistic ability but an imaginative mind.

True Creativity

When creativity is defined in terms of originality, most children are not as creative as dreamers. In general, doer children are more practical than creative. They can take someone else's idea and expand on it with an eye to function and efficiency. In the arts or business, doers are gifted at perfecting techniques. They can be technically gifted, but they are not inventors. Singers, but not songwriters. Artisans, but not true artists.

Many doer craftspeople will be the first to tell you that there is something qualitatively different about dreamers. Doers may be more successful because of their common sense, but they know whether or not they are true innovators. When we describe the dreamer cognitive style as poetic, we always receive knowing looks from the audience. The tortured youth Mozart as depicted in *Amadeus* was no doer.

Being a poetic dreamer does not have to be synonymous with experiencing failure and pain. All of us can think of great inventors, novelists, photographers, songwriters, playwrights, actors, and poets who have achieved celebrity status. Of course, not all dreamers would consider wealth and celebrity the signs of true success. Men and women of faith are often dreamers. Before David the poet and David the king, there was young David the righter of wrongs and giant slayer (see 1 Sam. 17).

Imagination in Childhood

Because all children are made in the image of a creative God, all have creative moments. Some creative drivers can be especially inventive. But most doers do not experience the constant bombardment of new ideas that are the blessings and curses of dreamers. Dreamers say that they have forgotten some of their greatest ideas when another idea intruded before they could write down the first one. A dreamer friend tells us that she wrecked her car in high school while trying to write down a fleeting thought about the school prom decorations.

So exactly how does this creativity manifest itself in childhood? First, dreamers are gifted at understanding abstract concepts from an early age. Focusing on things of the spirit more than on possessions or activities, dreamers think about truth and beauty when their peers are thinking about bats and balls. Using intuition to connect ideas in new ways, dreamers express insightful perspectives on the relational and aesthetic aspects of life. Even without adult creative role models, dreamers' innate abilities blossom in the preschool years.

> **Dreamers think about truth and beauty when their peers are thinking about bats and balls.**

Preschool dreamers enjoy imaginary play and are more likely than their peers to have imaginary friends. If imagination is nurtured, dreamers can especially enjoy discussing their ideas with adults and are often more articulate and entertaining in conversation than their age-mates. Dreamers enjoy discussing their perception of the abstract. Ideas such as God, angels, demons, good, evil, right, and wrong swirl in their heads.

When Candice was three, she was concerned that she might have to go to heaven alone. Already aware that parents often die before their children, Candice wanted to go to heaven, but only if Mommy could go with her. Hearing that Mommy would be there waiting for her did not comfort her. The journey itself worried her. She didn't want to make that trip alone.

From a developmental standpoint, Candice's questions about heaven came two years or more earlier than those of her bright doer sister, Hunter. And when Hunter, though three years older, seriously contemplated heaven, she showed little concern over the relational aspects of death that three-year-old Candice wanted to know about. The doer asked questions about the positive, concrete aspects of heaven like, "What does it look like?" and "Are animals there?" while the dreamer's questions were more abstract and potentially fear producing. Discussion of Candice's concerns helped the parents to know what she was thinking that might be scaring her.

Unable to fully separate fantasy from reality, preschool dreamers can have dangerous thoughts ("I can fly off the garage roof"), scary thoughts ("Monsters are in my closet"), and painful thoughts ("My parents divorced because I was bad!") that will affect their behavior, relationships, and self-esteem. During the fantasy stage of cognitive development, dreamers' fantasies are wilder and more vivid than those of other children.

For most children, the fascination with fantasy ends during early childhood, but for dreamers, it is only beginning. Because dreamers have the ability to make imagination into reality, they continue to engage in fantasy play well after the preschool years.

Dreamers also attribute personhood to loved objects. During carpool one day, doer Martha invited dreamer Beth to play after school. Beth said that she could not come because her stuffed dog was sick and her mother would not allow her to leave her sick dog any longer than was necessary.

Martha was astounded. "Stuffed animals don't get sick and mommies don't care about them!" said the frustrated doer. Beth began to cry. Having not intended to hurt her friend, Martha then whispered to her mother, who was driving the car, "Do I have to pretend that the dog is real?"

Just as Beth probably had been thinking of her stuffed dog all morning and had imagined him into a deadly illness, dreamers can engage in play in their minds. Such internal play is considered daydreaming, but it is different from the preoccupation with thoughts about real life that doer children experience. For doers, daydreaming may be a sign of stress or anxiety about family, school, or friends. For dreamers, daydreaming may be a pleasurable escape from the mundane world with all of its limits. Some fantasies involve the imaginative expression of deep-seated feelings of anger (revenge fantasies), inadequacy (dreamer-as-hero fantasies), attraction (romance fantasies), or fear (frightening fantasies). But many dreamer fantasies are neutral, such as imagined adventures.

Ron shares this high school experience: "My favorite subject in school was social studies. During history classes, I often daydreamed and put myself into the minds of historical figures. I imagined how I might respond if I were in their places. I remember one day being so embarrassed when the teacher called on me during one of my exciting adventures. There I was, a Rebel on the battlefield defending Kennesaw Mountain as a part of the Confederate army. The Union forces were attacking in their drive to capture Atlanta. I was looking out my trench facing the bayonet of a Yankee soldier advancing toward my position. All of a sudden Mr. Bagwell said, 'Ronnie, what do you think about . . . ?' I didn't have a clue what we were talking about. Drifting into my own world was fun, but it sometimes distracted me from what I was supposed to be focusing on."

Imagination and the Aesthetic

Dreamers use imagination to explore the aesthetic world. To encourage creativity, you can provide your child with a variety of materials for artistic exploration and allow him to use the materials in any way he desires. Picture books with excellent artwork, age-appropriate music and drama, storytelling, creative writing with the child "dictating" stories to the parent, and problem-solving games foster dreamer development.

Provide your child with a variety of materials for artistic exploration.

Books like *Amazing Grace* about a girl who loved to tell stories give us a glimpse of the dreamer's life. Openness to books and music that appeal to your child can say, "I appreciate your interests. Your ideas are important."[1]

Two-year-old Pat found a friend in Princess Molly the Messy in *Tumble Tower,* novelist Anne Tyler's first book for children. When this dreamer saw that Molly liked to sleep in her bed all "lumpy and knobby with half-finished books," she laughed in delight. A soul mate! That's exactly the way she liked to take a nap—dragging a dozen or more books into bed, looking at them, then sleeping sprawled out on top of them.[2]

You may be thinking, *I don't want to encourage my disorganized child to stay that way.* We can understand that completely. But if you are too quick to criticize a child's natural tendencies, interests, or activities, you can squelch creativity. Correcting the child's artistic or problem-solving efforts and setting rigid limits to experimentation can create such a strong fear of failure that the dreamer will never take the risk to express himself creatively again. A grandparent of seven-year-old Ross told him, "You can't carry a tune in a bucket!" and he hasn't opened his mouth to sing since.

Harry Chapin's song "Flowers Are Red" poignantly describes the impact of criticism on creativity:

The little boy went first day of school
He got some crayons and started to draw
He put colors all over the paper
For colors was what he saw
And the teacher said, "What you doing young man?"
"I'm painting flowers," he said.
She said, "It's not the time for art, young man
And anyway, Flowers are green and red.

There's a time for everything, young man,
And a way it should be done.
You've got to show concern for everyone else.
For you're not the only one."

And she said,"Flowers are red.
And green leaves are green.
There's no need to see flowers any other way,
Than the way they always have been seen."

But the little boy said,"There's so many colors in the rainbow
So many colors in the morning sun,
So many colors in a flower,
And I see every one."

The teacher said,"You're sassy,
There's ways that things should be.
And you'll paint flowers the way they are,
So repeat after me ..."

And she said,"Flowers are red.
And green leaves are green.
There's no need to see flowers any other way,
Than the way they always have been seen."

But the boy said,"There's so many colors in the rainbow,
So many colors in the morning sun,
So many colors in a flower,
And I see every one."

The teacher put him in a corner
She said,"It's for your own good.
You won't come out till you get it right
And are responding like you should."
Well, finally he got lonely.
Frightened thoughts filled his head.
And he went up to the teacher
And this is what he said,

He said,"Flowers are red.
And green leaves are green.
There's no need to see flowers any other way,
Than the way they always have been seen."

Time went by like it always does and
they moved to another town.
And the little boy went to another school
And this is what he found:
The teacher there was smiling.
She said, "Painting should be fun.
And there are so many colors in a flower,
So let's use every one."

But the little boy painted flowers
In neat rows of red and green.
And when the teacher asked him why,
This is what he said,

He said, "Flowers are red.
And green leaves are green.
There's no need to see flowers any other way,
Than the way they always have been seen."[3]

Rigid limits can strangle imagination.

It's tragic that anyone would discourage creativity, but it happens. Like this little boy, all dreamers have ideas that aren't naturally limited by rules and conventions. Rigid limits can strangle imagination.

An encouraging teacher, however, may be able to nurture the very tendencies that others are trying to squelch. Leah drew a beautiful dragon for her first-grade teacher. The dragon's tail went off the page at one point and then reappeared at another. What she envisioned in her mind's eye was so real that it was not limited by the size of the paper. Her teacher was delighted.

Dreamers enjoy doing things from the heart, and they are especially gifted in activities that draw on emotion, such as drama, creative writing, poetry, song lyrics, painting, photography, and sculpture. They can be innovative where an ideal or abstract concept is the focus, such as in the creation of worshipful music, dance, and drama or the production of visual arts that communicate an ideal or portray the destruction of an ideal.

Imagination and Problem Solving

Because dreamers enjoy compassionate expressions of creativity, many envision solutions to people problems. An ironic fact is that dreamers are often better at solving other people's problems than their own. Dreamers are never totally able to separate themselves from the feelings of others, yet they can be objective enough to analyze the needs of others and develop innovative solutions.

When dreamers come up with solutions, they may employ a process that is cryptic to the casual observer. Faced with the probable slaughter of her friend, Wilbur the pig, by Farmer Zuckerman, the character Charlotte in *Charlotte's Web* retreats to her web in the barn rafters to think. Within a few days, words appear in her web, strategically positioned directly over Wilbur's pen. First, *Some Pig.* A few days later, *Terrific.* Then, *Radiant.* And finally, *Humble.* To the practical mind, her messages seem pointless at first. But soon people come from far and near to see Zuckerman's famous pig. And Wilbur becomes so well known that Mr. Zuckerman wouldn't think of killing him come winter.[4]

Like Charlotte, dreamers may develop solutions not limited by personal experience. They may hold tenaciously to the practicality of solutions even when the solution is based on childish logic or fantasy.

At age seven, Alex decided to build a rocket ship. He went to the junk pile out back and started putting something together. He found pipes and pieced them together with duct tape. When he finally completed his masterpiece, he headed for the garage to get some gasoline. His mother saw him out the kitchen window and averted catastrophe.

Check out Peter Spier's book *Bored—Nothing to Do!* if you want a picture of dreamer ingenuity. This delightful children's book shows how two boys build an airplane from parts in the barn and a few things borrowed from the car, the phone, and the baby carriage. As the boys are sent to bed early after a day of building and flying, their parents say, "Some boys. Clever, too!" Upstairs their sons sullenly state, Bored—nothing to do."[5] It can be dangerous to leave dreamers with nothing to do or even to say to them, "It can't be done." Dreamers eventually seem to find a way to do anything if they try long enough or think long enough.

Imagination and Writing

The same love for mental manipulation of the abstract that leads to many inventions can lead to interesting writing. Not all parents know how to nurture writing ability and may jump too quickly to correct spelling or other details that from the dreamer's perspective are insignificant in comparison to the ideas being expressed. Often very good at creative writing from an early age, dreamers may be frustrated by the process of putting ideas onto paper during early childhood when they learn how to write or type. An encouraging parent will assist the child in getting ideas onto paper at this age without criticizing the child's limited fine-motor ability, spelling, or grammar.

Dreamers also enjoy other types of writing that require critical thinking, such as journalism, criticism, and editorials. Although they dislike criticism from others, dreamers can be excellent at finding flaws with institutions and society in general and pointing them out in original and thought-provoking language. Equally willing to examine themselves as long as they are the critics, they excel at journaling and writing self-reflective poetry. Dreamers are insightful in their writing that relates to people, relationships, and emotions.

Imagination and Social Acceptance

Among peers, dreamers may be perceived as fun and inventive, taking the role of class clown, prankster, artist, or imaginative playmate. But they are just as likely to be perceived negatively.

At age ten, Tracy alienated her peers by unintentionally making them feel dumb. If anyone answered incorrectly, Tracy was all too quick to chuckle and state the correct response. Though deeply sensitive, she ignored the feelings of her peers because she perceived them as popular, without need of her sympathy or sensitivity. Tracy did not associate their rejection of her with her behavior; she thought that she was attacked because of her appearance and other unchangeable traits. It was a revelation to Tracy to hear that it is best not to state everything you know about something unless others ask for more information. Dreamers can teach when peers have no desire to learn.

Some dreamers who experience problems in relationships, for this or other reasons, withdraw into their imaginations or become absorbed in books, computers, and computer games that give them positive feedback and immediate rewards for imaginative problem solving. Separating themselves from the peer group only accentuates their uniqueness and can lead to more difficulties.

> **Some dreamers who experience problems in relationships withdraw into their imaginations.**

More confident dreamers tend to have a wide variety of friends, compassionately trying not to ostracize the underdog while enjoying socializing with many types of people. Using their originality to parlay their way into spheres of influence, dreamers seek involvement in creative activities such as the yearbook and the school paper. Upon graduation, dreamers may be named wittiest and most creative while rarely being selected most dependable.

Anna was on the yearbook staff at her high school. She was in charge of the senior superlatives section. Being a dreamer, Anna thought that the traditional superlatives were boring. She developed an expanded list including shadiest character, wildest imagination, and best practical joker. Although the sponsor axed some of the categories, that year a lot more dreamers made the superlatives section of the yearbook.

Imagination and Fears

Because dreamer children do not have to experience something for an event to become real to them, there is tremendous potential for the development of fears. Whereas doer children tend to be fearful of things they have directly experienced or things that they have seen on the news, dreamers can fear monsters, aliens, angels, and demons. We have seen doer children who can separate fantasy from reality before the age of six and who are not in the least bothered by the flying monkeys in the *Wizard of Oz*—a sure sign of a fearless child! Dreamers, on the other hand, go in and out of fear phases throughout childhood and are very much affected by films or TV shows they have seen.

Bob's mother tells of a period in her son's life when he suddenly begged for a twin bed instead of a double bed. One could not get him to explain why. Three years later, after attending a seminar on dreamers, Bob's mother said, "I don't remember you having a lot of fears. Do you?"

Her son reminded her of his desire for a twin bed. "I never told you this," replied Bob, "but I saw a movie in which a troll got into a bed with a child and the bed in the movie was a double bed. Somehow, I thought that if I had a twin bed, I'd be safe."

This tendency to imagine themselves as a part of the plot can lead to fears. Dreamers can re-create the experience repeatedly, weeks or even months after seeing something that frightened them. And what they find frightening may not be what parents would expect. Historical dramas where people are trudging through the snow may be relived with dreamers among the trudgers: desperate, cold, and hungry. Or they may be frightened by scenes that were intended to be funny but that involve someone getting hurt. They may also fail to be sad or frightened when parents might expect it while becoming distraught over a minor incident.

Dreamer children have an intuitive ability to sense problems among people around them and understand parts of conversations that adults wrongly believe will be completely over their heads.

Sally lost a baby brother to sudden infant death syndrome (SIDS). Hearing that the baby stopped breathing, Sally put two and two together. At school, she told her teacher that her parents had smothered the baby. What fears this child must have been experiencing! What would happen to her if she displeased her parents?

Imagining all the possibilities never stops being frightening. Twenty-four-year-old Doug is afraid to fly. In his profession, Doug supervises toxic waste cleanup. He talks about being in the middle of a cleanup site and seeing birds drop dead right out of the sky; then in the same breath, he'll say he doesn't want to get on an airplane to go to the next job. Why doesn't toxic waste scare him more than flying?

In terms of chances of injury or death, statistics are probably on the side of the airline passenger. But because Doug is a dreamer, he can't find much comfort in statistics. He is scared of the plane because he is not flying it. On the cleanup site, he knows what precautions have been taken. In the plane, Doug is imagining a flock of geese headed straight for the engine; a pilot behind the cabin door who's drunk, leaving a flight attendant to fly the plane; and a mechanic on the ground saying, "Oops! Why is this main wing bolt still sitting here?"

Imagination and Sleep Disorders

For children with such an imaginative cognitive style, nightmares and night terrors are common. Dreamers' vivid dreams can be wonderful or horrible. Many have nightmares related to a fear of death. In his book on sleep disorders in children, Dr. Richard Ferber writes that children around age five or six "have serious concerns about falling asleep and never waking again."[6] We have found that because of their awareness of the abstract, dreamers have these nightmares about death at younger ages than other children, often as early as age three or four.

Dreamers can have nightmares about monsters and other imaginary threats. As a preschooler, Grace had a recurring nightmare in which she was eaten by a giant daddy longlegs. Like Jonah in the whale, Grace was alive inside his belly. She spent the dream trying to fight her way out. She awakened to find herself in a dark room filled with spiders. Or so she thought. She could "see" them all around her in the dark. Closing her eyes brought no escape, so she shrieked until Daddy or Mommy came to her room. On some nights, Grace gathered up her courage to run down the long, dark hall leading to their bedroom. But even when her parents let her snuggle in between them in bed, she could not keep visions of spiders from dancing in her head.

Ferber believes that children develop fears of monsters by using their imaginations to develop explanations for their undefined feelings and anxieties. Although the monsters are not real, the feelings are, and they should not be ignored. The middle of the night is probably not the best time to discover the source of the anxiety. The next day, talking about events in the child's life may illuminate the source of the problem.[7] We believe that because dreamers are more imaginative than other children, they are more likely to explain their anxieties through fantasy objects and beings.

During periods of anxiety, a dreamer may experience night terrors or sleep terrors. "He may talk, moan and cry all at the same time in a confusing and nonsensical way. During the episode he will not recognize you or allow you to comfort him. . . . he will have no memory of a dream or that he was yelling and thrashing about," according to Ferber.[8]

Sleep terrors are not dreams; they occur during the nondreaming phase of sleep. Children who have sleep terrors are difficult to awaken and are no longer fearful once awake. In contrast, nightmares often cause the child to wake up, are vivid in the memory, and cause fear after the child is awake. Sleep terrors generally occur in the first few hours of sleep while nightmares usually happen during the last few hours of the night just before the new day begins.

During a nightmare, your child may lie very still because of the depth of sleep. Because night terrors occur during the light sleep cycle, your child may thrash around in the bed and make lots of noise. He may suddenly sit up in bed or jump out of bed. Sleep terrors are associated with sleepwalking and other behaviors that involve disorientation and movement during light sleep.

Ron recalls how his son was affected by this form of night terror: "Until Adam reached age ten, on many nights during the first few hours after retiring for bed, we would hear a loud cry that caused me to jump out of bed ready for action. I would then encounter Adam walking in the house, talking as if something was terribly wrong. He would look at me and carry on a nonsensical conversation. I would direct him back to bed and lie beside him until he was settled again. The next morning he would have absolutely no recollection of his adventure during the night. We didn't make a big deal of these incidents and even joked about it within the family. Being knowledgeable of night terror episodes prevented me from becoming overly concerned. I have to admit, though, being startled out of my sleep was unsettling."

In the preschool years, sleep terrors can be a normal part of development as your child's sleep stages mature. But if sleep terrors appear for the first time in an older child or a teen, there is generally a psychological cause of the behavior. The cause could be something that is in reality harmless, or it could be something real and troubling. Teens with this sleep disturbance may have difficulty talking about their feelings or may not be allowed to talk things out. Teens tend to have more violent sleep terrors than younger children and may let out bloodcurdling screams. Fortunately, the intensity of the sleep terror does not necessarily correlate directly with the level of anxiety.

Because dreamers are more emotionally sensitive, they can be more prone to the types of anxiety and emotional turmoil that trigger nightmares and night terrors. In our experience, because creative children tend to go in and out of fear stages throughout childhood, the potential for sleep problems related to fears is never totally outgrown.

> **In the preschool years, sleep terrors can be a normal part of development.**

Starry-Eyed Dreamers

What a wonder is the imagination! Despite the fears they can create, few dreamers would part with their imaginations in exchange for a good night's sleep. Dreamer children don't always realize that others have less of an imaginative bent. Observers think they are being daring when dreamers are only being themselves.

Luke tells this about himself in high school: "My little brother told me how much he admired me for walking down the halls singing out loud, without being afraid of what other people thought of me. I had to laugh because I wasn't aware that I was singing, and I had no idea that anyone would find singing in the halls unacceptable."

One of the dreamiest dreamers in all of literature is the delightful Anne Shirley of *Anne of Green Gables* by Lucy Maud Montgomery. The orphaned Anne goes to live with unmarried Marilla and her bachelor brother Matthew.

Anne and Marilla have just met and are riding in a buggy when the extroverted Anne says,

"I've made up my mind to enjoy this drive. It's been my experience that you can nearly always enjoy anything if you make up your mind firmly that you will. . . . Oh look, there's a little wild rose out! . . . Isn't pink the most bewitching color in the world? I love it, but I can't wear it. Redheaded people can't wear pink, not even in imagination. Did you ever know anybody whose hair was red when she was young, but got to be another color when she grew up?"

"No, I don't know as I ever did," said Marilla mercilessly, "and I shouldn't think it likely to happen in your case, either."

"Well, there is another hope gone. My life is a perfect graveyard of buried hopes. That's a sentence that I read in a book once, and I say it over to comfort myself whenever I'm disappointed in anything."

"I don't see where the comforting comes in myself," said Marilla.

"Why, because it sounds so nice and romantic, just as if I were a heroine in a book, you know. . . . Are we going across the lake of shining waters today?"

"We're not going over Barry's pond, if that's what you mean. . . . We're going by the shore road."

"The shore road sounds nice," said Anne dreamily. ". . . Just when you said 'shore road' I got a picture in my mind as quick as that! And white sands is a pretty name, too. . . . How far is it to white sands?"

"It's five miles . . . you might as well talk to some purpose by telling me what you know about yourself."

"Oh, what I *know* about myself isn't worth telling," said Anne eagerly. "If you'll only let me tell you what I *imagine* about myself you'll think it ever so much more interesting."[9]

Do you know who your child imagines herself to be? To truly know and enjoy your child, peek into her imaginative world by taking the time to play, listen, and observe. At times you may need to guide your child's use of her original thinking, but do so gently. Much potential is unrealized due to nothing more than a lack of encouragement.

Chapter 6

Sailing over the Bounding Moods: The Emotional Ups and Downs of Dreamers

Our sincerest laughter
With some pain is fraught;
Our sweetest songs are those
That tell of saddest thought.

from "To a Skylark"
by Percy Bysshe Shelley

"Are boys supposed to be this moody?" Mike's dad asked. "I could handle the bad temper, but he cries anytime another child teases him even a little. And sometimes he seems to wake up angry. Other days, you would think he'd been elected president by the elation he experiences. I feel like I'm on a roller coaster following him up and down through life. Mike wants to play football this fall. What will the other boys do to him the first time he falls apart when he misses a pass?" Mike's dad's unspoken question is, "How can I help my deeply sensitive son successfully navigate the rough spots of life?"

It's stormy sailing out there, particularly for an emotional dreamer like Mike. As a parent, you can't protect your child from the squalls that are whipping up all around him—or even the tempest inside.

Sailing over the bounding moods is a learned art—one that must be mastered by a dreamer's parents and, eventually, by the dreamer. But it can be gut-wrenching to watch your child ride out some rough years.

Some Emotional Children Aren't Dreamers

Because dreamers aren't the only moody and emotional children, distinguishing them from those other relators, the diplomats, and from emotionally troubled children is important. First a word about diplomats. These children are sensitive, and although not as moody as dreamers, they have their highs and lows. Diplomats are generally more self-controlled than dreamers, fearing the repercussions of anger. They may seem more up than they actually feel, since cheerfulness is more socially acceptable. Though better than dreamers at masking unhappiness, diplomats can be unhappy nevertheless. If you create a nurturing home environment, diplomats feel freer to express sadness and anger.

> **Does the child have dreamer traits that are not related to emotions, such as imagination?**

In contrast to diplomats, emotionally troubled children—whatever their cognitive style—are less likely to contain negative emotions. To distinguish a dreamer from an emotionally disturbed child, think through these questions: First, does the child have dreamer traits that are not related to emotions, such as imagination? If the child is not clearly imaginative, he is probably not a dreamer, and persistent explosiveness may stem from trauma. Likewise, if a child suddenly becomes sensitive after years of driver-type behavior, she is likely to be experiencing something painful or traumatic. Sudden personality change should always be taken seriously in a child over six years old. If you know that your child has been verbally, physically, or sexually abused, or has experienced a trauma such as the death of a close relative, do not attribute the emotional changes to simply being a dreamer.

Second, does the child have ups as well as downs? Dreamers can be joyful as well as depressed, but children with emotional problems may be down all the time. Developmental problems such as learning disabilities may be accompanied by low self-esteem and lack of emotional control. Some children have neurological causes of emotional disturbance; symptoms may include the repetition of rituals like hand washing, rocking, head banging that lasts for more than a year, or arm flapping. Such ritualistic and self-stimulating behaviors are rarely seen in normal dreamers.

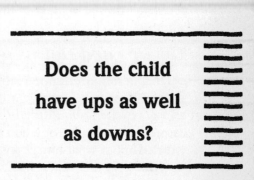

Does the child have ups as well as downs?

Third, is there a known history of depression or mental illness in the family? Few in the family may remember what the mentally ill relative was like as a child. Emotional problems that appear to be inheritable include depression, manic-depressive disorder, obsessive-compulsive disorder, and schizophrenia.[1] If you suspect emotional disturbance, whether due to environmental or physiological causes, you should seek a professional evaluation.

Is there a known history of depression or mental illness in the family?

A child who can look very much like a dreamer emotionally, and yet not be imaginative, is a child with attention deficit disorder (ADD). Some children with ADD are dreamers, but many are not. Children with ADD can be emotionally volatile because they have low frustration tolerance and high impulsivity. Because many dreamers are incorrectly thought to have ADD, we have devoted chapter 11 to that topic.

A dreamer who has experienced trauma will be doubly emotional. The focus of this book, however, is on normal emotional development in dreamers and how they differ from their doer peers. When dreamers are not suffering from serious emotional problems, they should have "high highs" and "low lows."

The Ups and Downs of Life

Dreamers experience elation that is rare in other cognitive styles. When they observe a driver, dreamers think, *Doesn't she ever get excited about anything?* When they get excited, dreamers can really have fun. They don't try to contain their joy and aren't worried about what others will think. They just *feel* it.

Three-year-old Laura was at an outdoor family concert. Suddenly, her parents noticed that she wasn't with them anymore. Laura hadn't strayed far. She was dancing alone on a small hill, feeling the music. This usually somewhat introverted dreamer was totally lost in the joy of the moment.

Perhaps this deep experience of joy is one reason that dreamers make such wonderful actors. Although drivers are naturals at acting out anger and diplomats communicate sadness poignantly, dreamers are gifted at expressing the full range of emotion in all its extremes with little or no dramatic training.

Five-year-old Cammie went to a baseball game with her family and some friends. When her mother looked back at some pictures taken that night, she saw an almost comical change from one picture to the next. In the first picture, Cammie was definitely angry. In the next, joyous. In the next, she was almost in tears. In the entire roll of film, it seemed that no emotion was repeated.

In the blink of an eye, dreamers can swing from joy to deep sadness. Compassionate and strongly attached to friends and family, dreamers are especially prone to grieving over lost loved ones, the death of a pet, and the suffering of people around the world. Parents have brought dreamers for counseling because they were grieving family members who died before they were born. Able to imagine what a relationship might have been like with a grandfather, the child genuinely grieves the loss of the relationship. Less-relational drivers cannot imagine such feelings.

Judy recalls the death of her neighbor's dog, Thatcher, whom she frequently had for sleepovers at her house. After her mother told her the mixed breed collie had eaten poison and died, eleven-year-old Judy retreated to her room, sobbing. When she could cry no more, she went to her shelf, pulled off a porcelain figurine that closely resembled the dog, and put it on the floor of her room. Then she pleaded with God to bring the dog to life by turning the porcelain dog into her Thatcher. When that didn't work, Judy wrote a poem in tribute to her friend, which moved her mother and the neighbors to fresh tears over the dog's death.

The Ideal of Kindness

Dreamers hold strong personal beliefs about many things from theology to politics to education. But no ideas affect their emotional state more completely than beliefs about human behavior. Being more abstract than concrete or literal, dreamers more than any other cognitive style focus on the subtle, underlying meaning of communication. Always attuned to the affective aspect of behavior, idealistic dreamers expect a lot from their parents and teachers.

Dreamers expect all adults to meet the ideal of kindness. Although they may not treat others with kindness, dreamers want to be treated kindly and respected at all times. They want to be *asked*, not *told* what to do. That is not always possible because asking implies a choice that may not exist. Still, how things are stated is important. Your child may perceive constant reminders as nagging and may refuse to cooperate.

Sometimes a child gets into a pattern of interaction with parents in which the child responds only when the parent raises his or her voice. This pattern is created by parental inconsistency and failure to take action on the first warning. If your dreamer is in this pattern, his behavior will change only when your behavior changes.

For some parents, talking in "serious softness" is helpful. Rather than becoming louder to let your child know you mean business, try using a quiet voice or even whisper in the child's ear when you give your one warning. Keeping things quiet prevents humiliation and keeps her from being able to focus on your anger rather than on her lack of cooperation. If you yell, your child says internally, "See, I'm not so bad. My *mother* isn't being nice."

In trying to be both kind and consistent, you need to remember that even when being lovingly guided, dreamers sometimes protect their sensitive spirits by blaming others. They usually know that they are at fault, and they blame themselves internally while pointing a finger at others in an effort to keep your approval. But some children, especially very young dreamers, protect their self-esteem by imagining themselves to be innocent of the offense. The depth of the young dreamer's imagination often results in some interesting stories.

> **Dreamers sometimes protect their sensitive spirits by blaming others.**

When Sandy was five, she wanted to see a particular doctor in a group dental practice, even though that dentist was not in. She was a little afraid of going to the dentist, so to psych herself up in the car on the way she repeatedly said, "I get to see my Dr. Jones today." Her mother, realizing she would be disappointed, kept telling her that Dr. Jones would not be there. The dreamer became belligerent: "I *will* get to see my Dr. Jones today." When they arrived at the office, Sandy went happily into Dr. Smith's office and came out smiling, much to the mother's relief. Back in the car, she said, "I got to see my Dr. Jones today." Astounded, her mother said, "That was not Dr. Jones!" To which Sandy screamed, "Yes, it was! Yes, it was! He just had a different head!"

This mother could have punished Sandy for yelling and lying, but she did not. It was all she could do not to burst out laughing. Sandy was not lying in the classic sense. She believed what she was saying. Had Mom yelled at her, the mother would have acted unkindly and unfairly in the dreamer's eyes; in her mind, she had her facts straight. Parents may unwittingly respond in ways that seem completely brutal by dreamer logic. Because of their sensitivity, these painful events are more damaging to dreamers than to other children.

The Ideal of Justice

As sensitive as dreamers are about how they are treated, they can be equally sensitive about how others are treated. If dreamers see another child being spoken to unkindly, they tend to rally to the side of that child to provide comfort. Some even retaliate for another, having a bit of the vigilante spring from their idealism. When adults mistreat another child, dreamers can become enraged. Your dreamer child may be more outwardly upset than the victim. When adults violate dreamer ideals, dreamers can confront the adults with amazing audacity.

When Ben's father was unfairly fired, the teenager went to the father's place of business and yelled at the boss. When filled with righteous indignation, dreamers can be fearless.

If a dreamer does not defend the innocent or the underdog, she experiences tremendous guilt. In the fourth grade, Rita was included in an "in" crowd of girls led by a mean-spirited driver. In what was treated as a game, the leader would select a child to be out of the group for a week or so, and the others would go along.

One week, Rita's best friend was ousted. Not wanting to be outside the popular crowd, Rita was afraid to confront the ringleader. She was racked with guilt and began to have stomachaches. After a few days of misery, Rita finally confessed to her mother her silent participation in the vicious activities of the group. The dreamer then went to her friend and apologized, ignoring the popular girls. Soon, others still within the group stood up to the group leader, and the in/out game was abandoned. Everyone benefited when this dreamer's deeply held ideals overpowered her need for popularity.

In all aspects of life, fairness and kindness become intertwined for the dreamer. Fairness without kindness is not enough to earn a dreamer's respect. Even when you are kind, a dreamer youngster may not understand fairness in the way you as an adult do. You have a better perspective on time and realize that equal treatment overall does not always mean equal treatment moment by moment. The dreamer, who so loves being favored, sees a sibling receiving special attention and is all too quick to say, "That's not fair!" Although doers make this comment, too, practical children are more likely than dreamers to intentionally manipulate a fairness-conscious parent. Practical children often have a realistic understanding of give-and-take. Dreamers know only how they feel at that moment.

Becca's parents say she was a "thunderstorm" as a child. Every mood came suddenly—first the hail, then torrential rain, and then the sun shone through. One day, four-year-old Becca injured her younger brother and older sister, albeit unintentionally. But when her mom stopped her cleaning to comfort the siblings, Becca was deeply offended. "You never snuggle me!" she cried. "You never give me hugs." Despite Mom's reminders of several instances that day when she had been loved and hugged, the little "thunderstorm" could not recall the tender moments.

Reactions and Overreactions

Because they hurt so deeply when their ideals are not met, dreamers are the most emotionally reactive of all cognitive styles. We've talked about their tendency to react stubbornly, but they can also react with extreme joy to beauty, play, personal achievement, and moments of wonder. Whether dreamers meet glory or tragedy along life's road, they cannot keep from reacting with strong emotion. Telling a dreamer to "ignore your feelings and don't respond" is like telling an Alka-Seltzer not to fizz. It's going to fizz every time.

When Jack was six, he and his younger brother Jared were playing in one corner of the room, while their baby brother Lawrence was playing on the bed. Lawrence was three and should have known not to dive off the bed onto his face. When Jack saw the blood everywhere from Lawrence's lip and nose, he began to cry. Although his parents didn't think that Jack was responsible for the accident, he felt guilty because he wasn't watching Lawrence. Later that night, after the other boys were asleep, Jack's parents could hear him crying softly and talking to himself, "Why wasn't I watching him? It's all my fault!"

Just as dreamers can feel guilty over the problems of siblings and peers, they also can be hurt by other children. Their sensitivity can make them almost a magnet for teasing and verbal harassment. Some dreamers react to teasing with tears, while others try to bully their way through difficult social situations.

Dana told a dreamer child who felt rejected by his peers, "When children tease, it is often because they are unhappy and hope to feel better by making others miserable." He thoughtfully responded, "I am the unhappy one who makes others miserable." Like this child, dreamers can try to lash out at others before they can be hurt. This action may keep peers at a distance for a time but results in an escalation of social problems.

Dreamers react strongly to discipline if they perceive it to be harsh or unfair. Some react tearfully with blaming statements such as, "Why are you yelling at me?" or self-blaming statements like, "I'm so stupid!" Others are openly angry and can go from anger to rage in a matter of seconds. Feeling hurt and angry, dreamers become stubbornly entrenched. When they feel rejected, some fantasize revenge; others respond passive-aggressively.

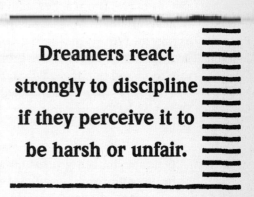

Dreamers react strongly to discipline if they perceive it to be harsh or unfair.

Passive-aggressive behavior is an intentional nonresponse to adult instructions. Your child may not appear angry. You may wonder if the passive-aggressive child has a hearing problem. This silent treatment is an expression of anger, as is slow response to an instruction. As a form of protest, dreamers can drag their feet when they believe a rule is ridiculous, whether or not they are angry with the person who made the rule.

George's family moved to a new house with a white kitchen floor. The new rule was to take off your shoes at the garage door. George thought that the rule was absurd, and he completely ignored it. He was the only one in the family with a particular type of shoe, and his shoe marks could be seen day after day. George's parents wondered if he was unable to remember the rule. He never openly said that "floors are meant to be walked on" and that he thought taking off your shoes was "stupid," but that was what he was communicating by refusing to remove his shoes.

Or perhaps we should say, that was what George *thought* he was communicating. Dreamers believe that they are making a point with a passive-aggressive response when their parents or teachers are not clued in to their message. Several dreamer children we have known have used passive-aggressive approaches as revenge against their perceived mistreatment by teachers.

A ten-year-old was asked in counseling, "What do you think that the teacher is thinking when you don't turn in your homework?"

"She will know that I am angry," was her response.

Of course, the teacher didn't know she was angry. Her teacher believed that she was lazy. This view of passive aggressive children as lazy and irresponsible is a common one. But if you discipline for laziness when anger is the problem, your dreamer will feel misunderstood and her anger will mushroom.

They'll be sorry for treating me this way! thinks the dreamer. When Mark Twain's Tom Sawyer was wrongly punished by Aunt Polly,

> he knew in his heart that his aunt was on her knees to him, and he was morosely gratified by the consciousness of it . . . he refused to recognize it. He pictured himself, lying sick unto death and his aunt bending over him beseeching a forgiving word, but he would turn his face to the wall and die with that word unsaid. Ah, how would she feel then? . . . She would throw herself upon him, and how her tears would fall like rain, and her lips pray God to give her back her boy and she would never, never abuse him any more![2]

We have seen dreamers who spend hours picturing or plotting revenge against a parent, teacher, or peer. Although most never act on the plans, pent-up anger can explode at any time. Sometimes when the dreamer verbalizes these fantasies, others laugh at them or brush them aside. No matter how far-fetched the ideas, you should listen to your dreamer's feelings because they are a clue to her emotional state.

In describing his Fifth Symphony, Gustav Mahler wrote, "It is the sum of all the suffering I have been compelled to endure at the hands of life."[3] What would you expect the symphony to sound like? A dirge perhaps? Sad and sentimental? When Phillip and Dana heard the symphony, Dana remembers thinking, *If that is about his sufferings, it is obvious that Mahler fought back.* The symphony is filled with mood swings from joy to anger. There is little that could be called sad or sentimental.

Like Mahler, when dreamers feel misunderstood, they can become extremely angry. If your dreamer decides he cannot please you, he will not make an effort to please you. He may purposely displease you if he thinks you are unreasonable or unfair. Dreamers make decisions about who is being unreasonable by listening to *what* is said and *how* it is said, by listening to tone of voice and observing facial expressions and body language.

When Meg was four, she and her mother visited Mrs. Grey, who had a baby, Zach. The baby was sitting on a small table. Meg, knowing that babies aren't supposed to be on tables, went over and pulled Zach off by yanking his feet. His head barely missed the edge of the table, and he landed on his bottom. Meg's mother and Mrs. Grey gasped. When she saw the look on Mrs. Grey's face, Meg was sure that her mother's friend hated her. Although Mrs. Grey told Meg that it was fine to get the baby off the table in another way and that she knew that Meg was only trying to help, Meg felt rejected. When she and her mother got into the car to go home, Meg threw her shoe angrily across the car. Her mother took Meg back into the Greys' house and asked her friend to reassure Meg. Mrs. Grey hugged Meg and said, "I love you very much." In the car on the way home, Meg got mad at her mother because she wouldn't stop for French fries and exclaimed, "I want to go live with Mrs. Grey!"

Getting Dreamers to Accept Guidance

Despite your child's explosive reactions, fear of making him angry should never keep you from setting appropriate limits. To reduce the potential for anger, use positive language when you give your child instructions. Instead of saying, "You aren't going anywhere until this room is cleaned up!" try, "As soon as this room is cleaned up, you can go outside."

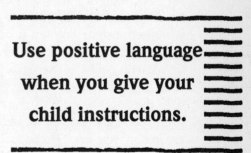

Use positive language when you give your child instructions.

Also use positive language whenever you address a group of children. Dreamers take group commands or reprimands personally. "The teacher hates *me*!" is a fairly common response to a teacher's reprimand of an entire class. Those with low self-esteem are prone to taking a group statement as a personal attack.

Even when not being disciplined, dreamers constantly observe the behavior of others and look for hidden meaning. Dreamers are sensitive to laughing by others in their proximity, assuming that they are being laughed at. Young dreamers do adorable things that they take very seriously. You may be tempted to laugh at your child too often. We have met dreamers who have vivid memories of being laughed at in their early years and who are still hurt by the experience whenever they think about it.

Linking Their Moods to the Moods of Others

Dreamers take the pain of others to heart. Particularly good at reading unhappiness in others, dreamers ride the waves of their own emotions and fears, and they also move up and down with others around them. They may not understand why someone is unhappy and may examine themselves to be sure that they are not in some way at fault. When dreamers are in dysfunctional families, we have found that they are rarely able to be objective about the problems and they may purposely place themselves in the middle of the conflict by attempting to be the peacemaker or allowing themselves to be the scapegoat so that parents won't fight.

By failing in school, eight-year-old Martin managed to get his divorced parents to work together on the same team. Whether or not he was doing it consciously, he began to fail several subjects whenever communication between his parents broke down. They would then rally together, go to meetings with the teachers, and ally once more for Martin's sake. This pattern of failure followed by intense parental attention and cooperation was not broken until a school counselor pointed it out to the parents and they began to work out their own communication problems. They finally realized that Martin could not separate himself from their conflict.

As a parent, when you experience stress that has nothing to do with the family, your dreamer child may read too much into the situation. Be clear and allow him to ask questions, but don't be too evasive. If you say, "There are problems at work and I am upset about them. I am not angry with you," he may feel happy that you are not angry. But he may wonder about the problems at work: *Is Mom about to lose her job? If she loses her job, will we lose our house? Will we be like those homeless people on TV? Will I have to go to a foster home?* and so forth. This train of thought may seem far-fetched, but with a dreamer's imagination it's possible.

If you attempt to protect a dreamer from difficult situations, she may perceive the stress anyway and imagine a situation far worse than the reality. At age five, Denise had seen ads on TV for mental hospitals. When her parents told her that her dad had to go to the hospital, Denise panicked. She thought her father was losing his mind when he was only having hernia surgery.

No matter how young, children can experience stress. Dreamers, therefore, have to deal with the stress that they soak up from the family and the stress from school and friendships. If you want to know whether a dreamer is experiencing stress at home, at school, or in the neighborhood, you can observe his changing emotions. The reactive dreamer is even more volatile when under stress.

Not all stress is caused by problems or unhappiness. Your child could simply be doing too much. Dreamers who are involved in too many activities begin to fall apart emotionally. Physical symptoms of stress include exhaustion, stomach problems, fevers, headaches, nausea, and susceptibility to viral illnesses. Emotional symptoms of stress involve increased emotionality and include weeping, tantrums, clinging, raging, destructiveness, and aggressiveness. When a dreamer experiences stress, especially if everyone else in the family is stressed, her emotionality can provoke anger in other family members. Then the provocative dreamer ends up angry and bitter over things said at a stressful moment.

Keeping a Long List of Wrongs

We want to think that children's lives are happy-go-lucky and that they are resilient. Dreamers are not resilient. They can be bitter because they have an amazing memory for feelings. They may remember more vividly the way the event felt than the event itself. The imaginative dreamer may even add details that did not occur.

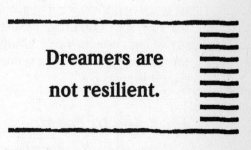

**Dreamers are
not resilient.**

If someone slights him, a dreamer may label that person unkind or unfair and then have difficulty moving beyond the label. This reaction is ironic, since a dreamer despises being stereotyped. He realizes when he is being labeled but may not realize that he is doing the same thing to others.

When Steve was eight, he was playing in a summer baseball league. After one game, his father noticed that he was kicking the dirt and wouldn't leave the field. When his dad reached him, he could see that Steve was upset. "Did you see that number twenty-one on the other team? He hates me!" said Steve.

"How can you know that he hates you?" responded Steve's dad. "You don't even know him."

"Well, he ran right past me and almost knocked me down."

Steve's dad, trying hard not to laugh, said, "But, Steve, you're playing second base!"

Because dreamers are observant, they look for patterns in the behavior of others in order to answer the "Does this person like me?" question and to decide whether the relationship has potential or should be avoided. As a defense against rejection, dreamer children with low self-esteem sometimes choose to avoid confident and successful peers because dreamers perceive them as popular and stereotype them as shallow or self-centered. Such labeling becomes a self-fulfilling prophecy because insecure dreamers constantly look for evidence to support their views.

Dreamers are less critical and more forgiving of people they think really like and approve of them. This can be a real saving grace in the family. If you make sure that your dreamer feels accepted, he may forgive times when you become impatient and lose your temper.

With peers, a dreamer may put up with almost abusive behavior from a "friend," wanting to see the best in that person and ignoring the rest. Your child may idealize family members who are unworthy of high esteem while villainizing someone who has been nothing but supportive. This tendency is especially likely when one parent is absent.

Learning to Forgive

If you want to encourage your dreamer to be forgiving rather than resentful, set an example by putting aside your detailed mental list of everything your child has ever done wrong. "Why do you always . . . ?" provokes the dreamer to retrieve her long emotional memories about you. This can escalate into arguments that severely hurt you and your child.

Because turmoil is destructive, try to create positive rather than negative memories. Begin by forgiving your child. Then when *you* make mistakes, use them as teaching opportunities. Asking for forgiveness allows you to show your dreamer the significance of contrition and the healing power of forgiveness.

Ron recalls an incident when he got angry with a teenage boy who was acting irresponsibly at his son Rich's party. He impulsively reacted and used a four-letter word in asking the boy what he was doing. "It got really quiet for a moment, but the boy shaped up fast. After I got home and reflected on my temper and my language, I knew an apology was in order. The next day, I called each of the boys who were at the party and asked for forgiveness, and I told their parents what happened.

"One boy said to my son later, 'My dad would *never* admit making a mistake.'" In this experience, Ron was able to teach his son something about going back and reconciling when emotions have been used in a way that doesn't bless another. To teach this lesson, he had to die to himself. Are you ready to model forgiveness and humility for your dreamer?

Chapter 7

Shelter from the Storm: Dreamers Need Some Tender Loving Care

For You have been a strength to the poor,
A strength to the needy in his distress,
A refuge from the storm.

Isaiah 25:4

When your dreamer hits stormy seas, you can be tempted to take the wheel, stand alongside like a friend, or jump ship. But a dreamer really needs you to be a shelter from the storm.

Being a shelter from life's harsh storms begins with listening.

Periodically examine what you are doing to help your dreamer weather the storms of life. Parents who provide effective shelter tend to share several qualities. They are good listeners, encourage confidence, accept the child's emotionality, and let the dreamer know that being different is wonderful!

Trying to change a child into another cognitive style does not help her face life realistically. Rather than stimulating success,

parents who try to toughen up a dreamer may contribute to the child's feeling of being a failure for not being strong. In contrast, if you provide the emotional protection and encouragement your dreamer needs, there will be more good times ahead for both of you.

Being a shelter from life's harsh storms begins with listening. To be a good listener, you need to focus on feelings, not just words. Because a dreamer does not always say what he means, reflect the feelings and thoughts you are hearing so that he can clarify both.

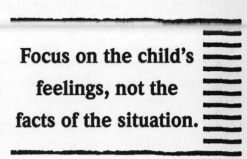

Focus on the child's feelings, not the facts of the situation.

We'll deal in detail with some examples of positive listening later. For now, let's think through a few key points about listening skills.

First, focus on the child's feelings, not the facts of the situation. Allow the facts to come to light gradually as your child feels safe to reveal them. Your child can't process the events fully until he deals with the feelings.

Second, be sympathetic to your child's feelings without going overboard. If your child has been called a name, for example, try saying, "It upsets me that anyone would use that word about another person. I know that must have hurt."

Third, communicate that you have confidence in your child's ability to handle the situation. Although you may not feel totally confident, dreamers do much bet-ter if they hear, "You can do it!"

Fourth, affirm your child's com-passion and ability to be kind in the face of adversity. Your affirmation

Be sympathetic to your child's feelings without going overboard.

creates an environment in which your child will be more likely to desire and initiate reconciliation rather than react with stubbornness and anger. Avoid giving advice to a child who has the resources to solve the problem for herself.

No matter how supportive you are, however, there are problems that your dreamer cannot solve alone. Some situations permit your intervention and some are beyond your control. For example, your child might be rejected because he thinks and acts differently. You will never be able to change the dreamer's inborn cognitive style to help him be better accepted.

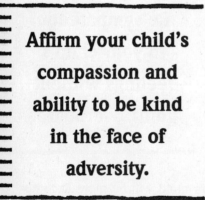

Communicate that you have confidence in your child's ability to handle the situation.

Your child may tell you how much she wants a certain girl or group to like her. Respond with statements about how to accept and value her own uniqueness. Avoid overreacting or overprotecting because your anger over the treatment of your child feeds her anger.

Selfish Anger and Righteous Indignation: Teaching Dreamers the Difference

We know that some members of our profession say that all feelings are good. In our view, plenty of feelings are downright destructive. Among these self-defeating emotions are self-pity and selfish anger of the type: "I want what I want and I have a right to it!" In listening to your child, you want to be sure that you aren't encouraging childish selfishness and self-pity. Let your child know you heard him, but don't reward his selfishness by giving in. Because of the tendency to become angry over circumstances, a dreamer needs to learn the difference between selfish anger and anger over injustice. If anger over injustice is encouraged, selfish anger can lose its stronghold in your child's life.

Affirm your child's compassion and ability to be kind in the face of adversity.

Whether or not your child's emotional state is justified, she may not be teachable when she is mad. Anger and hurt are often intertwined, and a hurting child can be overly sensitive to anything you say at that moment. Dreamers are more receptive to new information or confrontation if they don't realize at first that it has anything to do with them.

Do you know the biblical story of Nathan and David? Nathan was a prophet sent from God to confront David about the murder of Uriah the Hittite, husband of Bathsheba. Nathan started with this story:

> "There were two men in one city, one rich and the other poor. The rich man had exceedingly many flocks and herds. But the poor man had nothing, except one little ewe lamb which he had bought and nourished; and it grew up together with him and with his children. . . . It was like a daughter to him. And a traveler came to the rich man, who refused to take from his own . . . herd to prepare one for the wayfaring man who had come to him; but he took the poor man's lamb and prepared it for the man who had come to him." So David's anger was greatly aroused against the man, and he said to Nathan, "As the LORD lives, the man who has done this shall surely die!" . . . Then Nathan said to David, "You are the man! . . . You have killed Uriah the Hittite . . . ; you have taken his wife to be your wife" (2 Sam. 12:1–14).

David was a dreamer and Nathan knew it. He knew that David was a compassionate man whose defenses would drop if he thought Nathan was talking about someone else's unjust behavior. David judged himself.

Tools for Gently Teaching Life's Lessons

Although dreamers learn best from experience, stories and parables are powerful teaching tools because they touch the hearts and challenge the minds of dreamers. Nathan used a story to show David his error. Jesus used parables like that of the seed and the sower to communicate spiritual truth (Matt. 13:3–9). Why not tell your child Bible stories, hypothetical tales, and fables from time to time rather than give a lecture? If you use stories to teach, don't point out the moral. Intrigue your dreamer child by letting him guess the meaning.

Role playing can also be a teaching method. Suppose that your daughter has decided to be kinder to the bully in her class. Part of you wants to say, "Avoid that kid. You'll only get hurt." By saying that, you are discouraging compassion in a child who can only ignore insults when she has sympathy for the person insulting her. Try praising your daughter's courage and character. Then to add some real-world experience in an emotionally safe setting, role-play the next meeting with the bully to give her confidence and an idea of what could go wrong.

When jazz singer Ernestine Anderson was a child, she suffered racist taunting from white children. She remembers how her grandmother helped her learn to handle it:

> Whenever I had a problem, I would always go to my grandmother, and somehow the problem would get solved. . . . There was something about sitting in this swing and swinging back and forth, that just sort of calmed me down, with her talking to me. So I came home in a rage this time saying, "I hate 'em, I hate 'em." And she sat there and started swinging me back and forth until I calmed down, and then she said in a very soothing voice, "Before you go to bed tonight, I want you to say a prayer for those people."
>
> I loved my grandmother so much, but I found myself saying, "I can't do it."
>
> And she said, "Well, you have to, because you can't carry hate in your heart for anybody, for any man."[1]

This grandmother appealed to her granddaughter's compassion. She never excused the racist acts. She never told her granddaughter not to hurt. She used the child's dreamer strengths to help her cope with difficult people.

Want to know how much your child already understands about human relationships? Make the most of teachable moments like Ernestine Anderson's grandmother did. Use events you observe at the mall or other impersonal examples to test your child's insight. She may understand far more about successful social behavior and tough issues like forgiveness than she is able to act on in the heat of the moment.

Helping Dreamers Handle Harassment

Ernestine Anderson's grandmother was able to give her skills to help with the harassment she experienced. Some situations will arise that require more active intervention. Any child can be a victim of peer harassment, but the reactive dreamer makes an interesting target for the insensitive or angry peer. A friend of ours, Melanie Harrison Wofford, has written her story of harassment and how her parents responded:

Seventh grade is an awkward time for many young girls, and most of my friends were no exception. For me it was extremely painful. Gawky, peering through glasses as thick as soda bottles, I had no self-confidence. My bright red hair was not considered an asset either!

A couple of the boys in the class decided to make me the class joke. I've learned since that as a dreamer my sensitivity made me a magnet for this type of teasing, but at the time I thought, *What have I done to deserve this?*

The boys barked at me as I passed them in the hall. I would walk into the classroom and scrawled on the board would be, "Harrison is ugly!" or "Harrison is a dog." Sometimes it was written on my desk as well. Several teachers saw what was happening, but did nothing.

I kept thinking that if I didn't react this would stop. I chose alternate routes to classes and hid in the bathroom during lunch. Once I bit my lip severely to keep from crying. All attempts failed and my obvious pain encouraged the ringleaders. One Saturday I awoke to find my yard had been rolled with toilet paper. I had a glimmer of hope. In our twisted seventh-grade society this action was usually the highest form of flattery. As I surveyed what I assumed was the end of the long siege, I saw that they had written "UGLY" in huge letters. I was crushed. I begged my brother to help me clean it up before my parents saw it. Too terrified to tell them what was going on at school, I was sure that my parents would do something to make things worse.

In our small southern town, we still had social dancing classes. Everyone in the seventh grade took social dancing from Mr.

Lawrence, who had taught all of our parents to waltz, rumba, and foxtrot before us. The classes were held in a large church basement that had support pillars inconveniently scattered throughout. Week after week the boys would scramble for the most popular girls. Last man out got Harrison.

One night Mr. Lawrence decided to mix things up a bit. At several points during our dance he would say, "Next partner," and each boy was to rotate around the circle to the next girl in line. At last, I wouldn't be singled out as the booby prize!

But the boys had a plan to foil Mr. Lawrence. They all agreed that every time a boy rotated to me, he should dance with one of the support posts and not even look at me. I felt so betrayed by all my other classmates who laughed. At first, the teacher didn't notice their little game. I stood painfully alone watching tears fall onto my shoes as boy after boy danced with the post. Suddenly Mr. Lawrence *did* notice. He was irate! He immediately yanked the two ringleaders outside and expelled them from the class.

I managed to hold myself together during the excruciating carpool ride home. Barely making it to the door of my home, I exploded into tears. Both my parents held me as all the pain and shame rushed out. My father was livid. My mother was distraught. I begged them not to call the boys' parents. They managed to calm me down, and then my mother called every family.

Most of the boys were grounded indefinitely and the harassment immediately stopped. My parents' wisdom, tenderness, and foresight amaze me now. They resisted the urge to rush me to forgiveness. My father allowed me to see his outrage, knowing that his reaction would in part determine the behavior I would accept from men in the future. My parents never told me that it was time to get over it; they let me grieve at my own pace and listened endlessly to my feelings.

My mother recognized my need for belief in my physical beauty. Knowing that it would not meet my need, she did not try to convince me of my inner beauty. Instead she retold the story of the ugly duckling and promised me that one day I was going to be a beautiful woman. I placed my hopes in a lovely fairy tale, and Mom placed hers in an all-powerful God who could make her promises come true. As I look back at my seventh-grade picture, I smile. I'm sure she felt He was going to need quite a lot of that power!

During the next two years I experienced a metamorphosis. The braces came off, the glasses were replaced with contacts, and suddenly my body was not quite so shapeless. Later, during my senior year in high school, I was voted homecoming queen.

That same year God gave me the ability to express forgiveness to the boys who had hurt me. I went to the ringleader and said, "I want you to know that I forgive you." He was shocked. It was the beginning of a friendship that has lasted to this day.

I am a grown woman now, with two young daughters of my own. It is only through the experience of loving them that I fully understand the precious gift my parents gave to me during that most difficult time in my childhood.

My very humble and practical parents are not so impressed by their actions. In retrospect my mother says simply, "You do what you must for your child." I marvel at her and wonder if she knows the greatness of her gift. Eighteenth-century American painter Benjamin West once said, "A kiss from my mother made me a painter." How well I know. A kiss from my mother made me a swan.

Several key elements of this story point to guidelines to help you know when to intervene. First, is your child able to handle the situation alone? In this case, Melanie had made every effort to address the situation by ignoring it, but it had not improved. Second, are other parents unaware of their children's behavior? Although some parents are defensive, most want to address their children's character flaws, not ignore them. Third, have other adults been aware of the problem and failed to take appropriate action? If another adult is not doing his job, that is the place to start.

Your Role with Other Adults

Another classification of problems absolutely requires your intervention. These are situations in which the harassing party is an older child, a significantly larger child, or an adult. If an adult, even a family member, is ridiculing your child, you should not tolerate it. Or if an adult is behaving like a child by arguing, criticizing, or teasing, you should intervene.

Because dreamers respond so strongly to emotional stress, there are times when your dreamer will be the first child in a group to experience problems that are affecting others. Consider the needs of other children. Don't pull your child out of the situation without attempting to address the problem or inform other parents.

Harry was showing signs of low self-esteem because of a negative group of older boys in his school. His driver mother thought that he, being so sensitive, was overreacting to normal teasing. Later she found out that the harassment of another child, Don, was so severe that he was unable to cope and had become suicidal. Had this mother made more of an effort to validate her son's experiences with other parents she might have been more sympathetic to Harry and could have addressed the problem with school officials.

Other Ports in a Storm: Teachers, Coaches, and Youth Leaders

If you are going to allow your child to fall flat, you need to create a safe place for him to tumble. Teachers, coaches, and youth group leaders can dole out consequences for your dreamer child. Unfortunately, a few may do this vindictively or cruelly. Selecting the right people to surround your dreamer child is crucial.

For example, you can pull him from the team that has a verbally abusive coach. Realize that if you leave your child in a bad situation just because he is gifted at the sport, soon he may be losing his temper as much as the coach does. And then the coach will yell at your child for yelling at the referee. What a terrible learning environment!

If your dreamer demonstrates poor sportsmanship, you want the coach handling that problem to be self-controlled and respectful of others. The words have meaning from a coach who shows maturity when he speaks to a player.

Whenever possible, look for adults who are willing to adapt their leadership style in the classroom or on the ball field to the cognitive styles of the individual children. Ron tells how his son responded to one coach:

"Adam loves basketball. On his school team, the coach saw Adam's potential and was trying to work with him to improve his play. Unfortunately, whenever Adam or any other player made mistakes, the coach would loudly point out those errors in front of the teammates. Adam was convinced that the coach didn't like him. Although his mom and I emphasized that his coach genuinely wanted to help him, Adam was not convinced and never responded well to this coach's style."

Many teachers and coaches see the need to adapt their style to the unique needs of children. However, if your dreamer has unusual difficulty with a coach or teacher, a private conference between you and the adult may produce positive results and keep the problem from escalating.

Getting Family Members on Your Team

We have seen a few grandparents and other family members who have a tendency to create poor learning environments for dreamers. Some are concerned with the child's sensitivity and are too lenient. Others see the child's behavior toward parents and say to themselves, *Just give me that child for a few days and that would stop! I'll let her know who's the boss!* Either extreme creates an unproductive environment for learning from life. In the lenient home, the child learns how to manipulate, whine, and demand, with the overarching lesson being "all behavior is acceptable." In the authoritarian home where failure is not allowed, the child learns to fear, sneak, and repress, with the overarching lesson being "behavior is bad if you get caught."

Many parents depend on grandparents or other extended family members to care for children while they work. In most cases, that is a good choice. But if your extended family undermines your strategies for dealing with your child, why not consider other alternatives? When a dreamer falls, the right person should be there to pick her up.

Just as you can change, so can your family. We have had families come in, grandparents among the group, and try to develop a consistent approach for encouraging and disciplining a dreamer child. Try sharing a book like this one that explains the needs of your child. Say to your family, "I'm trying to do something about my child's behavior. It's important that we all understand him better. Can't we get on the same team and work together?"

Learning from Life

Children can learn some meaningful lessons through difficult situations and be empowered rather than scarred by the experiences. Since dreamers learn lessons in life better from direct experience than from verbal instruction or from observation of others' mistakes, creating situations in which dreamers can safely fall on their faces leads to some hard, but well-learned lessons. This allows you to pull out of the bad guy–punisher role and move into the shelter-comforter role. If you try to control every detail of your dreamer's life, you may breed resentment and never allow your child to experience productive failure.

> **Creating situations in which dreamers can safely fall on their faces leads to some hard, but well-learned lessons.**

When learning is painful, dreamers can experience for themselves the reality that even though there are bad times, eventually there are happy times again. Children's failures usually have an ending and can teach about healing. If your child is not constantly reminded of the failure, he can move forward. However, some events are so traumatic that progress is slow.

At sixteen, Laura had been protected during much of her early life from failure. If she wanted anything, she got it. She had never experienced any significant disappointment. Then one day a boyfriend broke up with her. She threatened suicide. Why? Because having never felt that kind of pain before, Laura did not believe that she would ever feel better.

When a dreamer is in the midst of situational depression, telling her, "You will feel better," never has the same impact as previous personal experiences of pain and recovery. A dreamer who can point to difficulties that worked out in the past is likely to have a sense of hope.

Some parents can't allow their child to fail, not because of the child's feelings, but because of their own. Have you ever said, "Why do you always embarrass me like this?" to your dreamer? A dreamer who discovers your fear of being embarrassed can be adept at acting out in public. You should never humiliate a child. But as long as the consequences come from life and not Mom and Dad, a dreamer with moderate to good self-esteem can handle a little embarrassment. The question is, can you?

Letting your child experience natural consequences means that sometimes you have to swallow your pride and stop worrying about what other people think. You should develop your own strategies for nurturing the character development of your child. An occasional failure can be a part of that process.

Raising a responsible child sometimes means stepping back. If you are really controlling, you might get a moderate amount of compliance from the dreamer at home. But as soon as your dreamer has any freedom, he may rebel and reject your values. It is better for a dreamer child to learn the hard lessons of life while he is young so that you can provide shelter and comfort. If you want him to learn that your rules and insights are wise, let him test those rules and insights at an age when the consequences of experimentation will not have lifelong implications.

Raising a responsible child sometimes means stepping back.

Sensitivity Turned Outward

Not all dreamers turn their sensitivity inward. And those who do can change. Many are deeply sensitive and empathetic toward others, wanting to be the shelter from the storm for their friends and family. By high school, your dreamer should begin showing greater sensitivity toward others than himself. If you want to nurture your dreamer toward this goal, notice and praise his compassionate spirit.

Having compassion also means feeling the pain of others. This pain moves the dreamer toward greater emotional maturity. You can play a key role in giving your dreamer appropriate outlets for compassion so that he does not end up expressing his need to be needed by attaching himself only to deeply troubled peers.

> **Appropriate opportunities for dreamer caregiving can be found through volunteer work.**

Appropriate opportunities for dreamer caregiving can be found through volunteer work with small children, older people, and people in hospitals. Service-oriented diplomats need little prodding, but dreamers may be fearful of an unfamiliar environment and may need coaxing to become involved. Many schools now require community service, and families can, too. Dreamers should have a choice of service, but it's okay to have a family rule that everyone must be involved in volunteer work.

Volunteerism can bring a dreamer in contact with dreamer adults who are not only compassionate but also successful and goal oriented. These positive models let your child know that dreamers can make a difference. That is especially important for a teen who believes that "there aren't *any* adults like me" and seeks models only from the peer group.

Dreamers and Their Hurting Friends

Even with outside activities, a dreamer will focus to some degree on the emotional needs of friends. Your child needs balanced friendships. Some hurting friends are okay if there are also some emotionally healthy friends. You can't force this balance, but you can gently guide her in this direction.

By making your home an inviting place where your child or teen will want to bring his friends, you will know what is going on among the peer group. If things seem to be out of balance, casually mention other options. Help your dreamer see that it is unkind to dismiss old friends or new acquaintances simply because they aren't like him or don't have obvious needs. Use feeling language and talk about being genuine and caring toward all types of people to encourage a variety of relationships.

In encouraging healthy friendships, don't push your dreamer toward any one peer because the person may then look somehow less appealing. And don't criticize your dreamer's current friends or his compassion for them.

If you attack your child's friends, you are triggering his need to protect them. He might have been considering severing the ties, but your criticism will send him back into his knight in shining armor role of defending the innocent. Instead, affirm him. Say something like, "You are really good at helping others. It can be draining at times, I'm sure. I hope you'll take some time out for yourself, to get recharged. Maybe spend some time with an old friend just to catch your breath."

Affirming and nurturing your child's emotional sensitivity lets her be who she was created to be. Providing shelter from life's storms communicates, "I understand."

Chapter 8

Getting the Big Picture: How Dreamers Learn

It is better to know some of the questions than all of the answers.

James Thurber

Rex transferred to a new school as a tenth grader. An introvert, he didn't immediately find friends. He went back to an old coping mechanism: reading. In every class, even shop and PE, he read. He particularly loved the fantasy of J.R.R. Tolkien. Soon, he began dressing like a medieval character. Everyone treated him as a "weird" young man, but academically, he was a star. He aced every class while reading books on completely unrelated subjects during the lectures. It was obvious that Rex could think about several things at once. And somehow, he blocked out the social isolation by filling every crevice of his mind. He didn't love school, but he loved learning.

> **All dreamers are born with a natural love for learning.**

Not all dreamers are academic successes, but all dreamers are born with a natural love for learning. A case in point is an outgoing eighth grader named Harold. "Harold has always been an under-achiever," began Mr. Todd. "He's very bright and he says that he likes school, but you'd never know it by his work. He seems to learn almost by osmosis. I stand right over him when he takes the tests and he finishes quickly. His test grades are excellent, and he is an active participant in discussion. But Harold never turns in the homework, except an occasional project. The day-to-day practice assignments that should take a bright child no more than a half-hour are apparently never done. I can't just excuse him from the work that the others are required to do. Besides, Harold needs to learn how to work, or he'll never make it in life. Not everything will come easy to him in the future.

"Harold's parents have been cooperative whenever I've contacted them," continued Mr. Todd, "but I refuse to mail all the assignments to the parents of an eighth grader. He's too old for that type of hand holding. His parents say they feel helpless because when they ask, he always says he has no homework. Should I let him eke by like this when I can see that he has so much potential?"

Perhaps you are surprised that we would use Harold as an example of a dreamer who loves learning. Yet, remember how Mr. Todd said Harold learned "almost by osmosis"? If he loves learning so much, why won't Harold do the homework? All over America, indeed all over the world, teachers like Mr. Todd are asking that question. A certain spark in a dreamer child lets teachers know the love for learning is there. What parents want to know is: How do we fan that spark into a blazing fire?

> **How do we fan that spark into a blazing fire?**

Global Learning

When we talk to parents, many ask, "Are dreamers right-brained?" Ever since the popular book *Drawing on the Right Side of the Brain* was published in 1979, there has been more of an awareness of the role that brain hemispheres play in learning and creativity.[1] In general, dreamers are more right-brained than left-brained. They gravitate toward the right-brained skills of color sensitivity, singing and music, shapes and patterns, art expression, visualization of images, and emotional expressiveness. But dreamers can also be gifted in language and reading, which are left-brained skills.

In her book *Unicorns Are Real,* Barbara Vitale offers suggestions for teaching children in a right-brained fashion. Although she addresses issues of dreamers who are so right-brained that they struggle with learning to read and do math, her approach is appropriate for any dreamer child. She includes intriguing activities with titles such as "Eating Color," "Intuitive Reading," "Air Writing," "Rainbow Letters," and "Singing Spelling."[2]

> **Dreamers tend to learn from the general to the specific.**

But understanding hemispheres of the brain doesn't tell the whole story. In learning style, dreamers are global or conceptual learners. The term *global* has been used to refer to the "big picture" cognitive style of dreamers. Seeing the big picture first, dreamers tend to learn from the general to the specific, rather than the specific to the general. They must understand the overarching concept to understand how the concept can be applied to specific situations. For the doer majority who must see specific examples to understand general concepts, this global thinking style is perplexing. "I understand what you're saying about teaching the concept," said one doer parent, "but I don't know *how* to teach the concept."

Before learning how to teach concepts, doer parents must first understand how truly global the dreamer's thinking is. When Dana was five, she and her parents learned something about her brother's cognitive style: "My mother told us that our male Siamese cat would be away for a few days to help a mommy cat make kittens. I didn't understand why a boy cat was needed for kittens to be born. My mother saw that I was going to persist until she answered the bigger question of how babies are made. She asked my older brother Marshall to leave the room. Marshall insisted that he wanted to hear, too. Confused, my mother responded, 'Your dad has talked to you about this.'

"Marshall replied, 'Oh, I know about people. I just don't know about cats.'"

Dana's parents assumed that in explaining about people, their son would generalize from that specific example to other mammals. If Marshall had been a doer, he probably would have made that generalization automatically. Nonglobal, doer learners gather specific examples and look for patterns that might indicate an overarching rule. These children accumulate information in a step-by-step process: A, then B, then C. This nonglobal processing is called *linear* or analytic logic.[3]

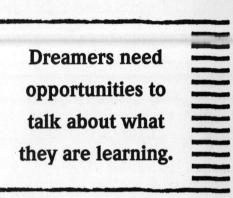

Dreamers need opportunities to talk about what they are learning.

Dreamers, on the other hand, are less concrete in their learning style. When they understand the global concept, thinking can jump from A to C, B to D, or even D to A. Because dreamer cognition depends on global concepts rather than available facts, original thinking can occur. The dreamer cannot always explain the source of the new ideas. It is indeed like a light bulb turning on or what has been called the "Aha!" experience.

The How-Tos of Global Learning

How do you teach global concepts if not by collecting facts? No two dreamers learn in exactly the same way, but a few general principles do apply:

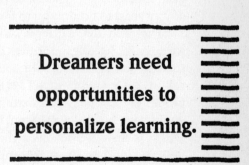

Dreamers need opportunities to personalize learning.

- Dreamers need opportunities to talk about what they are learning.
- Dreamers need opportunities to personalize learning by developing examples of applications of the subject matter that are relevant to them.

• Dreamers need individualized instruction. With that, your child or teen can move on after he has learned a concept or step and can spend more time on something he doesn't understand. Although dreamers do not learn new concepts well from practice assignments, homework can be helpful to you when you want to get a picture of what your dreamer does and doesn't comprehend. Examine the specific items missed rather than look at grades alone. A dreamer may make a careless mistake, being less interested in concrete details, and yet fully understand the general concept.

> **Dreamers need individualized instruction.**

Dreamers and Tests

Many dreamers do well on standardized achievement tests. Their excellent performance is a double-edged sword. High scores that mean placement in challenging classes may cause your child to be labeled an underachiever.

One mother told this story about her thirteen-year-old: "Olivia was coming up to the end of the seventh grade and it was time for the school Awards Night. As it happened, Olivia was failing two subjects, not involved in any clubs, and not playing any sports that year. It made logical sense to me that Olivia wouldn't be receiving any awards, so I didn't go to the program.

"The next day a friend called and asked why I wasn't at the Awards Night. She informed me that Olivia had received one of the top school awards. She had scored higher than anyone in the school on a standardized achievement test—in the ninety-ninth percentile overall. I was stunned! I knew Olivia was smart and could have been doing better, but this was astounding to me. Now, Olivia is grown and has a master's degree. I would *never* have believed it when she was thirteen."

Olivia had a knack for test taking. But she didn't score in the top percentile just by being a quick reader and a savvy guesser. She was retaining more of the academics than her grades indicated. In contrast to Olivia's experience, there are dreamers who test differently from other children and don't get the credit on standardized tests that their answers merit.

A university student gave four-year-old Eve an intelligence test. Because it was a test for children not yet able to read, all the questions were asked using pictures. The college student showed Eve a picture of a bird in a bird cage and said, "What is it?"

"Sad," Eve responded. She received a zero for her response. The testing company listed the only acceptable answers as "bird" and "cage."

Dreamers may respond in an unexpected manner to tests and teachers. In many grading systems, half or more of a student's grade is based on homework because turning in daily work is considered an indication of motivation and self-discipline. Practice assignments are an effective learning tool for linear thinkers. But since dreamers don't learn well from practice, they either already understand the concept and find the homework boring, or they don't understand the concept and find the homework impossible. By seventh or eighth grade, some dreamers stop doing all practice assignments. We'll suggest alternatives in chapter 9.

Learning Modalities

General learning styles, such as the dreamer's global style, are only one aspect of learning. There are tremendous differences within any cognitive style in how children learn. One aspect of learning that complements general learning style is what Cynthia Tobias has called learning modality or effective modes of learning.[4] One dreamer learns best in one mode, while another dreamer is strong in another learning modality. For this reason, it's helpful to understand the primary modes of learning: auditory learning, visual learning, and kinesthetic learning.

Auditory dreamers learn best by repeating auditory information to themselves. The information can be in the form of words, music, or other sounds that have meaning for them. Auditory dreamers read aloud, talk to themselves, put "boring" information that must be remembered to music, and enjoy talk radio and books on tape. If your child has remembered all the words to songs from a young age, you probably have an auditory learner. Those attracted to drama who have an easy time learning dialogue also demonstrate an auditory bent.

At age four, Jeremy was getting a ride home from the airport with his grandparents. They had flown all the way to France to get him for the summer. To help pass the time on the two-hour car trip to his grandparents' house, his grandmother put in the tape of the Broadway musical, *Fiddler on the Roof.* By the time they arrived at home, Jeremy had memorized the words to every song. Not only that, but he understood the story. He kept telling his grandparents about the girl who was going away to be with her boyfriend who was in prison. "But she *wanted* to go," he emphasized.

Visual dreamers learn by observing visual information and by making mental pictures. Deborah tells us that since childhood she has noticed a particular symbol whenever it is woven into fabric, can be seen in a tile pattern, or is in a diagram. She hesitates to describe her experience to others because she fears they may think she's kooky.

This experience is not unusual for visual dreamers. The symbol is a basic concept that they find applied to many apparently unrelated specific situations. Visual learners notice such patterns and use them as memory cues. But dreamers may not notice the "meaningless" concrete visual information that stands out to linear learners. For example, visual doers often say they notice any scrap of trash on the side of the road, yet no matter how visual dreamers are, such concrete details can escape notice.

Visual dreamers have one advantage over visual doers. Because they have an easier time inventing mental pictures, dreamers don't need pictures in books as learning cues. No matter how visual, doers can't always visualize the story when reading. For them, pictures are essential. But dreamers need no pictures. When a novel has been made into a film, it's dreamers you hear in a movie theater whispering, "The house shouldn't look like that. She's too tall to be Emily. What were they thinking when they cast *her* as Anne? The hair is all wrong!"

For people who learn in a hands-on manner, the modality of choice is called the kinesthetic mode. *Kinesthetic dreamers* enjoy moving about and manipulating their environment. These dreamers are in constant motion. Building, experimenting, sculpting, drawing, and cooking keep kinesthetic dreamers involved in active learning.

Kinesthetic dreamers may seem less "dreamy" than their auditory and visual counterparts because they rarely sit and daydream, but they are just as imaginative and sensitive. Their tactile senses can be acute; for example, a dreamer remembered differences in types of rocks by recalling their texture.

At age four, Christopher was sensitive to the way his clothing felt. It was an indication of a kinesthetic bent, rather than a way to control his mom, because he did everything in a kinesthetic manner. At that age, he could build almost anything, including clothing, with Legos. Much of his play involved building with or manipulating three-dimensional objects. It made sense that he would be so three-dimensional because his mother is a sculptor. But she says she did little to direct his play. She provided Christopher with materials, and he took it from there.

If, like Christopher, a child learns best when engaged in hands-on projects such as making three-dimensional maps or conducting chemistry experiments, he is likely to be a kinesthetic learner. If a child cannot sit still, but does not seem to be learning from all that activity, she may not be kinesthetic. Children and teens with an attention deficit disorder with hyperactivity (ADHD) are moving but may struggle to concentrate on anything long enough to learn to their potential (see chapter 11).

Teaching Styles for Different Modes of Learning

Some dreamers have strengths in more than one modality, while others are strong in only one learning mode. Understanding the three modalities helps when trying to teach a complex concept. For example, many parents assume that if a child is not understanding a concept, a slower step-by-step presentation is the answer. But if a presentation has been ineffective once, going slowly is more likely to frustrate the boredom-sensitive dreamer than to teach the concept.

Many dreamers have told us that when they are having difficulty understanding something, it is helpful to present the information using a different modality. Changing from auditory to visual, or kinesthetic to auditory, can help the light bulb click on for your dreamer child.

In her book *Unlocking Your Child's Learning Potential,* Cheri Fuller provides insightful suggestions for teaching according to your child's learning mode. We won't go into too much detail, but here are a few of Fuller's principles. Visual learners normally have good reading comprehension. But they also need to be taught using pictures, maps, charts, and other visual cues. Auditory learners like audiotapes, discussions, information put to music, and guest speakers as teaching tools. And the kinesthetic learners need to be able to move around while they learn. Learning centers, movable chairs rather than stationary desks, and hands-on projects are adaptations a parent or teacher can make to the kinesthetic learner.[5]

Many other aspects of learning can be helpful to you in teaching a dreamer. To read more about the diversity of learning issues, we recommend *The Way They Learn* by Cynthia Tobias. Far too rare are dreamers who are being taught in the way they learn. Don't try to address too many learning issues at once. No one can provide a perfect educational experience for any child. Learning style information is simply one tool among many that you can use to enrich your dreamer's life and understand him better. With dreamers, a little understanding goes a long way.

Chapter 9

Turning the Spark into a Flame: Dreamers in School

Education is not the filling of a pail, but the lighting of a fire.

William Butler Yeats

Does the following student sound like one of the dreamers we've been discussing?

He hated the strict discipline, the learning by memorization, and the unwillingness to consider new ideas. It was too "Prussian" for the dreamy, thoughtful boy who wanted to be left alone. . . . Later, he called his elementary school teachers "sergeants" and his high school teachers "lieutenants."

Being forced to learn without questioning made him suspicious of all authority. He would criticize and doubt what his fellow students took on faith. This was probably the best preparation for his later work. It gave him the inquiring mind that would not accept something because some great name in the past had said it was so. . . .

. . .The teenager still refused to believe anything he read until he had proved it for himself. He questioned everything. "How do we know this is true?" and even "What is truth?" he asked.

The boy had a great mind. It is said that "he could hold an idea in his mind for months. He could examine the problem from different angles and make daring guesses as to the answer." Despite his rebellious attitude toward authority, this teen sounds like the class valedictorian, right? Think again. He left high school before getting his diploma, and his parents feared he had forfeited any hopes of a decent career. He left his native country and applied to a technical school that did not require a diploma, only the passing of an entrance exam. From all the clues, you probably know by now the man of whom we speak: "With his expulsion from high school and his inability to pass the examination for technical school, the future did not look bright for Albert Einstein."[1]

A genius has a better chance of overcoming a disastrous school experience. Nevertheless, the lesson of Einstein's early life is a point well taken. Don't estimate the dreamer's future success based solely on what his school experience has been. He may surprise you.

Dreamers Take Boredom Personally

Although kinesthetic dreamers have the greatest difficulty sitting still, all dreamers handle boredom poorly. Mary describes her elementary school experience this way: "I could spot a boring lecture from the first few sentences, and it would almost be like a switch went off in my head. 'Oh, no! Another boring lesson!' and I would begin to think about lunch or a book I had read. Daydreaming was a favorite pastime, but usually I tried to keep one-quarter of my attention on what was being said, in case I was called on.

All dreamers handle boredom poorly.

"One day I glanced up to see my name written on the board. I was aghast! Only bad children's names went on the board. The teacher called me into the hall and told me that I was being 'rebellious.' I was in shock. What could she mean? All my assignments were always turned in on time, and I made 100 on most tests. *She must know something about me that I don't,* I thought. I felt ashamed and began crying when I realized that she was upset that I didn't enjoy her lectures. By the next year, though, I was less concerned with pleasing the teacher and more frustrated by any boring assignment.

"I remember how disappointing school was to me. In the second grade I heard that we would soon be starting science. I was so excited! But when the teacher began with methods of identifying clouds as cumulus, nimbus, etc., I felt betrayed! Who cares what you call them. I wanted to know: *Why* were clouds so beautiful? How did they get there? Why does it rain? The teacher, of course, was trying to keep things on the second grade level. Because the teacher appeared to be refusing to teach the things that interested me, I shut down. I made my first F. This embarrassed me terribly, but not because people would think I didn't know science. I could have cared less about that dumb science class. I was only embarrassed because my sisters passed that subject when they were my age and because I didn't think I should be failing stupid subjects. If it had been a challenging subject, a failure might have been okay."

Meaning Makes Learning Fun

What Mary described is a common experience among dreamers. At the core of many school problems is the dreamer belief that all learning should be fun. Any child enjoys having fun, but not all children assume that learning *should* be fun. For dreamers, anything short of this ideal is an outrage, an insult to their intellect.

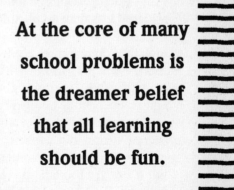

> At the core of many school problems is the dreamer belief that all learning should be fun.

Because dreamers are born with a natural love for learning, a well-intentioned parent or teacher who insists on pushing the idea that "life isn't always fun" can damage this love for learning. But if the love for learning is not squelched during the school years, dreamers are lifelong learners. Dreamers can be happy to get out of a particularly rigid academic setting, but they are not trying to escape learning.

For dreamers, meaningful learning is fun. Dreamers want to learn things that touch their hearts and souls. Their questions are rarely related to "How will I use this in life?" Instead, dreamers want to know how and why things work the way they do. They seek abstract principles in the subject matter being studied; their learning and thinking cannot be reduced to a mechanical model of feeding the information in and spitting the information out.

The Dangers of Input-Output Teaching

If you try to slow down a dreamer to force her into a mechanical input-output model, behavior problems can occur in the classroom or at home during homework time. This acting out can range from daydreaming to open disrespect to organized efforts to enlist others in active rebellion against the teacher. Adults who teach in a manner that the dreamer finds boring violate the dreamer's passion for learning. Feeling this offense deeply, the dreamer could respond with passive-aggressive behavior, openly expressed anger, or a unique solution to the problem.

Young Johann Sebastian Bach took organ lessons from the village organist. But Bach didn't like the pace of study. At night, he secretly copied the texts from more advanced composers so that he could learn them. Doesn't sound like Bach was a lazy youth, does it? Yet he wouldn't follow the teacher's approach and was considered less than an ideal student.[2]

Eventually, if dreamers become disillusioned with lessons or school, they may express less anger and more cynicism, deciding, "School isn't my thing." When Sarah was in kindergarten, her teacher thought she was too active and inattentive. Why she wouldn't even hold her pencil right! Each day, the teacher went over the same things, but stubborn Sarah resisted. In class she appeared strong, but every day after school she cried all the way home. Her flame almost went out.

But it's never too late to reignite the fire. One good teacher can recharge a disused dreamer mind. When Sarah was in the seventh grade, she had a teacher who was more interested in her ideas than her penmanship. When graded for content, not neatness, Sarah did well. She began to express herself much more in writing, although she still didn't hold the pencil right.

Albert Einstein, like Sarah, had one teacher he remembered fondly. A biographer describes the teacher this way:

There was one teacher in the gymnasium, named Ruess, who really tried to introduce the students to the spirit of ancient culture. He also showed them the influence of these ancient ideas in the classical German poets and in modern German culture. Einstein, with his strong feeling for everything artistic and for all ideas that brought him closer to the hidden harmony of the world, could hardly have enough of this teacher. He aroused in him a strong interest in the German classical writers, Schiller and Goethe, as well as in Shakespeare....

The fact that in the midst of all the mechanical drilling he was sometimes able to spend an hour in an artistic atmosphere made a great impression on him. The recollection of this class remained very vivid in his mind.[3]

It's little wonder that later in life, Einstein said, "It is the supreme art of the teacher to awaken joy in creative expression and knowledge."[4]

Focusing on things that interest a dreamer can jump-start a sluggish child. Dreamers want to know, "Why is this subject important to people in my family, my community, or the world at large?" As we have said, by "important," dreamers do not mean useful. Their concerns are with the hearts and minds of others. This concern for humankind leads to an interest in subjects such as social studies, psychology, sociology, and religion. Other "fire-starter" subjects include art, music, and literature.

But what about more objective subjects? Can dreamers become interested in mathematics, chemistry, or physics? Einstein did. Dreamers find almost any subject interesting if it is presented creatively, conceptually, and with an eye for the meaningfulness of the topic to people and their relationships. For example, a bread-making machine may seem frivolous to the dreamer. But if the machine is discussed in terms of the aromas in the home or the shared enjoyment of the family—in other words, not in terms of efficiency but in terms of its impact on lives—the machine becomes more interesting. Learning how the machine works becomes fun for the dreamer.

All subjects can be personalized. For the teacher who has limited time and specific texts to use, making the material personal may seem too much to ask. And yet, it is the only way to engage the dreamer in the subject.

In high school, Jess had a drafting teacher who made the subject come alive by allowing the class members to design their own solutions to interesting problems. They might have to design a bridge across a canyon or a tunnel under the sea. It was a class that Jess thoroughly enjoyed. When he went to college, his first major was economics. But he quickly became frustrated, feeling that he couldn't help others enough by forecasting events. Then he thought back to that drafting class. Jess changed his major to engineering, believing that as an engineer, he could make a difference in people's lives.

Making Sure the Building Blocks Are in Place

Just as any subject can be made personal, any subject can be made impersonal and dull. As Mr. Barber, the world history teacher, explained the rise and fall of the Soviet Union in monotone, Bill was daydreaming. Because he learns conceptually, building one concept on another, Bill couldn't move forward, having missed the building block concepts needed to understand the complexities of Soviet history.

Dreamers who have gotten behind, whether due to their daydreaming, an ineffective teacher, or a boring textbook, may use defense mechanisms such as saying, "It's just a stupid subject," or "The teacher stinks," or "I understand it. I just wasn't trying," to mask personal feelings of inadequacy. In contrast, if a subject comes easily to dreamers, that alone can give the subject personal relevance.

When a dreamer is naturally good at a subject, it is too easy to say, "Well, we won't have to adapt the materials to him in this class." Trying to force a dreamer into being a linear thinker ties him to the ground. If you want him to soar, teach to his strengths in every subject whenever possible.

For example, many dreamers are good in abstract mathematics but cannot explain in a linear fashion exactly how they got their answers. Lana came up with her own method of doing division.

Mrs. Gardener, her third-grade teacher, expected all the students to use her method. Although Lana's answers were correct, her method really bothered the teacher. When Lana tried to explain her logic, the mere fact that it was not the established method frustrated Mrs. Gardener, so she kept trying to get Lana to conform. She appealed to Lana's sense of justice, "It wouldn't be fair to the others who have to show their work, step by step." Lana interpreted Mrs. Gardener's frustration as disapproval, which angered her. She decided that she hated mathematics and showed only marginal interest in the subject after that.

Just as children can shut down if they decide "this subject is not for me," dreamers can buckle down if they find a subject interesting. Dreamers often do better in difficult classes than in something they find easy but boring. When you move an underachieving dreamer out of a more difficult class and place her in a general class in an effort to help her succeed, she may do worse. *I'm dumb in this subject,* she may think, or *I can't stay awake in that new class.* But if a dreamer is placed in a challenging class and clearly told, "You have the ability to succeed," the dreamer will often work very hard to meet that expectation. Dreamers will work for teachers who believe in them.

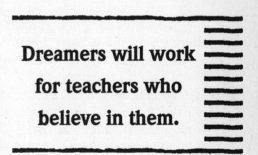

Dreamers will work for teachers who believe in them.

Why Dreamers Learn from Discussion

One way that teachers can express confidence in dreamers, in addition to directly saying, "I believe in you," is to affirm their ideas during discussions. Dreamers learn well in a discussion format because discussion focuses on concepts rather than on facts alone. Dreamers see the relevance of the information introduced through discussions and have a better memory of the details.

Discussions effectively teach abstract concepts and the deeper meaning of issues. Because dreamers don't think in a black-and-white manner, before they will change their position on anything, they have to understand the reasons why the information they believe to be correct is incorrect. Discussions can challenge your dreamer to hone his thinking skills. Reasoning through the information and self-correcting his errors teach him what no lecture could.

In addition to the learning aspects, dreamers enjoy discussion because it is relational. They like to hear what others think and observe the interaction of the group. Learning is enhanced because dreamers often remember who said what. Despite the help that peer interaction lends to memory for information, teachers should use caution when relying on student-led discussions. Dreamers need the structure a teacher gives. Without that guidance, dreamers tend to dominate a discussion, especially if they perceive things to be headed away from truth toward "shared ignorance."

When the discussion is thoughtful or thought provoking, dreamers delight in debating. However, the rest of the class may not share their enthusiasm. Playing devil's advocate, dreamers may ask questions just to spice things up. But if the discussion becomes heated, so may dreamers. What began as a fun exercise may become too personal, resulting in hurt feelings. If dreamers feel hurt or feel they are losing the debate, they may have an overwhelming need to have the last word. A teacher who is gifted at leading a discussion can usually prevent this.

Sometimes not just the dreamer and his fellow students feel the pain. "In high school discussions, I would disagree for the sake of disagreeing," admitted Carl. "Many of my teachers thought I had good ideas, so there was that tension—they wanted to hear from me, with my good ideas, but when it turned argumentative, the discussion was painful for them." He challenged a physics teacher about something he said, and it turned out Carl was right. "The teacher couldn't disagree with it, so all he could do was get angry."

Many dreamers rail against the limits of a linear, traditional American education. But their love of discussion makes a British classical approach to education, like that at Oxford or Cambridge in England, a perfect fit. In a British classical education, the student reads classic and modern books or articles in a given field and is expected to develop her own ideas on the subject matter. In tutorial or small class sessions, the student must be prepared to defend her ideas in the professor-led discussion. The British classical approach can be adapted to younger ages and is as "back to basics" as what we consider traditional.

Why Dreamers Love Problem Solving and Projects

Projects may seem too detailed for dreamers. Not so! Most dreamers love projects and have several personal projects going at one time. They are notorious for waiting until the last minute to start a project, yet still coming up with an interesting and original product.

Once they begin, dreamers love the process of a project. They enjoy planning it in their minds or brainstorming with others about ways to present ideas. They are less interested in processes that involve long-term commitment to detailed data collection. Gathering samples every day for several weeks to compare in a science project is not nearly as fascinating as inventing something completely new. Planning an advertising campaign is more fun than selling a product. Some hate making collections where they have to kill the flowers, bugs, or whatever because the projects are both boring and heartless. Dreamers like projects where they can be original.

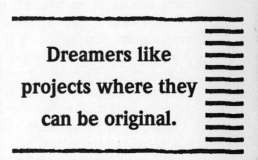

Dreamers like projects where they can be original.

What Happens When Dreamers Work in a Group

Extroverted dreamers fare well in group projects. If someone else can put all facts on note cards, while the dreamer designs the display or plans a creative oral presentation, all the better. Although the dreamer can benefit from a team approach, there are potential problems. If a driver is pushing the project in a different direction from the dreamer's vision, conflict may arise. Or the dreamer may keep her mouth shut and inwardly feel angry or hurt. The dreamer needs ideas to be valued, and sometimes the realists in the group can't see the value of a dreamer's big picture.

When a team is not cohesive, even if dreamers are valued, most of them will want to jump ship and work alone. People problems tend to interfere with the creative process. Also, if your dreamer child or teen is intimidated by the conflict, he is not going to say much to contribute to the project. He may try to mediate disagreements, but only if he isn't part of the disagreement. In classrooms where cooperative group learning is the norm, dreamers who are unpopular or who lack confidence will function poorly within the group. Some say too little, keeping their creative ideas to themselves. Others say too much, trying to get a positive reaction from the group while actually annoying everyone.

A teacher recalls a school folk-singing group; of the four teens, three were in it mostly for the fun. But not Trudi. She was in it for the music. She had the vision; she knew how great this little high school group could be, and she was frustrated that her fellow musicians didn't grasp the big picture.

The choral teacher overheard them practicing one day, and the session was punctuated by the dreamer's remarks: "No, no, no, you've got it all wrong." Trudi could hear every discordant note. The teacher realized the other kids weren't going to have any fun in the singing group if Trudi kept that up. So he tried to intervene by asking her to give the other kids a chance to speak up.

Shocked, Trudi turned and looked at the group. "Anyone want to say anything?" she asked.

"No, whatever you say, Trudi," they replied as one. The teacher knew that Trudi wanted the group members to like her; but more than that, she wanted them to make beautiful music. And so her vision clouded her ability to work within the group. Sometimes, when a dreamer dominates the discussion, the group can react more strongly than this group did to Trudi. One too many put-downs and a dreamer child may feel such deep hurt that she can't concentrate enough to learn anything.

Whether working in a group or independently, dreamers benefit from open-ended, flexible projects. Those projects with a single correct outcome, like a typical chemistry lab project, are less effective teaching tools than projects where the teacher encourages students to find their own solutions to a problem or issue. Many teachers are being trained in college and continuing education seminars to ask more open-ended questions. But we have found that some teacher's aren't open to more than one answer.

Joan's third-grade teacher asked her class to measure the perimeter of their desks using a ruler. She specifically stated, "Measure it in your own way and come up with an answer." The first several students gave their answers in total inches. Then Joan raised her hand and gave an answer in feet and inches. Even though the teacher had not specified total inches, she told Joan that her correct answer was incorrect. She assumed that she had taken a shortcut by using the foot unit. In terms of cognitive maturity, however, the answer in feet and inches indicated a better understanding of the concept of measurement. Joan glowered at the teacher. Under her breath, she quietly but firmly said, "But my answer was right!"

The Teacher's Impact on Dreamers

Dreamers like Joan need to feel accepted and appreciated by the teacher or they may not reach their potentials. Even Einstein, who had so many negative experiences with teachers, had Mr. Ruess. A teacher who enjoys global learners and knows how to encourage them will be respected and loved by a dreamer child as long as the teacher is also fair and kind. Social style is significant, too. Teachers perceived as cold are not received well by dreamers, especially in the younger years.

Remember that dreamers need to feel special, even favored, to be confident. Nowhere is this more true than in the classroom. It is not so important that the teacher actually favors the dreamer as that she *feels* favored. When we use the term *favored,* we are not recommending favoritism but simply an attitude of blessing. Whether the teacher presents a dreamer with extra work by saying, "This is something special I want you to do because I've noticed that you are gifted in social studies," invites her to take a test early, or places her in a more advanced art class, the message to the dreamer is, "I'm special and this teacher knows it." That critical question for the dreamer, "Does this person like me?" is answered by favored treatment.

When he feels favored, a dreamer will probably remember it for years. "My third-grade teacher thought I was a genius," said David. "I was her favorite, no question. She sometimes gave me a lot of extra work that was too hard. And although she corrected me, she also inspired me." Even though David felt favored, he wasn't seen as a teacher's pet by other students because he had to do all that extra work.

Special Encouragement in the Early Grades

Young dreamers crave affection. They will have a better day if it begins with a kind word and a hug from a teacher. One principal, a dreamer, understands this need. He stands outside the school in the morning and gives each child a hug. His affection is given in front of the parents, leaving no room for misinterpretations or false accusations. Starting out the school day happy helps moody dreamers because unhappy dreamers are poor learners. They can just shut down.

In third grade, Barbara had a critical teacher. She was not the only child who was suffering. School officials refused to move her from the classroom because they had too many other requests to transfer children away from the teacher. Before she was placed in this class, Barbara's handwriting was excellent. By two months into that school year, her handwriting was almost unreadable. When she turned in sloppy papers, the teacher criticized her in front of the class. The teacher also corrected Barbara for the nervous habits, such as hair twirling, that began to appear. Clearly the critical teacher emotionally affected the child. With appropriate testing, Barbara's parents were able to get her removed from this classroom, and she made a rapid academic recovery. Her self-esteem healed more slowly, however.

Most teachers do their best to create a positive learning environment. But acceptance by the teacher is not always enough to make a dreamer happy. Too many teachers feel they are being placed in the role of parent or counselor with a dreamer who arrives at school with emotional problems. Because a dreamer soaks up everyone's pain, a dreamer whose parents, siblings, or friends are experiencing trauma may learn poorly.

Some dreamers become counselors to their school friends and bear the burden of dark secrets, such as a friend who is being abused or one who is suicidal. Other dreamers serve in the role of punching bag or class joke for an unhappy peer group. Teachers may try to help the dreamer child cope because they understand what the group is doing, but we have encountered a few teachers who blame the dreamer entirely for somehow provoking the harassment.

It is sometimes true that dreamers unintentionally exacerbate the problem. Dreamers who are unpopular at school can do some irritating things to get attention. Even negative attention is better than no attention to them. Sometimes the child thinks, *If they would just notice me, they would like me.* If you see this pattern occurring, it is too easy to criticize the dreamer and ignore the harassment. Remember that dreamers receive advice poorly even when they have high self-esteem. A child with low self-esteem who is already being battered and bruised at school is vulnerable and must be guided gently.

Discouraging Dependency in the Classroom

Teachers worth their salt are willing to try to prevent the group's rejection of a child. When social problems plague the classroom, many teachers keep the dreamer close by so that negative statements from peers are discouraged. And when a dreamer is struggling emotionally with peer or family problems, that can be a good time for the teacher to show favor toward the dreamer child.

In showing favor, however, teachers shouldn't say, "Because your parents are divorcing, I want you to have this special privilege," or "Because the girls are being mean to you, I'd like you to help me out in the classroom during recess." These statements encourage a dreamer to seek teacher sympathy and almost create a desire to be miserable by giving too much attention to specific family problems and general moodiness. A child who thinks the teacher likes her only because she has problems will develop new problems to get attention. And showing too much pity feeds attention-seeking behaviors while communicating, "You need me to protect you. You *can't* take care of yourself," instead of, "You can handle this situation."

A dreamer named Killian had an operation during the middle of her sixth-grade year. All of her teachers were encouraging and sympathetic. When she came back to school, she was still weak and got extra attention. But after a few months, her teachers noticed that she had a new illness or family disaster every week. They soon labeled her a hypochondriac and ignored her. She then began telling peers that she had cancer, her mother was beating her, and her father had lost his job. Killian had learned how to get attention for being sick, but she didn't know how to be well.

Although teachers need to be observant and willing to intervene if necessary, many feel overwhelmed by the amount of harassment and don't attempt to stop it. Although we understand that dilemma, standing up to the bully—and even to his parents—tells the dreamer, "You matter." If teachers take no action, without saying a word, they communicate, "You don't matter." As a parent, acknowledge the difficulty of the teacher's position and ask how you can work together as a team. Parents who become frustrated with a teacher or a school regarding how a dreamer is being guided and protected at school often consider changing schools or taking the child out of school and teaching him at home.

Home School for Dreamers

> **Dreamers can thrive in home schooling, but only if it is creative.**

More and more parents are home schooling their dreamer children. Many parents who teach at home dispense with textbooks, using literature, library books on science, projects, and field trips as teaching tools. Dreamers can thrive in home schooling, but only if it is creative. Just removing your child from the social stresses of school without providing a superior education is likely to drive a wedge between you and your child. It's hard enough to be misunderstood by teachers and peers at school. If you teach at home in a linear way, you are communicating, "I don't understand you either."

In her book *For the Children's Sake,* Susan Schaeffer Macaulay outlines her philosophy of education based on the work of educator Charlotte Mason.[5] Read this book and/or others on home schooling before undertaking this option. You need to have a clear philosophy of education before you embark into teaching. Although home schooling is not appropriate for every child or every family, it is an option that allows for the individualized approach a dreamer needs. If you try home schooling, make sure that you are teaching in the way he can really hear.

As Henry David Thoreau said, "If a man does not keep pace with his companions, perhaps it is because he hears a different drummer. Let him step to the music that he hears, however measured or far away."[6]

Chapter 10

Finding That Passion: Academic and Career Identity in Dreamers

Since I first gained the use of reason my inclination towards learning has been so violent and strong that neither the scolding of other people ... nor my own reflections ... have been able to stop me from following this natural impulse that God gave me.

Juana Inés de la Cruz

They were an Oak View tradition, Mrs. Minton's predictions. Every year, as the eighth graders graduated and went on to high school, the teacher gazed into their futures to tell them what she saw. After all, she had been with them all year, and she considered herself a pretty good judge of character.

She began with Katie: "You will graduate from college magna cum laude." Most of the students stared at their teacher blankly. "Which means with high honors." Katie smiled, smug with satisfaction.

Some prediction, Mandy thought. *Anyone could have told you that. Katie always has straight A's.*

Next, Mrs. Minton turned her steady gaze to Mandy's best friend, Marla. "You, my dear, will be the first to appear on the society page."

The society page? The students were stumped again. "Which means you'll be the first to get married." A lot of giggling from the other girls and groans from the boys. Marla blushed.

Oh, no, Mandy panicked. *If she said that about Marla, what will she say about me? First to drive a station wagon?*

"And you, Mandy Parker," Mrs. Minton gave her a long, searching look, then pressed on, "you will be studying and going to school for the rest of your life."

A few snickers. What did that mean? That she'd never graduate?

After an interminable pause, she answered the unspoken question: "For you, my dear, are in love with learning." The other students looked at Mandy, confused. She certainly wasn't the top student in the honors class. And she certainly did her share of goofing off with Marla, the bride-to-be. Why would Mrs. Minton say that about her?

The soothsayer of Oak View saw something no one else saw. Though she didn't say it in so many words, this teacher knew a dreamer when she saw one.

Later that day, Mandy was still confused but pleased. *It must have been that independent study on the social repercussions of using nuclear weapons at Hiroshima and Nagasaki,* she thought. *She did say that it was a pretty ambitious topic for an eighth grader.*

What had Mrs. Minton given Mandy? It was a blessing. The teacher had shown Mandy who she could be. Mrs. Minton had articulated what was to become a significant part of Mandy's school identity.

School Identity in High School

By high school, dreamers often have a well-established school identity. It may be a positive identity, "I'm good at school," or it may be a negative identity, "I'm bad at school." Most teachers at the high school level are not dreamers. Consequently, dreamers may not relate well to the teachers or their linear teaching style. This often leads to problems because how much the dreamer likes the teacher directly relates to how much effort she makes to learn in the class.

We have seen report cards where we could say to the student, "So, can we assume that you don't like your science teacher or English teacher this year? Last year science was your best subject. Now it's your worst."

The typical teenage dreamer will respond, "My science and English teachers are boring! I can't keep my eyes open in those classes," or "That science teacher is out to get me because I refuse to color all those silly work sheets. I think she must be best friends with the English teacher. The English teacher frowns at me every time I enter the room. There's no pleasing either of those teachers."

Variability in grades from teacher to teacher perplexes most parents. "Just learn what the teacher wants and do it," says the doer parent. This advice is completely illogical to the dreamer teen. "Didn't you hear me?" says the dreamer. "The teachers don't like me. I'll never please them, so why try?" We have heard this discussion repeatedly in our counseling offices. Whether due to sensitivity, personality conflicts, frustration with boredom, or low self-esteem, dreamers often underachieve in high school. This poor performance can cause the teen or the school counselor to think that the dreamer should forget about college, reinforcing the negative school identity.

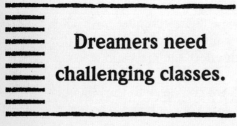

Dreamers often underachieve in high school.

Unless testing indicates below-average intelligence, guiding dreamers away from college is almost always a mistake. We have met many dreamers who did better in college than in high school. There may be little relationship between high school grades and academic achievement in college for dreamers. Mediocre high school students can obtain graduate degrees. The problem for parents, teachers, and counselors becomes, "How do I get this dreamer to do the work in the 'boring' classes that are required for admission to college? After all, this teen does not get going when the going gets tough."

Dreamers need challenging classes.

Although we will have a more detailed discussion of motivating teens in our chapter on adolescence, a few school guidance principles apply. First, because dreamers need challenging classes, they should not be placed below their potential even if their grades indicate a lack of motivation. Better to learn something in the tougher class than sleep through an easy class and fail anyway.

When dreamers are bored in class, there can be trouble. Larry's boredom in chemistry was so great that he and a friend set about creating inventions of great distinction. For example, Larry took notebook paper and created a balloon of sorts, which he filled with propane gas. Once it was filled, he thought he should light it. The stream of gas caught on fire, and the paper burst into flames in his hand. He threw it into the sink at his lab station, which was filled with trash from the lunch he wasn't supposed to be eating in class. "So now there's a miniature bonfire in the sink," he told us. "Meanwhile, there's a lecture going on." In classes that Larry found challenging, he did not go off on his own tangents. No mere goof-off, today, Larry has his Ph.D.

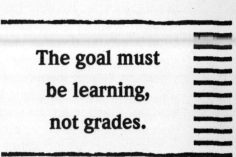

The goal must be learning, not grades.

Second, the goal must be learning, not grades. If a dreamer makes A's on the tests, the teen is probably learning, even if his overall grade is low because he doesn't turn in homework. If test scores are low, however, there's a problem. He may need extra help at home or with a tutor.

As Carol went into high school, she got behind in math. Her male teacher intimidated her a bit, so she never asked him for help. When her progress report came out at mid-semester, her parents became alarmed. Why wasn't she asking questions if she didn't understand? Instead of punishing Carol, they got her a tutor. This solution lessened the tension at home, created a comfortable environment for asking questions, and kept Carol accountable for learning the material. Once she was up to speed, her classroom teacher wasn't so frightening.

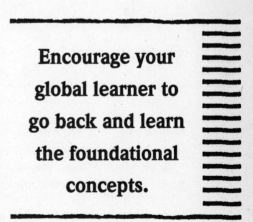

Encourage your global learner to go back and learn the foundational concepts.

Our third principle for developing a positive school identity is to encourage your global learner to go back and learn the foundational concepts. He may have done the work, but did he understand it? Without the necessary foundation, there will be nothing upon which the dreamer can build. For you to know what has and hasn't been learned, testing may be indicated. If your teenager has a negative school identity, or is close to saying, "I'm dumb," don't wait for standardized testing at school. You will need more specific kinds of information to make decisions about how to proceed than most group tests can give you.

Testing through a psychologist or learning center can help you identify missed concepts. Because a dreamer's response to grades is sometimes, "I wasn't trying," or "That teacher is lousy," the testing provides you with concrete reasons beyond grades to take specific actions. When a dreamer sees his potential spelled out in the results, he can be more motivated to learn the material. In a sense, the psychologist or learning center provides an objective viewpoint that takes the parent-child relationship out of the issue.

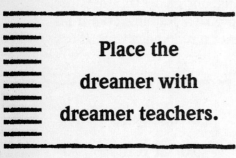

Place the dreamer with dreamer teachers.

A final key to dreamer success in high school is this: Place the dreamer with dreamer teachers or doers who use creative methods whenever possible. Creative role models who are enthusiastic about a subject can inspire idealistic dreamers to achieve academic success. If a dreamer likes or admires a teacher, he will want to please that teacher and will want to know what the teacher knows in order to be more like the teacher. The subject matter becomes personal because the teacher has made it meaningful.

When Jackie Torrance, one of America's foremost storytellers, was a child, she lacked confidence:

For the first fourteen years of my life, I was ashamed because I was fat, I had two sets of teeth in the roof of my mouth and I couldn't speak, and my classmates snickered at me.

My ninth grade teacher, Mrs. Abna Lancaster . . . says that she found me an "eagle among her chickens." She worked with me day and night and Saturdays to change my speech. She will tell you that she never taught school, she taught students.[1]

Sometimes a dreamer is purposely placed with a rigid teacher in an effort to structure the unstructured child or teen. This approach results in moderate improvement at best and an increasingly negative school identity at worst. School identity has lasting consequences. Because depressed teens and dropouts tend to have the "school is not for me" attitude, never underestimate the impact of one school year. Accepting your dreamer's strengths and weaknesses, and placing her with compatible teachers, increases school success.

When Dreamers Are Teachers

Dreamers who had negative school experiences sometimes choose to be teachers. They have an ideal picture of what school could be, and they follow that dream into the classroom. The fact that many dreamers had their most negative experiences with formal education in high school leads some to pursue teaching in preschool and the early grades. Perhaps because they often felt different in high school, they are not as attracted to that age group unless they can work with teens who are equally different.

Because dreamer teachers are more common in kindergarten and first grade where they may feel freer to be creative, dreamer children may not begin to experience academic frustration until they have more practical, linear teachers. With older children, dreamer teachers adapt their classrooms to their own global style.

One literature teacher told us that she completely ignores the school directives and paperwork requirements, shuts her door so no one can observe her, and teaches in her conceptual way. She is a very committed teacher who spends much of her free time taking her classes to see Shakespeare and other plays. Her students are learning, and so far, she hasn't been fired for ignoring the paperwork.

Relationships with students are essential to dreamer teachers. They take extra time after hours to conduct field trips, to sponsor clubs, and to coach athletics. They gravitate toward relational subjects, such as psychology, and use discussion and cooperative learning in their classrooms. Like most teachers, dreamers tend to teach in the way that they learn best, which isn't always ideal for linear students. But one thing dreamer teachers can do well with all children is inspire them to dream.

Dreamers in College

"At last. Other people like me!" College is heaven for many dreamers, especially once they have completed the core freshman requirements. Dreamers make up a higher percentage of the college population than of the high school population[2] because doers are more likely than dreamers to opt out of college to begin *doing* something immediately. Not loving learning for its own sake, doers usually choose college only when it fits into a specific plan to pursue a particular goal or to please parents. In contrast, dreamers love learning for its own sake.

The doer parent who hands a dreamer a college catalog and asks the dreamer to choose something to study may be surprised to find that his teen who didn't seem interested in anything in high school cannot narrow down her varied interests. Knowing that they become bored so easily, dreamers are often fearful of making a decision that they will be stuck with for the rest of their lives. At the same time, they enjoy imagining the possibilities. Dreamers tend to gravitate toward the liberal arts or more creative aspects of the sciences such as those that involve inventing, developing, researching, or problem solving.

If dreamers did not find a teacher to emulate in high school, they can probably find one in college. Most professors are dreamers or are somewhere on the creator continuum between dreamer and driver. Teachers at the college level tend to encourage and reward critical thinking skills. Dreamers are less likely to be bored in college, not only because the professors are more likely to be engaging, but also because they can usually drop the class if a professor is boring. Many dreamers change majors more than once, and they frequently pursue fields that require further education at the graduate level.

The dropping of classes and the changing of majors can frustrate doer parents, who want the dreamer to make a decision and stick with it. But to be able to focus on a specific career path and aggressively pursue that path, the dreamer must find a career that she can feel passionate about. Because dreamer passions are often caught from another dreamer, a professor-mentor can play a key role in helping a dreamer develop that passion. Parents who push too hard toward "sensible" careers with good job prospects may find that the dreamer rebels, sometimes dropping out of college, or tries to please (usually a firstborn) but then changes careers at a later point in life.

Dreamers in Careers

When dreamers head off in the wrong career direction, whether due to poor counsel or inadequate research, burnout quickly follows. If a dreamer is forced by burnout to make a career change, the later in life the change occurs, the greater the personal cost to marriage and family. For this reason, it is much better for dreamers to discover their passion early in the career preparation process.

We have met several dreamers who became accountants because they enjoyed math and someone said, "You could make a living at it." It turned out to be bad advice because dreamers enjoy abstract math, and accounting has concrete applications. Dreamers who love math are more likely to passionately pursue a career that involves abstract uses of math and problem solving such as computer programming, financial analysis, or research and development.

These birds need to fly. Turning a dreamer away from her passion can lead to a lifetime of misery for her and many missed innovations and insights for the rest of us. In the foreword to *A Whack on the Side of the Head*, Nolan Bushnell, the founder of Atari, Inc., Chuck E. Cheese's Pizza-Time Theater, Inc., and Catalyst Technologies, writes,

Innovative people have a passion for what they do. I don't know if this passion is innate or not, but it can be snuffed out in a person. Think about it: how much passion will Johnny exhibit if after every time he runs around the house and displays passion, he gets hit on the head and is told to "Sit down"? You're right, not much. This is one of the things that makes being a parent such a challenge. I see characteristics in my kids that in an adult would be fantastic, and yet occasionally they drive me nuts. Sometimes, I have to catch myself and stop and listen to them. If I just say no, they will probably lose the inventiveness and imagination they need to be creative when they grow up.[3]

Dana remembers seeing an article in a national newspaper that urged college students to look at the job market and not follow their hearts. Some dreamers follow such dreadful advice! Never, never, never separate a dreamer from his passion.

John Keating in *Dead Poets Society* (the book version) challenges a student and the status quo:

> "Now Mr. Pitts may argue that nineteenth-century literature has nothing to do with business school or medical school. He thinks we should study our J. Evans Pritchard, learn our rhyme and meter, and quietly go about our business of achieving other ambitions.
>
> . . . "Well," Keating whispered defiantly, "I say—drivel! One reads poetry because he is a member of the human race, and the human race is filled with passion! Medicine, law, banking—these are necessary to sustain life. But poetry, romance, love, beauty? These are what we stay alive for!
>
> "I quote from Whitman:
>
> *'O me! O life! of the questions of these recurring,*
> *Of the endless trains of the faithless, of cities fill'd with the*
> *   foolish, . . .*
> *What good amid these, O me, O life?'*
>
> Answer
> *'That you are here—That life exists and identity*
> *That the powerful play goes on, and you may contribute a*
> *   verse.'"*

In the silence of the moment, Keating repeats, "That the powerful play goes on, and you may contribute a verse." Then he asks, "What will *your* verse be?"[4]

That, for dreamers, is indeed the question.

Chapter 11

Is He ADD or Just Dreaming?: Attention Deficit Disorder and Dreamers

Sometimes a thousand twangling instruments will hum about mine ears.

from *The Tempest* by William Shakespeare

Are you concerned that your child

- is so easily distracted?
- has difficulty sticking to any task for more than a few minutes?
- can't seem to remember instructions?
- becomes frustrated when there is a lot of noise?

Each of these symptoms is found in children who have difficulty concentrating. This struggle to concentrate is called attention deficit disorder.

What Is Attention Deficit Disorder?

Attention deficit disorder (ADD) is a learning disability in which a child is easily distracted, has difficulty remembering, may be impulsive, and may have difficulty controlling emotions.[1] You may be thinking, *But that sounds exactly like a dreamer!* Well, it's not. Dreamers may seem to have ADD and yet have no true attention problem, at least not the kind of attention deficit found in children and adults with ADD.

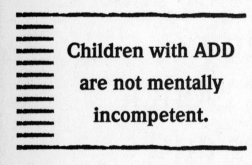

Children with ADD are not mentally incompetent.

The causes of ADD are not completely known. Like other physical qualities, it appears to be largely hereditary. We must point out that children with ADD are not mentally incompetent. ADD is unrelated to intelligence, although it can affect the ability to learn by disrupting the child's efforts to complete classroom assignments.

Everyone's mind wanders from time to time. Everyone acts impulsively on occasions. However, children with ADD have little control over their attention spans. Help in understanding this deficit and guidelines for treating and compensating for its effects are within the reach of every child and adult with ADD.

Ron tells of his experience with an attention deficit: "Looking back over my grammar and high school years, I exhibited a lot of the symptoms of ADD in addition to my many dreamer traits. My ADD characteristics made it difficult for me to concentrate in class, control impulsivity, and enjoy subjects that required memorization. Even though I struggled with an attention deficit, I was a student with an optimistic outlook on life and considered my strengths to be in the areas of personal relationships and athletics. On many occasions, I tried making up what I lacked in grades by relating to teachers and peers with humor and compassion.

"Academically, I especially recall struggling with subjects like math and English, which involved remembering numerous details and required prolonged levels of concentration. In English class, for example, I had difficulty recalling all the rules of grammar, completing compositions, and finishing reading assignments. I did, however, enjoy giving oral book reports on subjects I considered interesting or intriguing. The challenge for me with these reports was to read as little as possible and still be creative enough to compose a composition that was interesting and entertaining. I guess if I hadn't been a dreamer, I would really have been in trouble!

"The patterns I am admitting about myself are common among children with ADD. Like others who grew up in the 1950s and 1960s, I was never formally tested for ADD but found a way to compensate and complete school. I do, however, remember how hard it was for me to learn in a conventional way. I thought this pattern was normal until as an adult I saw my younger son, Adam, struggle with the same symptoms.

"Early in his school years, Adam got behind in reading. His lack of comprehension led us to seek testing by a developmental specialist and an interview with a neurologist. He was diagnosed with attention deficit disorder. A plan of action was put into place including medication and private tutoring to help him catch up in reading. In addition to this special help, his teachers gave him more time to read a book and prepare a book report.

"Too often, Adam would forget about a long-term assignment until the night before it was due. On one occasion, the teacher assigned an oral book report. He chose a book, made the report, and received a good grade. Everything was fine until another student made a report on the same book. The two reports were completely different! The theme, role of the characters, and conclusion did not match. Upon further exploration, the teacher discovered that Adam had not read the book, but had done an exceptional job of constructing his oral report using only the title, names of the characters, and general information from the book cover. His report was a complete fabrication. The dreamer in me found it difficult to be upset with Adam because even though he failed to read the book, his creative ability to develop his own story was amusing. As we say in the South, 'The acorn didn't fall far from the tree.'

"In most cases ADD appears to be inherited. I understand the pain many parents feel when they realize that they have passed on a trait that is creating frustration for their child. Many times, I've watched Adam trying to write a paper or complete his homework and wished that I could make things easier.

"A learning disability like ADD is not a disease. It isn't an outside invader, but is prewired within the brain. What I have to offer

Adam is what I have learned because of ADD. Learning to live with ADD has taught me how to accept problems as a challenge, learn from my mistakes, and persevere to come out ahead in the end."

Living with a Label

As with any learning disability, children with ADD have to contend with being labeled unfairly and treated differently. Some are thought to be spacey. Others are mislabeled lazy. Labeling can be rough on children during that time of life when they long for acceptance and a feeling of accomplishment. Children with learning disabilities need to understand themselves and face their challenges head-on so as not to hinder their future successes.

And these children do have successes. Paul is in graduate school. But when he was in high school, his mother wasn't sure he was going to make it. He was so impulsive. If the youth group went on a trip, Paul was the one who climbed on the roof. If the chemistry teacher left the room for a minute, he was taking chemicals out to make little bombs to throw in the field by his house. Paul was a B student who would have breezed through with little effort had he not had ADD.

All Paul wanted to do was fly planes, which scared his mother to death. *Well, at least it's legal,* she thought. When he turned sixteen, his mother let him take flying lessons. He was in heaven! He started making plans to go to college in aerospace engineering and was progressing nicely toward his pilot's license. Finally, it was time for Paul to take a fairly long solo flight. On the ground, then off the ground, and whoosh! He was having the time of his life. Then he looked down. There below lay his high school. *Yes!* he thought. *The football team is practicing and I'll just buzz down and scare the guys.*

At the end of that flight, the FAA investigator congratulated Paul on being the only student pilot ever to survive a flight that low over buildings and power lines. He was suspended from flying for four years. His impulsivity got the best of him and his dreams took a nosedive—at least temporarily. Today, Paul is preparing to go overseas as a missionary bush pilot. He'll soon be buzzing down between palm trees someplace far away. And there won't be any power lines.

Dreamer and ADD Similarities

In his book *Attention Deficit Disorder: A Different Perception*, Thom Hartman has called the child with ADD a "hunter in a farmer's world".[2] The hunter, always looking around and attuned to the slightest sound, isn't equipped for the slow pace of the farmer. Nor does the farmer have the quick reaction time needed to be a hunter.

Hartman claims that there is a correlation between creativity and ADD.[3] We have found, however, that ADD can occur in children and adults of any cognitive style. It does appear that adults with ADD gravitate toward occupations in which they work with dreamers, probably because creative people are more tolerant of the ADD traits of forgetfulness and disorganization. Although most dreamers do not have a neurologically based attention deficit, many have been misdiagnosed as having ADD.

Just as dreamers have some of the same characteristics as children with ADD, kinesthetic learners share some characteristics with them. But kinesthetic learners learn through activity rather than being distracted by it. Because kinesthetic learners, dreamers, and children with ADD have some similar traits, we will focus on the differences in the three.

Types of Attention Deficit Disorders

There are three types of ADHD (attention deficit/hyperactivity disorder) according to the *Diagnostic and Statistical Manual of Mental Disorders* (DSM-IV), the manual used by psychiatrists and psychologists for making diagnoses of psychological and learning disorders.[4]

First is the "combined" type. These children and adults are both hyperactive and inattentive, having at least six significant symptoms in each category.

Second is the "predominantly inattentive" type. These children and adults have six or more significant symptoms of inattention, but fewer symptoms of hyperactivity. This type, which can be confused with the dreamer cognitive style, is often designated ADD.

Third is the "predominantly hyperactive" type, having six or more significant symptoms of hyperactivity without being inattentive. These children share many characteristics with kinesthetic learners in that they are able to be attentive even though they are very active. Parents may be surprised to learn that children can be hyperactive without having an attention problem.

Hyperactivity without Inattention

To be considered hyperactive, a child must have a level of activity that is maladaptive and inappropriate for the child's age. The DSM-IV lists the following symptoms of hyperactivity-impulsivity:

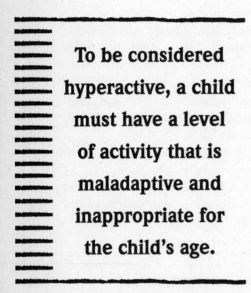

> To be considered hyperactive, a child must have a level of activity that is maladaptive and inappropriate for the child's age.

1. Often fidgets with hands or squirms in seat
2. Often leaves seat in classroom or in other situations in which remaining in the seat is expected
3. Often runs about or climbs excessively in situations in which it is inappropriate
4. Often has difficulty playing or engaging in leisure activities quietly
5. Is often "on the go" or often acts as if "driven by a motor"
6. Often talks excessively
7. Often blurts out answers before questions have been completed
8. Often has difficulty waiting turn
9. Often interrupts or intrudes on others

Kinesthetic learners who are not hyperactive should not have a maladaptive activity level, should be learning from the activity, should verbalize a normal amount or even be quiet, and should not be overly impulsive. Kinesthetic learners like to be moving when they are learning.

In contrast, the movement of children with ADHD tends to interfere with learning. They may fall out of the desk or drop all their books. Rather than enjoying fine-motor tasks like building and sculpting, ADHD children often have poor fine-motor skills and little patience for constructing elaborate models from Legos or Play-Doh.

Some kinesthetic dreamers have been misdiagnosed as having ADHD because of the combination of activity and daydreaming. Since many dreamers are visual or auditory learners, however, the inattentive child who is not hyperactive is most often confused with the dreamer. For this reason, we use ADD, rather than ADHD, when contrasting the two.

Inattention without Hyperactivity

According to the DSM-IV, *to be considered inattentive, a child must have the following symptoms to a degree that is maladaptive and developmentally inappropriate* (that is, a significant learning delay):

1. Often fails to give close attention to details or makes careless mistakes in schoolwork, work, or other activities
2. Often has difficulty sustaining attention in tasks or play activities*
3. Often does not seem to listen when spoken to directly*
4. Often does not follow through on instructions and fails to finish schoolwork, chores, or duties in the workplace (not due to oppositional behavior or failure to understand instructions)*
5. Often has difficulty organizing tasks and activities
6. Often avoids, dislikes, or is reluctant to engage in tasks that require sustained mental effort (such as schoolwork or homework)*
7. Often loses things necessary for tasks or activities (e.g., toys, school assignments, pencils, books, or tools)
8. Is often easily distracted by extraneous stimuli*
9. Is often forgetful in daily activities

A lot of these characteristics sound typical of the dreamer, don't they? But the dreamer without ADD should *not* have most of the symptoms that we have noted with an asterisk.

For example, symptom no. 2 mentions difficulty sustaining attention. Although dreamers are inattentive when bored, they are attentive to things that interest them. Dreamers without an attention deficit can read, work on a project, or discuss an issue for hours, oblivious to everything else happening around them. Children with ADD can focus on TV or video games that drown out other stimuli, but tend to have great difficulty reading or focusing on discussions even if they are interested in the subject matter.

In symptom no. 3, the "does not seem to listen" seems to describe a dreamer child. But ask dreamer children what was said and they will know, unless they were being given instructions while they were focused on something else, like a book or a song on the radio. Children with ADD can repeat the instruction word for word and then forget it before they get to the top of the stairs. Dreamers may pretend to forget because they object to the instruction, so parents may think that they have attention problems. Symptoms no. 4 and no. 6 are likely to appear in a stubborn dreamer. But a dreamer without ADD chooses not to perform the task; the child is intentionally passive-aggressive rather than inattentive.

The DSM-IV also mentions that children with ADD shy away from mental effort such as schoolwork. Although they may be very bright, children with ADD work slowly not because they are bored, but because they are distracted and have difficulty getting ideas onto paper. Children with ADD may spell poorly and have problems with proofreading because their eyes jump around the page. They tend to skip lines and miss portions of instructions.

Children with ADD can misread symbols and add when they should subtract, doing everything else in the math problem correctly, but getting no credit because the final answer is incorrect. This frustration with written tasks causes children with ADD to be reluctant to tackle mentally challenging assignments. In contrast, dreamers are drawn to mental stimulation, but resist routine and boring tasks.

Although other symptoms can look like ADD when they are not, symptom no. 8 should be found only in a child with ADD. Therefore, this characteristic most clearly delineates the child with ADD from the typical dreamer. Children and adults with ADD may report an inability to screen out extraneous stimuli. The child in the classroom hears the teacher at the same sound level as the lawn mower outside, the classmate shuffling papers, and the person walking down the hall. Background noises and visual background clutter such as bulletin boards or a messy room may distract the child with ADD. The sound of a clock ticking or the sight of rapidly changing images in a TV commercial may aggravate a child with ADD.

In contrast, the dreamer without ADD seems to be able to screen out distractions and become completely engrossed in imaginary play, reading, journaling, painting, clay, Legos, or just an interesting thought. Children with ADD may seem to be focused on an idea when they "zone out" and appear to daydream. But unlike the dreamer, who can recount the daydream in detail, the child with ADD reports an experience more like being in a fog with no particular train of thought.

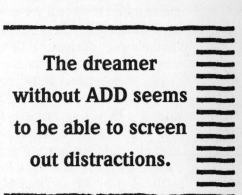

The dreamer without ADD seems to be able to screen out distractions.

As with other issues of behavior, evaluating dreamers by their overt behavior alone, without discussing why they do the things they do, can lead to a misdiagnosis of ADD. Teachers and parents may want to believe that the child *can't* do the task rather than *won't* do the task. They try medication for inattention and see no change in the dreamer, except perhaps a stimulant effect in which the child has more energy. (Ritalin, the most popular and safest drug for ADD, normally stimulates activity but reduces activity level in children with ADHD/ADD.)

No child or adult should be on medication when it isn't needed. Although most drugs given for ADD have good safety records, all drugs can have side effects. In addition to the problem of overmedicating, misdiagnosing a dreamer as inattentive can lower self-esteem or give the dreamer an excuse to avoid risks by saying, "I have ADD and I can't do that." Teachers often suggest ADD when a child daydreams, in part because teachers don't want to think that the class is boring.

Take Elizabeth, for example. She is in third grade now, and every year her teacher has said the same thing: "I don't think she's ADD *but . . ."* The teacher says Elizabeth can't seem to focus on what's going on enough to finish her classwork. It looks like Elizabeth is in a daze, but in reality she is daydreaming. She isn't underfocused; she is overfocused on her thoughts.

A school counselor told another mother that her fourth-grade son was probably ADD. She looked down the list of characteristics. "Inability to focus?" she said. "You don't know this kid." Brian builds elaborate projects with wood, nails, and all sorts of materials, and he keeps at it for weeks. And he doesn't just focus when he is alone. When he is building something, he drafts his friends as flunkies to perform some of the labor. Brian can focus intently and screen out external distractions if something interests him.

Just as dreamers can be misdiagnosed with ADD, some children are mislabeled as defiant or lazy who have a neurologically based attention deficit. Some parents reading this book may decide that true ADD is just dreamerness because they don't want to believe that the child has a learning problem. Remember, some dreamers have ADD. These children have a "double whammy" when it comes to disorganization and forgetfulness.

One other symptom associated with ADHD/ADD that does not appear in the DSM-IV, and yet is widely used by psychologists and psychiatrists when evaluating children, is emotionality. Mood swings, tearfulness, and flares of temper are generally considered characteristics of ADD. When a teacher sees a weepy boy, she may be too quick to think *attention deficit disorder* and may misdiagnose a dreamer.

If your dreamer continues to have significant attention problems, even when you do everything you can to nurture his dreamer cognitive style, he may need to be evaluated for ADD. Again, the difficulty with extraneous stimuli seems to be the best dividing line between normal dreamerness and ADD. Checklists will not always detect this symptom. At this point, you may be unsure whether your child has ADD or is a dreamer. Most neurologists we have worked with who specialize in ADD recommend that a licensed psychologist test children to assess neurologically based inattention.

Dreamers with ADD

When dreamers have ADD, they experience not only the "double whammy" of disorganization and forgetfulness but also double doses of other factors. One of the most problematic symptoms from the parent's perspective is that dreamers with ADD are doubly emotional. Their mood swings are extreme, and their level of rage can be frightening. The stress on the family may be tremendous. For this reason, seek outside support through professionals and parent support groups when caring for a dreamer with ADD. If you become frazzled, you are likely to overreact, which stimulates a dreamer with ADD toward more reactivity and less emotional control.

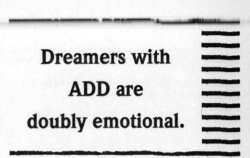

Dreamers with ADD are doubly emotional.

Dreamers with ADD are doubly restless. Take some dreamer intolerance of boredom and mix in ADD mental restlessness, and you get children who are constantly looking for something different to do. If dreamer creativity is mixed with impulsivity, mischievous behavior often occurs. These dreamers may talk a sibling or peer into acting on their imaginative plan rather than carrying it out themselves.

Dreamers with ADD are doubly frustrated by academic problems. Dreamers love to look good to others, and they tend to pride themselves on their intellectual capabilities. Difficulty in learning is very hard for them to swallow. Learning isn't fun anymore. Self-esteem often drops dramatically. Although some dreamers with

Dreamers with ADD are doubly restless.

ADD can develop alternative areas in which to shine, as Ron did in athletics, many children with ADD are clumsy and have poor gross-motor and fine-motor skills, which limits them in sports, art, and music. Being able to imagine something and not being able to get it onto paper either in drawing or in writing can be debilitating for the dreamer with ADD. This misery adds to the explosiveness.

Dreamers with ADD or other learning disabilities that interfere with their creative productivity need encouragement and adaptation in the classroom. By allowing these children to give oral rather than written reports, for example, the teacher can gain a more accurate view of their true ability. Of course, teachers need to watch those Braund boys to be sure that they have read the material.

> **Dreamers with ADD are doubly frustrated by academic problems.**

At home, allow your child to type on a computer that can check spelling or use a calculator to speed mathematical computation. She will still make some errors, but she can learn new concepts more quickly, reducing the chance of a negative school identity. More than anything, a dreamer with ADD needs to know that you believe in her potential to learn and express herself. As you nourish her mind, you validate her spirit.

Some people might discourage you along the way by telling you to be realistic about your child's potential. For such scoffers, we close with a quote from a nineteenth-century senator, Carl Schurtz: "Ideals are like stars; you will not succeed in touching them with your hands. But like the seafaring man on the desert of waters, you choose them as your guides, and following them you will reach your destiny."[5]

Chapter 12

Fear of Failure, Fear of Success: Helping Dreamers Take Some Risks

Public opinion is a weak tyrant compared with our own private opinion. What a man thinks of himself, that is which determines, or rather, indicates, his fate.

from *Walden* by Henry David Thoreau

We've all heard the saying, "If at first you don't succeed, try, try again." The dreamers of this world put another spin on it, which goes something like this: "If you're not sure you can succeed from the very first, don't try at all." But why?

In Dana's living room sat a group of dreamer adults who had gathered for a discussion of childhood. We were looking for some good stories for this book, but we were also looking for unusual trends: things several of them might have experienced that we might not expect. When we began to talk about fear of failure, an interesting trend emerged. Dana's husband, Phillip, said that when applying to colleges, he had not applied to the top photography/design program in the country because he had already decided that he couldn't get in. "Looking back, and looking at my colleagues who went there," he said, "I know now that I probably would have been admitted."

This story sparked discussion from the others in the group. "I did that, too," said Annie. "I wanted to go to Virginia, but I never applied. The schools where I did apply were as academically rigorous; they just weren't as *important to me.*" Two others in the small group admitted that they had not applied to the colleges of their dreams. All of them were good students and went to good colleges. They didn't apply to their top choices either because they had already decided (probably incorrectly) that there was no hope or because they weren't willing to risk a rejection letter from their dream schools. We were speechless. Even with all our experience with dreamers, this revelation shocked us. We were talking with confident, successful dreamers: the homecoming queen, the soccer star, and the president of the student body. If they wouldn't take risks, what dreamers would?

Our clients tell similarly surprising tales. "We can't get Elaina to try anything. It's been frustrating us for a long time because we know she needs to do something to build her self-esteem," said Mrs. Murray. "We've offered her every kind of lesson." "Made her take them, too," chimed in Mr. Murray.

"Yes, and that didn't work either," continued Mrs. Murray. "Elaina would complete the year of dance or piano and seem to enjoy it. But when it came time to sign up again, we'd try to encourage her by telling her the teacher thought she had talent and wanted to promote her to an advanced class or something, and she'd say, 'Dance is stupid! Please don't make me do it again this year.'"

"And I'm not paying for her to goof around and not practice like she did with piano," said Mr. Murray. "She never wants to do anything that involves work. It's as if she has to be perfect the first time she tries something or forget it. But if her sister does something well by working hard at it, Elaina will hear us praise Ruth and start crying."

"And Elaina's so pitiful, too!" exclaimed Mrs. Murray. "She says things like, 'I can't do anything well! I'm just a loser!' We try to be sympathetic, but sometimes it seems she's just lazy. I believe she would watch TV for the rest of her life if we'd let her."

Motivating Elaina has become an all-consuming concern for the Murray family. They don't want to favor her hardworking sibling, but comparing the two inevitably happens. When her parents don't make comparisons, Elaina does. And her comparisons tend to focus on the end product; she doesn't seem to grasp the effort Ruth has made to become good at things. In many respects Elaina is more naturally talented than Ruth, as evidenced by the enthusiasm of her activity teachers. Does Elaina think of herself as a loser because she doesn't achieve or because she doesn't self-motivate? If her self-esteem is low, why is she so eager to quit any activity at which she has been successful? Is quitting somehow related to the same fear of failure described by the dreamers sitting in Dana's living room?

Internal Perfectionists

Remember that dreamers are internal perfectionists, not external perfectionists. Rather than forcing herself, as an external perfectionist would, to face fears and drive to perfection, the demotivating thought of the internal perfectionist is, *If I can't do it well, I won't do it at all.* Because dreamers can mentally examine and vividly picture all possible outcomes, they don't need to have failed at something to fear it. Parents tell us about their dreamer children who were athletically gifted, but resisted learning to ride a bike until peers began to tease, or who refused to get out of the boat to try to water-ski after seeing a sibling fall.

In our counseling with parents, we find that many blame themselves for somehow creating insecurity in the child. "Have we put too much pressure on her?" they ask. "Have we discouraged him in some way?" It is hard to accept that dreamers, who don't drive hard to do things in a "perfect" way, have high self-imposed internal standards. No matter how much you encourage your child, you can never completely eliminate fear of failure. But you can learn to help him over the rocky road of self-doubt.

When Nothing Is Good Enough

Have you ever noticed that if your child thinks something he has made is flawed, no amount of complimenting and admiring will change his view? *You're my mom,* thinks a dreamer. *You have to say that.* Because a dreamer wants praise to be informed, not just heartfelt, the praise is generally more motivating if an "expert" like an art teacher, a coach, or a professional musician compliments the child.

Even when an expert's opinion is glowing, your dreamer will be able to find something that she could have done better. Being so hard on herself, she doesn't need another critic. If you give advice, your child will tune you out to protect her heart.

Having low frustration tolerance, a dreamer may get very angry with himself for his shortcomings. Not that he will admit that he feels this way, at least not to you. He projects his feelings of disappointment onto you, assuming that "Mom and Dad are just as disappointed in me as I am." For this reason, although a dreamer may not be immediately motivated by praise, it is still needed to dispel any generalized sense that you see your child as a failure.

If a dreamer decides that a certain person cannot be pleased, she won't even try. But a carefully worded compliment can turn this around. Remember, a dreamer is always looking for the underlying meaning in what you say. Watch your body language, tone of voice, and word choice.

Dreamers deal with their fears of disappointing others by attempting new things privately.

For example, the parent who says, "You played great! Much better than last week's game," has inadvertently put a negative ("You didn't play so great last week") into a statement that was intended to be positive. The teacher who says, "You had a good day today. Let's see if you can make every day a good day," has implied an expectation that the child will fail on a future day unless she works really hard. Again, a negative implication can destroy the positive intent. Never mix compliments with advice. Any comment that implies, "You did well, but _____," will hurt the sensitive dreamer. Dreamers need reassurance even about their greatest talents. Once they have had a series of successes, they become more willing to take risks without constant encouragement.

"I Want to Be Alone"

Some dreamers deal with their fears of disappointing others by attempting new things privately. Molly's mom told us about trying to teach her daughter to write. She stubbornly refused to write anything when Mom was in the room. But when Mom peeked back in later, after leaving Molly alone for a while, she found that the letters were written beautifully.

Although practice is a poor teacher of academic concepts, dreamers do learn motor skills such as handwriting, piano, or sports by rehearsing or practicing motor movements. Before trying out for the soccer team, twelve-year-old Tim practiced for almost a year, kicking a ball against his garage. A dreamer's need to practice privately can be frustrating. When you are around, your dreamer child refuses to practice anything. You can misread the situation and decide that you need to make your child accountable by standing over her. Our advice is to set limits and then back off. Set some standards, but let your child achieve those standards in her own way. And if she still refuses to practice piano or whatever, there can be a consequence, but only if she agreed to take lessons in the first place. Why punish a child for not wanting to follow your dreams?

> **Having time alone to think can help dreamers accept failure and move forward without fear.**

You may be concerned that backing off will result in failure, increasing your child's fears. A little failure can be helpful to the child's emotional development. He learns that he can go on, but he also learns that you were right about the benefits of persistence. Some failures, though, carry with them strong emotional baggage. If a child is humiliated in a public way, what was learned won't be worth the pain endured.

Having time alone to think can help dreamers accept failure and move forward without fear. What doer children can work through by action, dreamers must process through contemplation. Extroverted dreamers may not appear to be contemplative, but they are often reflecting while engaging in activities and play.

"I Don't Care" and Other Defense Mechanisms

Even the most talkative dreamers are not always good at admitting their fears of failure. Sixteen-year-old Melissa was invited to participate in a governor's honors summer program in the arts. The one stipulation was that a local artist interview her. At first she was proud and excited, telling everyone about her special honor. Then she began to think about the interview. Melissa became fearful that she might be rejected from the program and be embarrassed in front of her friends and family. Suddenly, to the surprise of everyone, she started saying that the governor's honors program was "dumb" and that she didn't want to be away for a month in the summer. She never said she was afraid of the interview, partly because she thought everyone would be disappointed in her, and partly because she was afraid they would make her face her fear.

Expressions of disinterest may be signs of hidden fears. This tendency is somewhat easy to spot when a child goes from excitement to disinterest in a matter of days. But it is not so easy to discern if your dreamer child or teen has never outwardly expressed an interest. As enthusiastic as dreamers are about their interests, a dreamer may be less willing to take risks at things he cares deeply about than at tasks or activities that hold only moderate appeal if he feels there is a probability of failure.

Everyone thinks I am a great dancer, thinks the dreamer. *If I blow that solo, I'll feel like a fool. But I don't mind being in a skit at church because no one thinks I'm a great actor or comic. If I'm not great at that, it won't matter.*

External perfectionists give their all to achieve the things that mean the most to them. But internal perfectionists need good reasons to face their fears. For example, when relationships become more important to them than embarrassment, dreamers can find the strength to face any challenge.

Esther had a wonderful third-grade teacher. She loved the teacher so much and would have done almost anything to please her. This teacher constantly communicated, "I believe in you!" One day the teacher told the class that the first student to say all of the multiplication tables through the nines in front of the entire class would get a prize. Esther saw an opportunity to prove herself to this accepting teacher. She studied constantly. Multiplication tables and other rote memorization tasks are hardly the favorite pastimes of dreamers, yet Esther practiced day and night until she could say them perfectly.

Although she is over thirty now, Esther still has the prize she won that day in the third grade. And she has fond memories of the teacher who inspired her. She was willing to strive for excellence with this teacher and face her fears because the teacher already accepted her unconditionally.

"Stop Pushing": Dreamers React to Pressure

When we talk about unconditional acceptance, we are talking about how it *feels* to the child. All of us notice things that children do that indicate a need for some major character improvement and growth. But what matters is that when your child thinks of you, she considers you more loving than critical, more encouraging than meddlesome. If you're thinking *lazy*, a perceptive dreamer is likely to see the words written all over your face.

If you want to help a dreamer overcome the fear of failure, keep it brief. Say, "I believe in you," without questioning the child's character. Never ask, "What is wrong with you that you won't try?" That approach communicates that you think the child has a serious character flaw.

Encouragement for the dreamer means helpfulness without pushiness. How can you know when help will be perceived as pressure? It's a fine line. When a dreamer is faced with a potentially risky situation, such as standing up in front of the class to try for a prize, asking him how he is feeling about trying or not trying lets your child know that you are interested in his choice and not your desires.

Before pointing out that a fear is unfounded, wait a moment to see whether the dreamer can discover that for herself. As you and your child lay out the options, "You could be great. You could miss some notes. You could freeze up and not be able to play," ask her the likelihood of each option and how she would handle it. Sometimes a dreamer knows intellectually that the likelihood of a particular disaster is small, but that knowledge hasn't moved from the head to the heart. Talking it out makes the possibilities less frightening.

Does this seem like a lot of talking and hand-holding to you? Do you just want to say, "Get over it"? Dreamers require patient attention. There's no way around it. If you stop listening and just shove, he won't take any responsibility for the outcome: "Well, I knew I wasn't ready, but my mother made me do it!" That doesn't make him more willing to take risks, and he can become dependent on you to push.

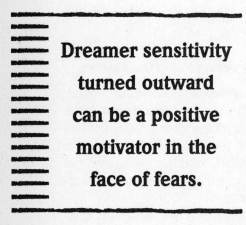

Dreamer sensitivity turned outward can be a positive motivator in the face of fears.

When you get the urge to give advice, start with an affirmation: "I'm sure you've already thought of this, but you didn't mention . . ." Get your dreamer to think about the feelings of others who might be affected by his decision. But don't focus on how you feel. Your child could perceive that as emotional manipulation. Instead, help your child to consider the feelings of teammates or the friends who could feel let down or abandoned when your child won't follow through. Dreamer sensitivity turned outward can be a positive motivator in the face of fears.

Sometimes she will choose to take the risk. Other times she will choose the safer path and experience the disappointment of seeing others succeed at what she wouldn't attempt. Letting a dreamer give in to fears is hard, but that, too, is a part of the learning process. Let your dreamer know that your love and acceptance are not based on her performance.

Are you ever tempted to point out the fun that others are having doing something your child chose not to try? Supporting your child means supporting whatever decision he makes. Later on, at a teachable moment, you can ask your dreamer what he has learned from the experience or how he is feeling about things now. You might be surprised with his honest assessment when you provide a supportive environment in which to assess himself and his choices. When your child or teen admits mistakes, affirm his character and the maturity shown in being able to learn from his experiences.

Wanting to Quit Before They Start: Encouraging Outside Activities

Does your dreamer tend to quit things before he starts? Allow him to choose from several activities, but then expect him to complete anything he begins. If he is being mistreated by a coach or his choir director is unwilling to take control of an extreme problem between peers, it may be reasonable to say, "You shouldn't have to deal with that. Let's explore other options." But by and large, a dreamer, like everyone else, shouldn't be allowed to bail out because things get a little tough.

Ron has firsthand experience coaching in youth basketball leagues. He has observed that on many occasions volunteer coaches don't consider the interests of all the players on their team. Therefore, the boys may get discouraged when they don't get the playing time they feel they deserve. Ron remembers one boy who was a dreamer and wanted to quit his team before the season ended. He felt the coach was not treating him fairly in playing time. "His mother asked for my counsel. My suggestion was to talk privately with the coach about her son's discouragement but insist that the boy remain on the team and not give up."

Some dreamers, like this boy, are naturally good at sports and will choose a physical activity. Others don't get enough exercise. In those cases, it's okay to say, "Our family values physical fitness so you must choose at least one physical activity." That means you need to get some regular exercise, too. When you require a child to be active, give the choice of team sports/classes or private lessons/classes whenever possible. Some dreamers choose the social atmosphere of the team or dance class. Others need the privacy to work on difficult skills provided by individualized lessons.

Provide as many options as possible, but tell your dreamer that *no action* is not one of the options. Because some activities involve money and deadlines while others do not, let your child know the deadlines and the default option. This can thaw out the frozen dreamer who otherwise would avoid any risks. If the dreamer refuses to sign up for a sport on time, the default physical activity might be aerobics. If the child puts off signing up for art lessons, the default activity could be continuing to take piano. You need to accept that from time to time the dreamer may miss out on things that require a quick decision.

Occasionally, it is permissible to make decisions for your child when a quick decision is required as long as the consequences for the dreamer are not long term. In the "it couldn't be helped" moments when you have committed your dreamer to something, explain the decision in dreamer language, such as, "Your Scout leader called and asked if you would want to go rappelling on Saturday. Because you weren't home I had to make a quick decision. I've already paid the money, and I'm sure you can do this even though some kids would be too scared to go," or "Jeremy called and wanted you to go to Camp Shakespeare with him tomorrow morning. It's only two hours long and he had to know right then. I said that you would probably enjoy it. I hope it's okay. I knew you wouldn't want to hurt Jeremy's feelings."

Sometimes a parent *must* make a decision that will be unpopular with a dreamer child. Ron recalls when he and Ginger decided Adam needed to go to cotillion, where boys and girls attend social classes to learn proper etiquette:

"When informed of our decision, Adam pitched a fit, became enraged, and declared he would *never* go. Instead of getting into a bargaining time or a power struggle with Adam, Ginger and I decided to be sympathetically firm. We told him that there are a few times when parents have to make decisions that are unpopular. 'You have permission to hate going to these classes,' we said. 'You can talk with the other boys and rag on us for making you attend. You can even be miserable. However, going is not optional. The choice to enjoy, endure, or be disgusted is your choice.'" He had to go, but he didn't have to enjoy it. That gave him some measure of freedom within limits, something dreamers cherish.

When work, not fun or learning, is involved, you would do well to talk it over with your child. Never commit a dreamer to work for someone outside the family, whether it's mowing lawns or baby-sitting, without his approval. In these situations, fear of failure is rarely the issue.

We understand the temptation to push, especially if your dreamer is a couch potato. You might be tempted to maneuver him into work without his knowledge, thinking, *I'll set something up with a neighbor and he'll be too embarrassed to back out.* He may not want to go back and tell the neighbor no, but you have just given him a weapon to use against you in the game of passive-aggression. He can delay and delay until the neighbor's yard looks like a meadow.

If you want your child or teen to do some work without having to be dragged kicking and screaming, let life teach the lesson. Make sure that your dreamer needs money and has no place to get it. The tried and true manipulation, "You'll embarrass me if you don't follow through," is not nearly as strong an encourager to work as a little real-world poverty.

Avoiding Flattery: Learning What Dreamers Need to Hear

How does your dreamer react to praise? Does she seem less than appreciative? Even when a dreamer takes risks and succeeds, she can perceive compliments as pressure. Take this comment: "I love that sculpture! It's so lifelike!" Certainly, the dreamer should hear a compliment, right? Well, not necessarily. It is equally possible that your child will look for criticism, thinking, *What you really mean is, "It's an ugly sculpture that looks just like that ugly person you used as a model."* Or the dreamer may hear an uninformed opinion like, *I don't know anything about sculpture, but I'd better say something.* Even if she feels that the comment is informed and positive, she may feel pressure: *Now Mom is going to expect everything I do to be this good. Doesn't she realize that this took a whole* month?

During most of his high school basketball games, Rick was on the bench. He had begun to wonder why he dressed out for the games. Then in mid-January, just before the play-offs, an outbreak of the flu hit the team. Three starters were out. Rick wouldn't be on the bench or making a brief substitution. For the first time, the team really needed him. His heart raced as he entered the gym for warm-ups. He was sweating like a fountain. The cute girl from his English class was on the front row. Yet for some reason, all Rick could see was his father's face halfway up the bleachers. His only thought was, *What will my dad say if I blow this chance?*

It was ironic. Rick's dad was supportive, but he had never pushed Rick into sports. Mr. Johnson didn't particularly like watching basketball. He went to the games only because his son might play. During the game, Rick kept glancing up to his dad to see if he could read any sign of disapproval. When Mr. Johnson left for a few minutes to get a soft drink, Rick actually played better. As the game ended without any major catastrophes, the Johnsons rushed down to congratulate their son. For the first time that night, Rick smiled.

What did Rick need to hear? What wasn't his dad saying at home that could have created that sense of pressure? Perhaps he needed to hear: "I just like being with you. It doesn't matter what we do."

A dreamer also needs to hear that you notice *her*—not what she does or how she looks. Look for the little clues she gives to discover what is in her heart. Does she pay special attention to a dying plant? Notice her green thumb. Does she like rearranging the furniture? Notice her eye for interiors and the ways in which she makes a room more comfortable and inviting. In short, find out what she cares about and make positive comments to your child.

Breaking the Cycle of Fear

Although all dreamers fear failure, the more risks a dreamer has taken successfully, the more willing she is to take risks in the future. To get your dreamer out of a negative fear cycle, help her to take some risks in areas where there is a high chance for immediate success. Instead of reiterating that "anything worth doing is worth doing well," which is a great platitude for the drivers and diplomats who don't need it, find something that she can do well with little effort. That is a starting point, not an admission that laziness is admirable.

After your dreamer has had some success, guide him gradually toward risks that will require greater effort. A little confidence goes a long way as your child enters the more difficult part of the journey. Each success becomes a building block toward a confident future.

To keep success in the forefront of your dreamer's mind, make special note of her accomplishments. Point out her artwork or trophies to others from time to time, not so often that she feels pressured and not so little that she feels ignored. Occasionally, watch videos of your dreamer's successes when others can share the joy. In Phillip's family, a brother and sister ice-skate. The parents proudly bring tapes of their children's competitions to family parties, and everyone enjoys seeing the videos and commenting on the children's talent.

In a few rare cases, we have seen dreamers who had so much success that they developed almost paralyzing fear of losing that success. Somehow they think, *Any day now, I'll be found out, and everyone will know that I'm not really talented at all.* More often, though, when a dreamer has had some successes and feels supported in success and failure, he begins to respond less extremely to failure when it occurs.

When you focus on who your child *is* and not what she *does,* as we have described, you will be doing as much as you can do to reduce fear. The rest is up to the dreamer.

Chapter 13

When External Perfectionists Meet Internal Perfectionists: There Are No Perfect Parents or Perfect Children

If all the good people were clever,
And all the clever people were good,
The world would be nicer than ever
We thought that it possibly could.

But somehow, 'tis seldom or never
The two hit it off as they should;
The good are so harsh to the clever,
The clever so rude to the good!

from "The Clever and the Good"
by Elizabeth Wordsworth

Now we get to a subject very close to our hearts. In our counseling practices, we have seen many painful family situations occur when parents are external perfectionists and children are dreamers. They are like oil and water. You see, external perfectionists and dreamers have very different agendas in life. No one is more "concrete detail" than an external perfectionist, and no one is more "big picture" than a dreamer. So this parent-child combination generally causes the most friction. But there are some exceptions. Not all external perfectionists expect others to meet their standards. Some have a real sense of humor about personality differences and are hard only on themselves. And some parents have learned to turn their perfectionism in a positive direction for the benefit of a dreamer child by saying to themselves, "I want to be the best parent I can be by learning what my child needs and doing it."

Take Deena for example. Her mother is an external perfectionist who doesn't really understand how Deena thinks. When Deena was a child and teen, her mother often missed the point of much of the child's communication, but she always tried to understand her. Deena didn't do her schoolwork in a conventional manner. She often stopped and started on school projects among her household chores.

One day Deena was cleaning out the bathtub and stopped to draw a portrait for a school report. When her mother found the bathtub half cleaned, she was angry. As Deena tried to explain, at first her mother didn't hear her. Then Deena shoved the drawing into her mother's hand. When she saw the drawing, Deena's mother ignored the bathtub and praised the picture. The mother was genuinely amazed by her daughter's talent. She then let Deena finish the bathtub on her own timetable.

From experiences like this one, Deena's mother learned to set general standards about chores and grades. She let Deena pursue tasks in her own way as long as Deena met the family's general standards. This mother encouraged the development of character in her daughter and set her priorities on the overall goals, even though she was frustrated or at least bewildered to see Deena's methods.

During Deena's elementary school years, her mother began to step back to see what her daughter would do given the responsibility for remembering projects and chores. She didn't completely comprehend how Deena got things done, but she was pleased with Deena's results. It became easier to focus on the product when she ignored the process, which took an extra measure of patience and a conscious choice not to interfere.

Despite her success in most areas, Deena's perfectionistic mother struggled to understand her daughter. But she didn't give up. As an external perfectionist, she wanted to do everything well, including parenting. She thought, *If I have to adapt a little, I'm willing to do it for Deena's sake.* And Deena thrived.

Sources of Conflict Between the Two Kinds of Perfectionists

Not all external perfectionists are so successful in discovering how to motivate dreamers toward their potentials. One discussion with some perfectionistic parents went something like this: "You know," said Mr. Tally, "what you said last time about passive-aggressive behavior may be what's happening at our house. Tara is definitely mad about something most of the time. I ask her to wipe off the counter, and she makes all these grunting and groaning noises. Then she makes a swipe at the counter. I make her go back and pick up every crumb, but it's a battle. Tara does everything halfway at best. She's never been allowed to manipulate us with this stuff. Why doesn't she just see that it would be easier to do the work right the first time?"

Like Deena's mother, Mr. and Mrs. Tally are external perfectionists with a dreamer child. On the one hand, it appears that they expect their daughter to be someone just like them, not accepting who God made her to be. On the other hand, they are trying to teach her skills that they know she will need in life. They interpret Tara's behavior through their doer glasses and come up with a negative picture of her. And perhaps her picture of them isn't so pretty either. Part of the internal perfectionism of the dreamer is the ideal of kindness toward others. External perfectionists who become perfectionistic, placing their standards on the child, are perceived as negative, critical, and unsympathetic.

Among all cognitive styles, dreamers are by far the least tolerant of nitpickers. As one dreamer jokingly said, "I believe that there is no such thing as constructive criticism." Some external perfectionists have a difficult time holding back comments that they consider helpful because they believe that dreamers will see things their way if the dreamers have *all* the information.

Perfectionistic parents who place their standards on others can be drivers who bellow orders at their children but are more likely to be diplomats who quietly and sternly pick at their children day after day. Diplomats who were constantly criticized as children, even though they rarely stepped out of line, grow up to fear any imperfection. As adults, these perfectionistic diplomats are too polite to openly criticize their friends, but they can be critical of anyone whose behavior or performance could reflect on them, whether that be a spouse, a child, or an employee.

Words like *lazy, irresponsible,* and *careless,* which come out in moments of frustration, let dreamers have some idea how perfectionistic parents perceive them. Although some parents also hear the dreamers' perspectives in angry moments, others have children who swallow their thoughts and feelings because they feel completely unable to communicate with Mom and Dad in the midst of criticism.

External perfectionists know when the dreamer child is not responding to their attempts to change her; but they may not realize that if an internal perfectionist believes that someone cannot be pleased, she will give up and do nothing. Because communication between external and internal perfectionists often breaks down, each needs to understand what the other feels and why.

The External Perfectionist's View of the Dreamer

Lazy is perhaps the word external perfectionists use most frequently to describe dreamers. Not all perfectionistic parents or teachers say this aloud to the child, but most think it. They are convinced that the dreamer could do things in a detailed way but is refusing to do so. This assessment is only partially correct. A dreamer can be detailed about the external world for brief periods of time. But external perfectionists expect detailed work from the dreamer child all the time. If the child works very hard to please the parent once in a detailed task, the external perfectionist doesn't realize the amount of effort required. Rather than appreciating how far the dreamer stretched to meet the standard, the perfectionistic parent sees the effort as proof he is lazy most of the time.

Some perfectionistic parents believe that their dreamer would sit around all day if she could, has no goals, and hates real work. By "work," external perfectionists mean manual labor such as housekeeping and yard work. The inventor Thomas Edison disliked physical labor, yet we know that he was quite productive. One biographer said, "Alva's imagination and liking for books were counterbalanced by an abhorrence of physical labor that would have made a sloth look like a long-distance runner."[1]

For dreamers like Edison, the effort needed to focus on tiny concrete details is much greater than that needed to be creative. Dreamers do become sloth-like around parents who "sweat the small stuff" because they are discouraged.

> **Global thinkers are less likely to read directions, listen carefully to the details of instructions, or do tasks in a step-by-step fashion.**

Related to the view that dreamers are lazy is the idea that dreamers are careless. Global thinkers are less likely to read directions, listen carefully to the details of instructions, or do tasks in a step-by-step fashion. Even calendars can feel too constraining to the dreamer child, who wants to keep all options open. "I know, I know," says the dreamer and then promptly forgets what was said without writing it down. Then the external perfectionist views the child as unteachable and the work done as mediocre.

Fiction writer Eudora Welty, in her autobiographical book *One Writer's Beginnings,* recalls her mother's take on her less-than-perfect schoolwork. She writes,

It was examinations that drove my wits away.... Being expected to measure up was paralyzing. I failed to make 100 on my spelling exam because I missed one word and that word was "uncle." Mother, as I knew she would, took it personally. "You couldn't spell *uncle*? When you've got those five perfectly splendid uncles in West Virginia? What would *they* say to that?"

It was never that Mother wanted me to beat my classmates in grades; what she wanted was for me to have my answers right. It was unclouded perfection I was up against.[2]

When perfectionistic parents and teachers want to give dreamers the benefit of the doubt, they tend to view dreamers as well-intentioned but forgetful. "She stops in the middle of a task as if she had been abducted by aliens. The cloth is on the counter. The counter is half wiped. And my daughter is nowhere to be found," the frustrated mom says. Dreamers are perceived as equally spacey about their possessions. They lose things, leave things, break things, and drop things on the floor. Dreamers will step right over something on the floor and then ask if you have seen the jacket or toy in question.

Being forgetful and not noticing details may frustrate your dreamer child. *What is wrong with me?* he may think. Even with something he cares a great deal about, like the family dog, a dreamer forgets to do the daily maintenance needed. Many a dreamer child has forgotten to feed the fish and cried bitter tears when the fish is found floating in the tank.

The Dreamer's View of the External Perfectionist

Just as external perfectionists have a negative view of their "lazy" and "spacey" dreamer children, dreamers have a few choice descriptions of their perfectionistic parents. We are not in any way implying that these perceptions are true. But you need to know what dreamers are thinking that they may not be saying. We have interviewed many dreamers, and certain themes emerge on their view of external perfectionists.

The key problem from the dreamer's perspective is that external perfectionists are shallow. When parents care about how things like clothes and appliances are taken care of, the dreamer views them as materialistic. "My parents care more about possessions than about people," said a dreamer. "They spend all their time worrying about how things will look to other people, and they never spend any time thinking deeply about anything. I'm worrying about ethnic cleansing in Europe, and my mother is only worried about cleansing the bathtub."

The view of external perfectionists as shallow begins early in life, well before the child knows the word *shallow.* Dreamers aren't able to accurately assess the depth of feeling or thought within external perfectionists because external perfectionists spend less time discussing their views and more time "doing." Many dreamers would be surprised at the depth of intellect and compassion of their doer parents. Yet, because most discussion in the family concerns the practical details of life, misperceptions persist.

For Eudora Welty, another perfectionist made a lasting impression:

> Miss Duling, a lifelong subscriber to perfection, ... was a dedicated schoolteacher who denied herself all she might have done or whatever other way she might have lived (this possibility was the last that could have occurred to us, her subjects in school)....
>
> She emerges in my perhaps inordinate number of schoolteacher characters. I loved those characters in the writing. But I did not, in life, love Miss Duling. ... I did nothing but fear her bearing-down authority, and did not connect this (as of course we were meant to) with our own need or desire to learn, perhaps because I already had this wish, and did not need to be driven.[3]

Dreamers see perfectionistic parents as obsessive, unable to free their minds of their "to do" list for a moment. *Everything has to be his way,* thinks the dreamer about a perfectionistic father. *He runs the house like a boot camp and treats everyone like a soldier, not caring about anyone else's feelings.* Most perfectionistic parents do care about other people's feelings, but they are trying to focus on character traits like stick-to-itiveness and desire for excellence in a detailed manner. They wrongly believe that by forcing the dreamer to be productive, they will nurture his self-esteem. In such families there is little room for the creative expression of ideas or experimentation with feelings.

Many external perfectionists assume that the child will respect the title "parent." They may have the Ten Commandments on the wall and assume that the child automatically will honor the parents by obeying. A dreamer doesn't have a natural respect for titles. If he views a parent or teacher as shallow or insensitive, he may fear, not respect, the adult; and if he views a parent as obsessive, he may have contempt for that parent. Respectful behavior must be earned by the parent and learned by the dreamer.

Are You Obsessive?

What do we mean by "obsessive"? Obsessions are thoughts that control a person's behavior. For example, suppose that you can't stand to go to bed without cleaning up the kitchen. It bothers you so much that you will stay up all night doing it, because if you get into bed, you won't be able to sleep. And suppose one night you did try to ignore the kitchen because you'd had a long day and when you lay down, the words, *Clean up the kitchen* kept coming into your mind; then you would be a person who struggles with obsessive thoughts. Everyone has an obsessive thought from time to time, but if you act on the thoughts compulsively, you may be what dreamers think of as obsessive.

Perhaps at this point you are wondering, *Have I become obsessive?* The following list gives true examples of external perfectionists who have gone over the edge into obsessiveness.

You know you're an obsessive parent if

- you command your toddler to sit up straight in his stroller.
- you receive a loving Mother's Day or Father's Day card from your seven-year-old, and you mark the misspellings and grammatical errors in red ink and return it to her to make corrections.
- you vacuum every time your child leaves a foot-shaped indention on your plush carpet.
- you avoid the urge to vacuum by not allowing your child to walk on your plush carpet.
- you make your teen wash her hands after she touches anything.
- you send your child to camp with all his clothes pinned together in matching outfits.
- you glue your decorative doodads and whatnots onto your tables so that your child can't knock them over or move them.

Obsessiveness is much rarer than perfectionism. The child feels as if the parent is walking around with a white glove all the time looking for a spot of failure to criticize. An obsessive parent may talk about how the child will reflect on the parent, saying things like, "Your room will embarrass me in front of my friends." Rather than appealing to the dreamer's fear of embarrassment and natural concern for the feelings of others, this statement results in less cooperation because the dreamer says to himself, "I'm just an embarrassment to my mother. I can never please her."

Because the dreamer feels hurt, she assumes that the obsessive parent is disrespectful of her feelings, and so, in turn, she shows the parent little respect. Some parents never point out what the child does right, only what she does wrong. Without encouragement, dreamers wither.

One family brought their fifteen-year-old son into counseling to be taught to be obedient. After an interview, it became clear that he was a dreamer. He had an inquisitive mind, but anytime he tried to explore different perspectives on life from those he had been taught in his family, his parents panicked. First the parents blamed the school, so they put him in private school. Then they blamed the neighborhood, so they forbade him to have contact with neighbors. At one point they decided that he was demon possessed. But the parents weren't willing to look at their behavior.

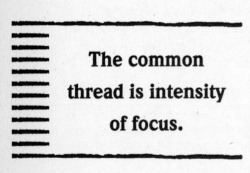

The common thread is intensity of focus.

By the time he was seventeen, the years had taken their toll. He didn't know who he was or who he wanted to be. He ran away and joined the marines, but before the end of basic training, he washed out. Now as an adult, to rebel against the identity his parents tried to force on him, he is a street musician. Though homeless, he feels free.

Common Ground Between the Two Types of Perfectionists

Two types of perfectionists with divergent worldviews: How can both be perfectionists and yet be so different? We believe that the common thread is intensity of focus. External perfectionists are focused on the concrete details of life. Dreamers are focused on the relational and abstract details of life. While the external perfectionist is giving a detailed list of instructions to the dreamer, the dreamer is contemplating the underlying meaning and philosophical implications of what is being said. Let's imagine some specific events and how the external perfectionist and the internal perfectionist (the dreamer) might perceive them.

Event	External Perfectionist's Thoughts	Dreamer's Thoughts
Dad says, "I'm sick of this mess!"	*I'm sick of this mess.*	*Dad is sick of me.*
Son says, "Oh Mom, give me a break. I just missed a few leaves. Nobody died."	*My son is so lazy. He does everything halfway. What did I do to deserve this?*	*My mother is so picky. Nothing I do is ever right. She acts like she hates me.*
Stepdad says, "Why don't you cut that hair? Who will ever give you a job if you look like a St. Bernard?"	*This kid needs guidance. He's going to be rejected all his life if he doesn't show himself in his best light. I hate to see such a great kid fail.*	*My stepdad thinks that people should be judged by how they look. If Jesus Himself walked in the door, he'd say, "Hey, don't You think You could use a cut and shave?"*

Parenting Style Adaptations

To raise a dreamer who is personally confident and who respects parents, teachers, and other authority, you must adapt your parenting to the dreamer's cognitive style, not the other way around. *Whoa, there!* you may be thinking. *I'm the adult. My child should adapt to me!* We aren't saying that you make the dreamer the center of your universe. But we do want to help you avoid exasperating your dreamer son or daughter.

> **No child can bend too far from his God-given personality and cognitive style without breaking.**

For your home to be one in which the dreamer thrives, you may have to be flexible. If you had a greenhouse, you wouldn't tell the tropical plants, "I don't like humidity, so you can adjust to a little less water." Well, you could say that, but your plants would die. No child can bend too far from his God-given personality and cognitive style without breaking. As an adult, you have a greater ability to understand and adapt to your child's needs than your child has to understand you.

Although you may not be an external perfectionist, you probably have perfectionistic moments. We have already mentioned some adaptations parents can make, such as avoiding nagging and criticism/advice. Knowing *how* to change can be more difficult than knowing *what* to change. You don't want to seem disinterested, so how can you show concern without giving advice? You don't want to be a nag, but how can you help a child who is so forgetful?

Ron's wife, Ginger, cited an example of how she responded to Adam's forgetfulness by imposing a natural consequence instead of nagging for his irresponsibility. Ginger had just purchased Adam a new jacket. In one day, he left it in two places. The first time he left it at the barbershop. They had to drive back to the shop and pick it up. Later he forgot to pick up his jacket after basketball practice. They had to drive back to the gym and get it. Instead of lecturing Adam, Ginger charged him for the gas and the time required to make the extra trips. Adam likes his money, so this approach made a lasting impact on his attitude toward his possessions.

Letting your dreamer learn from life doesn't mean that you don't set limits. Like all children, dreamers need to know what the rules are and what the consequences will be if they choose to step outside the limits. One way of reducing parent-child conflict is to set clear rules that apply to all the children in the family. Consistent rules keep dreamers from feeling that they are being compared negatively to siblings.

Many struggles could be avoided if dreamers would listen to parental advice. But because they are so sensitive and tend to learn best from experience, dreamers rarely take advice well until they are adults. Even as adults, dreamers accept advice only from people they feel genuinely care about them. If you start the "I told you so" routine, a dreamer child is less likely to take personal responsibility for failures and more likely to blame a peer, the teacher, or you.

Let your child take personal responsibility for as many tasks as are age appropriate. Then you can conserve energy to deal with the unavoidable battles over issues such as defensive or devious lying, stealing, cheating, using foul language, smoking, or drinking. Dreamers are no more likely than other children to engage in any of these behaviors, except for defensive lying, which we will discuss in chapter 15. However, when a dreamer has a perfectionistic parent or perceives the parent that way, he is more likely to choose to engage in self-destructive behaviors in defiance of the parent's standards.

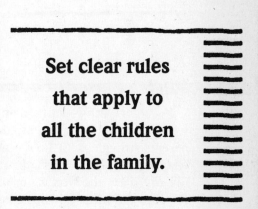

Set clear rules that apply to all the children in the family.

How to Avoid Giving a Dreamer Weapons of Rebellion

Many parents create opportunities for rebellion by showing an overconcern in a particular area of a child's life. If you openly worry about your child's diet, the dreamer who feels parental disapproval will refuse to eat healthy food as revenge. Of course, your child suffers ultimately. But you create the atmosphere for power struggles.

To avoid giving a dreamer weapons to use against you in a battle, don't harp on any one topic or group of topics. And be a person of integrity. In the heat of a verbal battle, every error you have ever made can and will be used against you. But if you set fair limits and avoid hypocritical behavior, you should be able to stand your ground effectively with a dreamer child when it really counts. To move to a deeper level of parent-child relationship, though, you must change not only outwardly, but also in ways that cause the dreamer child to feel that you are changing inwardly.

> **You create the atmosphere for power struggles.**

Moving Closer to a Dreamer Child

Dreamers value depth of person. How can your child know what is in your heart and mind if you don't communicate it? Many parents struggle with how real to be with their children: "Will it result in a loss of respect? In admitting my failings, will I be handing my teen another weapon to use against me?" Although a dreamer can bring up your admitted faults, she is far more likely to point out your unconfessed sins. Communicating at a deep level doesn't mean that you become your child's buddy. She still needs a parent willing to be responsible by setting and enforcing limits. The more genuine you are while maintaining the parental role, the more your dreamer will hear what you say about deeper issues such as values and faith.

Moving to this deeper level requires self-reflection on your part. You may ask, Why do I have a need for excellence? Is it because it was born in me or demanded of me? Is it that I want to be perfect or that I want my children to have an easier and more successful life than I have had? When you ask yourself these questions and face the answers honestly, there is hope for true communication with a dreamer child, who is interested in knowing feelings before facts.

A pronouncement like, "This is just the way that I am; and because I'm the parent, you should do things my way," can shut down communication. A feelings statement such as, "I never felt that I was good enough to please my father, and I guess sometimes I'm still trying to get his approval by having perfect children," can open the lines of communication to the compassionate dreamer. Stories and illustrations that paint a picture permit your child to see what motivates you and helps him feel less attacked.

Letting your dreamer child know "we want to be the parents you need" helps her see that you are still growing and haven't set yourself up as perfect. Teachers, coaches, youth leaders, and counselors can do the same. As different as external and internal perfectionists are, they can find common ground. Because dreamers are idealistic, it also helps them to know that the adults in their lives are trying to meet an ideal standard, such as pleasing God, that is not a superficial ideal. Your honesty about your fears of failure leads to greater honesty in the dreamer child.

Although a dreamer usually has less intimate knowledge of the fear of turmoil and chaos, perfectionistic parents who admit this fear allow the dreamer to be empathetic. Understanding your childhood and the resulting need for some sense of control can help the dreamer to be more patient, especially if you acknowledge her need for freedom of expression and variety in daily life. Some perfectionistic parents are critical when they are trying to be open and genuine. Saying, "I was just born with a natural desire to do things right the first time, and you are more in a dream world by nature," is not illuminating from the dreamer's perspective. The beginning of communication is not analysis. Later in the process, when she has come to believe in the parents' unconditional acceptance, the dreamer will begin to analyze the relationship dynamic for herself.

Helping the Dreamer Develop Respect for Adults

The honest communication we have been discussing goes a long way toward earning the respect of the dreamer child, particularly if you have a teenager who has shown little respect for you in the past. For younger children, the concept of respect for others can be taught using dreamer positive feeling language. Try saying, "One way we care for others is to treat them with respect, even if we are angry with them. We don't have to feel that we respect them to treat them respectfully. It's not being fake; it's being kind. Sometimes when people are gruff, it's because someone hasn't been kind to them in the past, and they think they have to be gruff to get cooperation."

Likewise, discussion about the child's reaction to Dad might be: "I know that you don't realize how sarcastically you said that. Why don't you calm down and think about what you want to say in response to your dad's question? I'm sorry if he upset you, but I'm sure that you can see how different that response was from your normal respectful tone of voice. It's so unusual for you to speak unkindly to anyone. Did you think that Dad was speaking unkindly to you?" Expressing openness to your child's feelings and acknowledging a positive view of him are keys to the development of respectful behavior in a young dreamer.

Part 3

PARENTING THE
DREAMER
CHILD

Chapter 14

The Age of Fantasy: Dreamers in the Early Years

What are you able to build with your blocks?
Castles and palaces, temples and docks.
Rain may keep raining, and others may roam,
But I can be happy and building at home....

from "Block City" by Robert Louis Stevenson

As your dreamer blossoms, you may be thrilled to discover you have a budding actress or the next great novelist. But at Terrance's house, they had the makings of a mechanical engineer. And the results weren't always so thrilling.

Four-year-old Terrance was impatient when people tried to tell him how things work because he wanted to figure it out for himself. If he could get his hands on it, he took it apart. He used watches, radios, and even the toaster for experimentation. But when he tried to put something back together, he often had a few extra parts left over. This frustrated Terrance enormously, but he wouldn't ask for help. And even though his parents punished him repeatedly for dismantling things, he could not seem to contain his curiosity.

If Terrance broke something, he never ran away to avoid the blame. He always stayed to fix his mistakes. One day, he decided that cars could probably run just as well on dirt as on gas. So, Terrance put dirt into the tank of his dad's new car. When Dad tried to crank it up and the car wouldn't start, Terrance knew that his hypothesis was flawed. Rather than confessing, as a diplomat might have done, or sitting stone-faced as some drivers do until confronted, dreamer Terrance wanted desperately to make amends.

What gets rid of dirt? thought Terrance. *Water!*

When his father came out of the house to wait for the mechanic, he found Terrance holding the garden hose in the gas tank. Terrance didn't know that water does more permanent damage to a car's fuel system than dirt does. His father's anger was confusing to this young dreamer. Because he was trying to be helpful, Terrance couldn't understand why he was in trouble. He was crushed.

Terrance ran away crying. He went to sit in a tree and think about things. When he finally came down, he told his father dramatically, "You just broke my little heart all to pieces!" His father scooped the boy up in his arms and gave Terrance a big hug while he explained why gas tanks were off limits. Dreamers like Terrance are vulnerable in the preschool years. If they are listened to and nurtured, they can enter the school years confidently. If they are treated harshly, they will enter the school years angry and discouraged. In between nurturing and harshness, there is a lot to learn about parenting dreamers.

The early years when the unique thinking patterns of the dreamer mix with the cognitive developmental stages of early childhood are called the age of fantasy.

Dreamers as Infants

It isn't always possible to distinguish dreamers from other sensitive children during infancy. We asked some parents of older dreamers to think back on their children when they were infants. They tell us that when their dreamers were infants, they were affectionate and enjoyed being held, showed a wide variety of emotion from joy and delight to sadness to anger, and were sensitive to perceived rejection or correction. The extroverted dreamers were more open in infancy to affection from strangers, smiling at everyone; and the introverted dreamers clung to familiar adults and were less expressive with strangers.

Dana's daughter Anna Kate is an extrovert. From her earliest days, she looked around to see if anyone was looking at her, and she would smile at anything that moved. People interested her, and she wanted to be liked by everyone. As an infant if an adult spoke to her sharply by saying something like, "Anna Kate, DON'T PUT THAT KEY IN THE WALL OUTLET!" she dramatically fell into tears and came for hugs and kisses of reassurance that she was still loved.

Anna Kate has a little friend who was an imaginative infant. He had a book with a picture of a train in it; he opened the book to that page and sat on it, while he made train noises as if he was taking a ride. Dreamer infants often use objects in original ways. They may pick up blocks and use them as airplanes or trucks, making the appropriate noises, even though they have never seen anyone use a block in that way.

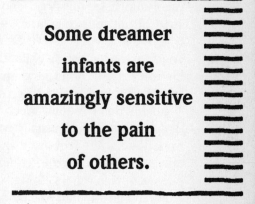

Dreamer infants often use objects in original ways.

Although all children have imaginative moments, dreamers are extreme in their inventive use of objects. If told by a peer or sibling not to use a toy or other object in a certain way, the dreamer infant is likely to have hurt feelings.

Some dreamer infants are amazingly sensitive to the pain of others. When David was an infant, he cried every time anyone else was injured. And it was clear from the way that he cried, he was truly heartbroken about the tears of his playmates. For months he couldn't stay in the church nursery because he was such an infectious crier that unless everyone else was quiet and happy, he was miserable. Early empathy is evident in many dreamer infants. And when a dreamer infant becomes upset over something that has happened to him or to another child, he can have difficulty calming himself down and can be very dramatic.

Some dreamer infants are amazingly sensitive to the pain of others.

Dreamer infants can also be infectious laughers. They are extreme in all emotions. Likewise, dreamers are extremely curious. They do a lot of exploring and dismantling. Some people say that boys are into everything, but we have found that dreamer girls can be just as curious and are sometimes dangerously quiet in their exploration.

Parenting the Dreamer Infant

All infants are somewhat perplexing because they can't clearly communicate thoughts and feelings. Dreamer children may be easier to fathom in infancy than at older ages. Most of us expect emotionality in infants and aren't so frustrated when we get it. Because during this early stage children determine whether or not others are trustworthy, we build a healthy foundation for their future relationships if we respond appropriately to the needs of these deeply sensitive children. This process begins with lots of affection.

Most dreamers enjoy hugging, cuddling, rocking, and sitting to look at books from time to time. Infants also need verbal affection. They may not understand the words, but the tone and body language communicate, "I love you very much!"

With affection there needs to be calmness. We don't mean lack of activity in the home. We mean calm parents. No yelling. None. We can't emphasize this point enough. Of course, we are talking about an ideal, but your child is an idealist and that's the world he lives in. If you know when you've blown it, and go back to apologize and comfort your infant or child, that goes a long way toward earning his respect. But don't give up striving toward the ideal! You'll be surprised at how much progress you can make in this area.

Infants don't require much discipline. When uncooperative, little Anna Kate could usually be distracted. But for biting, Dana sat Anna Kate a few feet away and firmly said, "No biting!" This time-out is a consequence intended to communicate that biting separates you from others. Biting is a behavior that can endanger other children and shouldn't be ignored.

Additional aspects of effective gentle discipline for infants include a firm tone and a serious face. Be calm, but clear. Warn once, and then act by removing the young child from the goal of misbehavior.

One final element of gentle discipline is the use of affection after a consequence. It doesn't make the discipline ineffective to reassure the infant while enforcing the limit. On the other hand, a child's tears should not result in his getting his own way. If you give in to a tearful or angry child, you are teaching the child that tears manipulate others. But reassurance isn't giving in. If daily life is sprinkled with generous doses of affection and a gentle discipline approach is followed, a dreamer infant develops a healthy trust of you and other adults in his life.

The Twos Transition

When children begin to become verbal, they are able to communicate their needs and wants more effectively and persistently. In general, what we are calling the twos transition occurs between one and three years of age during a time of rapid language development.

The introduction of language brings a new experimentation with ideas. They aren't just manipulating objects anymore. Dreamers learn how to manipulate their thoughts and how to affect the behavior of others through the use of language.

Barbara was having a moody day at mother's morning out. Her mother couldn't be there for an

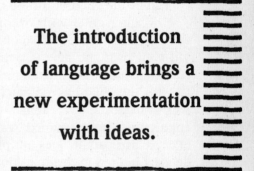

The introduction of language brings a new experimentation with ideas.

event that other parents were attending, and she was sulking in a corner when a teacher asked what was wrong. "My ditty dat and four dittens died!" said the forlorn child. This comment drew the sympathy of a group of teachers and parents.

When Joyce, a friend of Barbara's mother, noticed Barbara surrounded by consoling adults, she thought to herself *I don't think they have a cat.* She questioned Barbara about the truth of the story and was promptly kicked by a teacher. How dare Joyce question the poor suffering child! Joyce marched off to the phone and was able to reach Barbara's mother. Indeed, there were no "ditty dat and four dittens" and never had been.

This new level of dramatics makes it hard for you to know whether or not something is really bothering your child. Tall tales may mask real anxieties and disappointments or may be nothing more than playfulness. In Barbara's case, although there were no cats, she was genuinely sad that her mother wasn't at school that day. Young dreamers often create imagined reasons for their feelings. Your son may be in a bad mood but not know why. Or he may feel that his reasons for feeling unhappy won't be taken seriously, and a more extreme reason would be better.

As they move toward the preschool years, dreamers continue to be affectionate. But when angry, they may refuse affection. Anger is often caused by perceived rejection.

All children are more willful at this age because they are testing their abilities and their limits. The developmental task of all two-year-olds is to develop a sense of personal autonomy without social imbalances of too much control by the parents, too much control by the children, or too much isolation from adults.

A dreamer child with overly controlling parents may not develop a healthy sense of autonomy and could act like a two-year-old well past the age of two. Out-of-control, inconsistent, or passive parents can unintentionally encourage immaturity. In these families, the child has too much control and does not feel competent to handle the freedom. Autonomy that is inappropriate for a child's age, whether gained by emotional power struggles or given by a passive parent, does not produce a healthy sense of independence. Children in this transition need security with opportunities to test independence.

Emotions in the Transition Years

Even if you provide security and allow age-appropriate autonomy, the opposing desires for security and autonomy will battle within your child. Young dreamers go through normal moody phases, especially during physical growth spurts or periods of rapid cognitive development. During these times, the wide range of emotions and the speed with which the dreamer jumps from laughter to sadness to rage can be mind-boggling.

Like all two-year-olds, dreamers will throw a tantrum and be angry when they don't get what they want. Brooding dreamers may stay angry longer than doer children.

Despite volatility and moodiness as they express their independence, dreamers in this transition are delightfully playful and amusing. The imagination begins to blossom, although they may be hampered in demonstrating it while their language ability is growing. Fantasy play begins to engage more and more of their thoughts, but social savvy may lag well behind the desire to play creatively with peers.

Except for the most extroverted among them, dreamers at this age play well alone and generally entertain themselves better than more practical age-mates. Some prefer quiet activities such as books and puzzles while others prefer the grand stage of the backyard. If engaged in imaginative play, they won't be bored, although they may be destructive and break family rules in their exuberance and experimentation. Parents aren't always patient with such unrealistic play.

In the book *Little Bear* by Else Minarik, Mother Bear is initially less than sympathetic to Little Bear's desire to fly to the moon. He makes a marvelous space helmet and tells his mother about the trip he plans to make. She responds, "You are a little fat bear cub with no wings and no feathers."

Determined, Little Bear goes off to the moon anyway. He plays in his moon world alone until his mother decides to enter his imaginative play. "Are you a little bear from earth?" his mother asks. And she then tells him how much she misses her little bear who has gone off to the moon. Mother Bear stops trying to pull him into the real world and enters his dreamer world with words of love and acceptance.[1]

When they feel unaccepted, dreamers even this young can fantasize about revenge. Lisa at age three was playing in a pool with some older children. They started splashing, which she took as a personal attack more than a game. She started screaming at the older children: "My cousin big an' strong! He gonna come and t'row you in de ocean! De whales gonna eat you!"

Fears in the Transition Years

With the growth of fantasy and sensitivity comes the potential for fears. Although nightmares occur as the child tries to deal internally with fears of imaginary and possible dangers, what began as a real fear can become a tool to gain your attention. For example, once the sleep pattern is broken by repeated nightmares, a dreamer may awaken at about the same time on successive nights. Your child may then say that he had a nightmare and may believe it since he woke up. Wanting some help going back to sleep, your child can say he is frightened as an excuse for seeking your company.

The young dreamer learns from experience that more attention is paid to defined fears than to general loneliness or desire for affection. Tall tales can make us too quick to discount genuine fears. When an actual fear exists, the imaginative dreamer may relive the terror in vivid detail and will need help to work through the fear and anxiety. As language matures, a dreamer in the transition years is better able to communicate fears and feelings.

Discipline in the Transition Years

The general principles that apply to parenting infant dreamers also apply to children in the transition years. Calmness, affection, and playfulness continue to be important. Of new significance is your role as listener. While staying on an adult level emotionally, you can encourage discussion by getting onto your child's level physically by leaning down or picking him up. Because you are building the foundation for all future communication, developing an attentive listening style is critical.

There are times when it's okay to tell a child to hold a thought while you calm down or complete an interrupted task. But you must go back and listen to the young dreamer. Things that communicate "I am listening" include making eye contact, putting aside tasks, and turning on the answering machine. Not all conversations require focused attention, but don't try to guess whether or not an issue is significant to your child until you have heard his feelings.

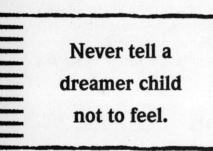

Never tell a dreamer child not to feel.

Many dreamers tell us that they can't remember how old they were when they stopped telling their parents how they really felt, but they must have been very young. To avoid this breakdown in communication, the listening parent focuses on feelings before facts and acknowledges the child's feelings without correcting them. A response such as, "You are feeling angry with your brother," opens communication, while a response such as, "You shouldn't feel so angry with your brother," closes communication. You may want to relabel a child's feelings, replacing *hate* with *angry*, for example, but never tell a dreamer child not to feel.

You also need to learn when to selectively ignore some behaviors. When your child demands a candy bar at the grocery store, that isn't the time for an attentive listening session. Although it's fine to try to distract your child first, you generally should ignore a child in the transition stage who whines and throws a tantrum.

If your child is in a pattern of losing emotional control in public places, you need to take control when the whining begins by stating the rule and the consequences. Try something like, "If you continue to whine, we will leave the store. You will have to go to Grandma's while I shop, and there will be no time to go to the park. Do you want to whine, or do you want to go to the park?" If your child just wanted an excuse to go to Grandma's, this deterrent won't work. But if the park is important and he isn't too tired, your young dreamer should be able to get emotional control and stop the whining before it turns into a tantrum.

Try making errands fun by playing games like "I spy." But when you go into a store, be preventive. The candy counter by the checkout looms in your future. Have something ready to give your child at that point, like a marker and paper. No one game or distraction works for long. We understand the desire to say to yourself, "Five more minutes. I know she's starting to lose it, but I need five more minutes."

Even when parents are preventive, calm, entertaining, and encouraging—in other words, perfect—dreamers in the transition stage can be uncooperative. Begin introducing natural and logical consequences at this age. Time-out is probably the most widely touted consequence these days. Many pediatricians and psychologists recommend one minute in time-out per year of age, followed by a hug. But time-out is really only logical for attention-seeking behaviors, so it doesn't solve all your discipline problems.

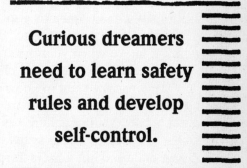

Curious dreamers need to learn safety rules and develop self-control.

Especially at this age, curious dreamers need to learn safety rules and develop self-control. Try adding one new limit and consequence at a time. If the issue is running in the street, for example, you could say, "From now on, if you run in the street, you will have to stay in the house for the rest of the day." A child of this age needs immediate consequences since he has no accurate sense of time. Setting one limit—and seeing how effective the consequence proves to be before adding new rules—allows you to gauge the child's maturity and keeps you from piling on too many limits and creating unnecessary power struggles.

Too often we can set limits on exploration when the dreamer is not in physical danger. Some parents let children this age go into the yard where there is a big, beautiful mud puddle and say, "Don't get wet!"

James at age three had an imaginative solution for getting wet. His mother told him not to get his Sunday clothes dirty by the creek. When she went out to find him, the clothes were in a neat row, and he was sliding naked into the creek for the whole neighborhood to see. But the clothes weren't wet.

In his dreamer fashion, James followed the spirit of the law more than the letter of the law. But by trying to keep his clothes dry, he was attempting to comply and thus exhibiting an early form of self-control. A dreamer wants to please you, so don't be too rigid. Give your child mud clothes for playing in the mud. If your vase is in danger, put it up. Punishing for exploration can communicate that curiosity is bad. You can also unintentionally send the message, "That vase is more important than your feelings." And guess what? In the future when your dreamer is angry with you, he is likely to start breaking the things you cherish the most.

Many parents want to know if within gentle discipline there is a place for spanking. Most of us were spanked as children and were not abused. Yet our culture has come to equate the two. Your decision to spank or not to spank should be based on what is best for your child and not what is the popular thing to do.

Parents of dreamers tell us that when they spanked a lot, they saw an increase in anger and disobedience. That means spanking had ceased to be discipline. Any consequence used too frequently will become ineffective. That is why logical consequences are nice. The consequence changes with the specific situation. If you choose to spank, just before and during the early talking stage seems to be the age when spanking used sparingly is most power-ful and least likely to produce bitterness.

One parent we know watched another parent choose not to spank a child who had clobbered his brother with a garden shovel. The observer commented, "I know he is feeling jealous of his brother, but I would have spanked him immediately to get his focus off his feelings and onto his behavior." If the child with the shovel was a driver, that approach might work. Being emotionally out of control isn't normal for drivers, and sometimes a little jolt brings the child back into emotional control. But get a dreamer's focus off his feelings with a spanking? It doesn't work that way. Dreamers often react to spanking, especially if it happens frequently or is done in anger, by becoming more upset and belligerent. Your setting off a chain reaction where he is increasingly out of control does not cause your child to accept personal responsibility for his behavior. Now he is mad at his brother and you, too.

A final word on spanking. If you were physically abused as a child, it is probably best for you to use time-out or some approach other than spanking. This choice protects you and your child. Every parent has been angry enough to hit a child too hard. If you have been abused, when you are angry you are more likely to impulsively act out the things that happened to you as a child. Instead of spanking at those moments, cool down and look at some other options. You do not have to neglect your responsibility as a parent if you choose not to spank.

Fun in the Transition Years

Now that your dreamer is talking, you can enjoy many new activities with him. One of the most delightful is storytelling. You already know that dreamers have an attraction to stories. They often entertain themselves with their own. Here are some ways that you can encourage that imaginative tendency in your child.

During these transition years, and even earlier, you may see clearer signs of the "dreamerness" of your child. She's telling tall tales? Then make the most of her knack for fiction, and try to develop her storytelling ability. It's never too early to pass on the oral tradition, the experts say, especially if your dreamer has an auditory learning style.

In *I'll Tell You a Story, I'll Sing You a Song: A Parents' Guide to the Fairy Tales, Fables, Songs, and Rhymes of Childhood,* author Christine Allison offers suggestions on how to tell stories. She includes all the classics, from Jack and the beanstalk to Aesop's fables, with all the details you may have forgotten—or have never known. And resources like this can give the confidence you need to help your young dreamer develop his gifts if you're not a natural storyteller.[2]

When you tell stories with books, be on the lookout for characters your dreamer child can identify with. His favorite characters will not necessarily be those you loved as a child. You may have been more of a Curious George[3] or a mischievous Madeline.[4] She may be more of an Angelina Ballerina. In the book by the same name, the little mouse "danced all the time and she danced everywhere, and often she was so busy dancing that she forgot about the other things she was supposed to be doing"—like cleaning up her room and coming down to breakfast. Sound like anyone you know?[5]

Some of the books your dreamer enjoys might strike you as bizarre. Look in the library for *Open House for Butterflies,* by Ruth Krauss, illustrated by Maurice Sendak, or one of their other collaborative projects. The steam-of-consciousness style skips around like a young dreamer's mind, with thoughts such as, "A little tree is a good thing not to be because you might grow up to be a telephone pole," and "If I had a tail I'd pull my wagon with it while I was picking flowers."[6] (The selected bibliography lists some additional books that dreamers love.)

Dreamers Three to Five

The latter preschool years when language is well established are the years of expressiveness. Social awareness of potential embarrassment is not yet fully developed, and dreamers at this age are likely to do or say anything. Your child may tell the clerk at the store that there is a baby in "Mommy's tummy," or that "our potty overflowed and made a *terrible* stinky mess." Whatever she says, it is certain to be full of drama.

Preschool-age dreamers have very expressive faces. When Kathleen was age four, if she stuck out her lip, lowered her eyes, and looked at the ground, the adult who just spoke to her was certain to have committed some grave offense against justice, truth, and all that is lovely and sacred. Such expressiveness makes the pain of the dreamer evident, whether or not the cause of the pain is apparent.

Storybooks that touch on feelings your child may be experiencing can open up discussion. In *Chrysanthemum* by Kevin Henkes, the title character is being singled out for ridicule because of her distinctive name. Despite her parents' constant encouragement, the sensitive Chrysanthemum wilts every time she faces the teasing of her peers at school—until she meets a wonderful dreamer teacher named Delphinium Twinkle who glories in Chrysanthemum's unique name, which not only stops the teasing, but helps the sensitive little mouse feel special again.[7] Books give you opportunities to talk to your child about love, friendship, and acceptance.

Perhaps because they are beginning to experience some of their own hurts, preschool dreamers show increasing compassion toward others who are hurting. Some parents of especially compassionate dreamers have told us that they saw their children gravitating toward the underdog even at this young age.

Imaginary Friends and Other Fantasy Play

Just as sensitivity becomes more well defined, so does the child's imagination. Able to more fully express ideas through language, the preschool dreamer is likely to have fantasy friends and engage in elaborate fantasy play. Dana's mother-in-law tells of Phillip's imaginary friend, Sarge, that he had at this age. He would say, "Oh, Sarge is here now," and tell her all about Sarge whenever they went for a ride in the car. On one trip from their hometown to Macon thirty minutes away, Phillip told his mother about Sarge's latest heroic deeds. When they arrived in Macon, Sarge was in the middle of a perilous situation. Phillip stopped in midstory and said, "That's all for today. More tomorrow."

Susan had imaginary baby sisters, John and Harold. No matter how hard her parents tried, she refused to change the names. She also had imaginary mice that she kept in a special box and that, unfortunately, some careless adult frequently sat on. All children of this age like fantasy, but imaginary friends are more common among dreamers.

Dreamers are more original and fantasy oriented in all their play than other children are. Some doers can't be Captain Hook without the right outfit, but dreamers don't need props. Although many children are somewhere between dreamer and diplomat or dreamer and driver, the parent should be able to say by age five whether or not the child is more of a dreamer or a doer. The dreamer is more interested in inventing and creating than in copying and producing. Imagination should be evident in problem solving, storytelling, or artistic creativity.

Imagination and Emotion

Fantasy can be seen in the way your child deals with anger and frustration at this age. Art had been told that he was not allowed to argue back when sent to time-out. So he decided that his toy lion could do his talking for him. One day when he was being sent to his room, he said, "Leo doesn't like you. He wants to bite your head off!"

"Oh, surely Leo doesn't mean that. If he bit off my head, I'd be dead," his mother replied.

"He wants you to be dead," came the angry retort. Neither Leo nor Art fully understood what it meant for Mother to be dead. But Art was angry and he found a way to express it.

With this increase in the positive side of imagination comes an increase in the prevalence and power of imaginary fears. Dreamer preschoolers know that monsters are real and parents can't see them. For dreamers, no amount of real-world proof changes the fact that there are things out there that they can't see and can't control. That makes the world a scary place. They also have fears about their performance in life and fears of disappointing people they love.

Although some internal perfectionism can be seen before age three, at this age the paralyzing effect of the dreamer's fear of failure becomes obvious. "I'm not sure what he can and can't do," said one mother of a three-year-old recently, "because I can't get him to try things."

The fear of failure is an indication that the dreamer's idealism is beginning to mature and more fully affect the child's worldview. Too often, the dreamer's ideal is an adult ideal of performance. If the child can't draw like an adult immediately, the dreamer won't attempt to draw at all. It can be the same thing with cutting, riding a bike, tying a shoe, or doing any other task that requires practice.

Listening to Your Preschooler

The general principles of a calm emotional climate and a gentle approach to discipline apply to preschool dreamers. They never outgrow their need for affection, although it may take a different form after the preschool years. Because the child talks all the time and has an unlimited supply of questions, you may want to say, "ENOUGH!" But now is the time for you to develop an active listening approach; that is, you become more involved in the listening process and encourage your child to talk about feelings.

Active listening is a concept found in many parent education programs including STEP[8] and Active Parenting.[9] An active listener listens for feelings and reflects those feelings back to the child without correction or advice. "Reflection without listening" is a rote repetition of what the child says. Repetition lets him know that you heard the words, but says nothing about whether or not you understood what he meant. Because dreamers so desperately want to be understood, *how* you listen is vital.

The dreamer says, "I hate my brother!" Don't give a correction like, "Now, dear, don't say that," or a rote reflection like, "You hate your brother." An active listening response would be, "You are feeling really angry with Michael right now."

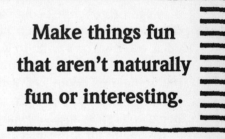

Make things fun that aren't naturally fun or interesting.

Active listening requires you to focus on your dreamer child. Feelings are more subtle than words and can be seen in body language and heard in tone of voice. Dreamers observe the whole person when they listen. Are you willing to try to become more like a dreamer in listening skills to discover the deeply rooted feelings motivating your child?

Fun as a Motivator

When your dreamer was an infant, you could do something fun to distract her from misbehavior. Now fun becomes a motivator. Dreamers can enjoy anything if it is made into a game. Many parents tell us that they get cooperation and enthusiasm by setting an egg timer and saying, "I think I can pick up these books faster than you can pick up those!" When you model creative approaches to routine tasks, dreamers learn a skill they will need to self-motivate in older years: How to make things fun that aren't naturally fun or interesting.

Incentives also make tasks more enjoyable for dreamer pre schoolers. No single incentive is an effective motivator for long. Try following a boring or negative task, like picking up the room, with a fun task, like reading a book together or playing a board game. Remember to state things in positive language. Say something like, "We can have popcorn as soon as you feed the dog," rather than, "If you don't feed that dog, there'll be no popcorn!"

Discipline for Preschoolers

We mentioned the use of a timer as a game, but it can also be used as a warning. "You have five more minutes to brush your teeth and put on your shoes. I've set the timer." Young dreamers respond well to this concrete way of measuring time.

"What?" you may say. "Are you saying that my abstract child will respond to a concrete approach?" Dreamers may not like it, but they can be concrete about some things. Your child needs to learn that, no matter how much he wants to wish it away, you mean what you say. For a child to get that message, you have to be consistent. You can count out loud as a warning, "If the puzzle is not put up before I count to five, then it will be put away for two days. One, two . . ." You have given your child ample time to comply. Being consistent and fair is important for the idealistic dreamer.

Discipline for a dreamer must also be gentle. Having your child make some form of restitution for misbehavior helps to keep her heart unscarred. One mother of a four-year-old tornado took money from her son's piggy bank after explaining to him that she expected him to pay for some broken candles. Knowing that he had a way to "make it right" helped this young boy to feel like less of a failure.

The dynamo who broke the candles was much more destructive with his sister around. Children are more destructive in groups, partly because they wind each other up, and partly because it's like a mob mentality—they give each other permission. For this reason, if two or more children are involved, there should be consequences for all.

For a child who uses passive-aggressive techniques like work slowdowns in response to consequences, conditional grounding can be an effective discipline technique to introduce in the preschool years. Rather than base grounding on a specific time period, restrict your child's freedom until a specific restitution is completed: "You can't leave the house until the rug is vacuumed." He can choose to sulk or get on with the consequence. If the child moves slowly, only the child suffers. Conditional grounding gives the responsibility back to the child for his actions without creating an angry confrontation.

Trauma in the Preschool Years

The preschool years are a time of rapid development. When basic developmental tasks coincide with emotional trauma, the dreamer can become stuck emotionally and may not be able to move forward without going back and experiencing the key emotional lessons that were interrupted.

For example, Lori was in the twos transition when her mother was killed in an accident. Somehow she associated the autonomy-seeking behaviors she'd been exhibiting with that abandonment. She regressed and became clingy. Her reaction was to be expected at first, during a period of grieving and confusion, but the dependent behavior did not subside two, four, or six years after her mother's death. A two-year-old can whine and cling, but by age eight, Lori's behavior was separating her from her peers. Because she had never successfully negotiated the development of autonomy, she did everything she could to keep people close through the use of dependent behaviors. But her classmates rejected her for those very behaviors.

Although few children of this age will lose a parent, far too many will experience an emotional trauma, whether divorce of the parents, harassment by peers, or child abuse. If you feel that your child is experiencing emotional struggles due to trauma, get a professional assessment. You may find that your child is experiencing a normal grieving process and time will be the healer, or you may discover that your dreamer has some underlying fear or anger that should be explored with a counselor. Some burdens are too heavy for you and your child to carry alone. Be willing to ask for help.

Chapter 15

The Age of Inventiveness: Dreamers in the School Years

Life rushes from within, not from without. There is no work of art so big or so beautiful that it was not all once contained in some youthful body.

from *Song of the Skylark* by Willa Cather

Teachers considered Al a problem child. He couldn't sit still in his seat, and his mind seemed to wander out the window. Once he and a classmate lowered a fishhook from the second story of their public school, and the bait attracted a live chicken. The pair pulled the squawking bird up into the air, making such a ruckus that it disrupted the whole school.

For a time his mother took him out of school and taught him at home. Al read rapidly and with interest. But even then, people told his parents that his mind was "too active for his body," and that they ought not let him read so many books.

People described him as reckless, undisciplined, and stubborn. He was a skeptic, who wouldn't believe it couldn't be done just because it hadn't been.

As a teenager, Al and a couple of friends hollowed out a log, filled it with gunpowder, and set off an explosion that blew the side off an icehouse. That time, he almost fulfilled his mother's prophecy: She told him more than once that they would blow their heads off someday. She also told him that work, not dreams, would help him make his way in the world.[1]

A dreamer? Yes. Mischief maker? Certainly. Addled? Hardly. The boy's full name, as you've probably guessed by now, was Thomas Alva Edison. And he went on to become the most prolific inventor in history, with more than 1,000 patents to his name.

Like Edison, dreamers of school age are industrious about what interests them, whether building model planes, drawing, making greeting cards, or building a dollhouse. At the same time, they struggle with self-criticism and fear of failure. How adults handle the dreamer's fear of failure during this period is a key to healthy development during the age of inventiveness.

Dreamers in the Early Grades

As children move into middle childhood, they no longer experience the rapid changes in cognitive ability that occurred in the first few years of life. Growth and development take a slower and steadier pace for a time. Children of this age are supposed to be more concrete than preschoolers, and in some ways dreamers are more concrete at this age. They have a better handle on the difference between reality and fantasy, for example. And they enjoy industrious activity such as building, inventing, and performing. It is a time for experimenting with all of their new abilities.

It is also a time when children become involved in activities such as lessons, clubs, and sports. Fear of failure creates invisible walls around dreamers that can seem insurmountable to both parents and children. Risking concrete, visible failure is much more difficult than playing mental games and experimenting with objects and ideas.

Never as concrete as their doer friends, who tend to develop their identity at this age based on their activities and skills, dreamers look for identity beyond performance, although they aren't quite sure where to find that identity. While things are very black and white to doers in terms of rules and values, dreamers see all the shades of gray.

On the other hand, school-age dreamers are very black and white about feelings and ideals. They feel loved or hated with little gray area in between. Because dreamers read things into the behavior of others, they are often hurt by peers, parents, and teachers, whether or not others intended to hurt them. This becomes evident in the early grades when the dreamer, perhaps for the first time, is with age mates nearly as much as with family. Suddenly, there are many people to watch and a lot of innuendo to watch for. The complexity of the social situation increases the likelihood that your child will misread the intentions of others.

Schoolhouse Fun, Schoolhouse Blues

As dreamers enter school, they have expectations of delightful new experiences and new friends. For many, there is much to enjoy in having a wider social circle and entering a stimulating learning environment. Learning the three R's increases access to the intellectual word and stimulates cognitive growth. Social growth is an important component of the school environment for dreamers.

With all their wonderful ideas, dreamers can be popular with less original peers who enjoy their playfulness. At the same time, they may not think of themselves as popular. And a lot goes on in school to make a child feel unpopular, especially a sensitive child. With all of the teasing and one-upmanship, if fifty percent of the slights the dreamer perceives are real and fifty percent are actions that had nothing to do with him, you can see how easy it would be for the dreamer child to feel disliked by everyone.

More than once parents have told us that the teacher and peer group in one classroom were very positive and the child loved school, but the next year the child had a stern teacher and negative classmates and the child hated school. "Isn't that true for every child?" you may ask. Yes, it is true that we all had good and bad years. But it didn't always affect our learning and self-image to the degree that it affects dreamers. If drivers are disliked by a teacher, they may sabotage the teacher, but they aren't likely to beat themselves up over it. If diplomats are disliked by the peer group, they may beat themselves up, but they will still please the teacher and won't react toward peers in a way that makes the problem worse.

Not so for a dreamer like Kathy, who told us of her painful third-grade year. Other children called her ugly. When we asked why she thought they called her ugly, her response was, "Because it's true. They wouldn't say it if it wasn't true." But it wasn't true! Kathy was an adorable little girl. She was teased because she reacted.

Reactivity coupled with a lot of social interaction can lead to a volatile child. This isn't inevitable. When dreamers are very popular from the outset because they are fun, funny, good-looking, or athletic or they have enough social confidence when they enter school to keep others from suspecting their sensitivity, they do well. But for dreamers who are insecure and less than the social ideal in humor, looks, or athleticism, the introduction to school can be an introduction to hard times.

Even when they feel disliked to some degree, most dreamers of this age have a lot of ups as well as downs. As their creativity develops, dreamers have many new ways to shine and fun activities to invent. Parents tell us about the elaborate home theatricals produced by their dreamers, many writing original songs or choreographing dances.

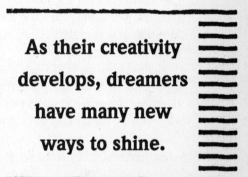

As their creativity develops, dreamers have many new ways to shine.

Dreamers can get encouragement from school at this age. They may win art or writing contests or be placed in gifted programs, and they can be tempted to brag to get attention. Needing praise from all sides, they can also look for creative ways to be noticed.

Daniel's pranks usually had an elaborate plan. In the sixth grade, his class was working on a large diorama of life in Egypt, with pyramids, palm trees—the works. When no one was looking, Daniel and a friend would take paper clips and bobby pins to create little finger traps. "You can bend them a certain way and they work like mousetraps," he said, laughing. "We'd place them under the surface of the sand, so when other kids would work on their areas, these little booby traps would snap their fingers—just ever so slightly. It didn't really hurt." Did people know who did it? "Well, it got to a point in my life where if something funny like that happened, people usually knew it was me," he said.

One saving grace of the early grades is the number of dreamers who teach at that level. Having a dreamer teacher who will encourage your child makes a tremendous difference in his emotional and educational well-being. But there seems to be a shift by fourth grade in which teachers are less likely to be dreamers. Some doer teachers see a child who needs affection and reassurance as immature and problematic.

One teacher, Mrs. Riley, kept telling Patsy's mother her daughter had serious problems because she sometimes played alone during recess. Patsy's mother didn't think that a child needing some time alone was a serious problem, but Mrs. Riley made her begin to doubt her instincts. Because she wanted Mrs. Riley to know that Patsy had friends, she told her about a time when Patsy had several friends over and from time to time went off by herself for a while. Mrs. Riley was horrified! Obviously, Patsy's problems were worse than she suspected.

Actually, introverted dreamers are a small, but normal subgroup of dreamers, who are perfectly content to be alone a good deal of the time. Because school forces them to be in a group setting for long hours, they need a reenergizing time of solitude. That is sometimes misunderstood by extroverted teachers or peers.

In general, girls tend to feel better accepted than boys at this age, probably because emotionality is not considered unusual for girls. But make no mistake, entering school can be less than a joy to any dreamer if there are peer or teacher problems in the classroom, on the bus, or on the playground. A child who has always been an optimist can suddenly become pessimistic if his self-esteem is suffering. Fortunately, a terrible year can be followed by a wonderful year if there are changes in the peer group or school. During the rough spots, many dreamers look to the family to be their shelter from the storm.

Family Life

Dreamers in the school years are still very much in need of family support and parental guidance. There are new skills to be learned and new emotional battles, such as those that occur in school, to be faced. Parents of children this age have many questions about their sensitivity and moodiness. They also ask us what to do about behaviors that they thought the children would have outgrown, like lying. And at an age when dreamers can be very industrious at pet projects, parents want to know how to motivate their dreamers to help around the house.

As your child gets older, it is reasonable to expect him to do more chores. Because chores most often have to be repeated week in and week out, the routine-resistant dreamer can be uncooperative. Your child might resort to passive-aggressive tactics and fantasy explanations for why something cannot be done.

Buster was a dreamer with a doer stepmother. She expected a lot of the boy, who had been the baby of the family until his father remarried and had more children. They lived on a farm, which meant chores for everyone. Buster always had a good explanation for why he didn't do his chores. One night he was supposed to feed the horses. Buster told his stepmother that there were a thousand owls on the roof of the barn.

"Now, Buster," she replied, "a thousand owls?"

"Well, nine hundred," said Buster.

The conversation went on for several minutes with Buster giving smaller and smaller numbers, but never veering from the basic story. Finally in exasperation Buster exclaimed, "Well, it's only one owl and you can just go out to that old barn and see for yourself!"

Relationships with Siblings

Buster's siblings tired of having to do his chores. Your dreamer child may work and play well with siblings or get into constant skirmishes. Part of this dynamic has to do with the cognitive styles of the siblings. Imagine the dreamer sharing a room with an orderly driver. The driver will be constantly trying to push the dreamer to keep the room clean, and the dreamer will respond with stubbornness, aggressiveness, or passive-aggressiveness.

But what if the sibling sharing the room is a diplomat? The diplomat doesn't want to be in trouble and doesn't want to fight with the dreamer. The diplomat may pick up the dreamer's things. Then the dreamer is likely to come out of the room wailing that she can't find anything because her sister moved all of her stuff.

Although some disagreements between siblings are inevitable, dreamers can be deeply attached to their brothers and sisters, an attachment that may not be fully returned. Idealistic about the family, the dreamer wants to be close to older and younger siblings. Many parents have told us about the love and care a dreamer gives to younger children. But if younger children are seen as favored by the parents, you may see as much revenge as nurturing.

When siblings fight, determining what is actually at the core of the conflict may elude you. A younger diplomat may slug the reactive dreamer and then cry pitifully when retaliation comes. Because the diplomat is rarely in trouble, the interaction may appear to be a one-sided attack. If a dreamer seems to get into trouble only when a driver or diplomat is around, consider the possibility that the other child is setting up the reactive dreamer to take the fall.

Learning Family Values

Being blamed unfairly, or at least one-sidedly, changes the dreamer's respect for you. But if you are fair and nurturing, during the early school years the dreamer should identify strongly with you and your values. It is the age of "my dad is better than your dad" for all children, and the age of "my parents' values are better than your parents' values" for idealistic dreamers. When other children are showing little interest in the news, dreamers are enthralled with political debates and their parents' reactions to them. They learn the parents' side of the argument about politics, economics, sociology, psychology, and religion. They may not understand what they are learning, but they know how to argue about it anyway.

You may be delighted that your child takes an interest in world events, or you may think that your child is worrying too much about adult problems. Either way, enjoy it now because soon he will be taking the opposite side of the argument to test your debating ability.

At this stage of development, your child needs to be able to identify wholeheartedly with you because she is acquiring foundational knowledge about values and desires a cohesive philosophy of life. But what if you and your spouse or ex-spouse don't agree about these fundamental issues? Your child may choose to identify with one of you and set about to convert the other. Never assume that a child who is trying to change your views to match those of the other parent is being put up to it. Dreamers set out on many crusades without any encouragement.

If both parents are equally accepting and nurturing, the dreamer at this age is likely to adopt the viewpoint of the same-gender parent. Although in later years the mother-daughter and father-son relationships can be strained, this is a time of strong identification with the parent of the same gender.

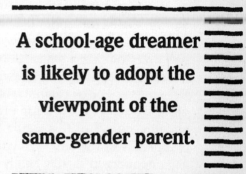

A school-age dreamer is likely to adopt the viewpoint of the same-gender parent.

Hobbies and Collections

Dreamers at this age tend to be very busy collecting things. A doer sibling is usually unhappy about sharing a room with the dreamer and his half-finished model planes, rocks, bugs, coins, baseball cards, soda bottles, and wood scraps.

Dreamers don't want to be limited to a single hobby. How boring! The collections are expressions of who the dreamer is at that moment, and any straightening is considered a personal attack. He may eventually throw it all out and start off in some other direction, but if you dispose of a single atom, you will be in hot water. You see, the dreamer collector needs to get the big picture by looking at it all at once.

The Inner Life

One of the most visible changes that occurs in dreamers as they enter the school years is the marked maturity of compassion and empathy. Less self-centered than in earlier years, dreamers show tremendous concern over the emotional and physical needs of friends, family, and strangers. They can anguish over a documentary they saw on TV and listen attentively to the sorrows of classmates. Their idealism "gets legs" as they think of specific actions they can take to alleviate suffering.

Robert remembers creating the Save Carter Johnson Club when he was in grade school. Some of Robert's classmates were picking on Carter Johnson, who was a social outcast according to the school pecking order. In his mind, Robert founded the SCJC, of which he was the only member. For months, he daydreamed about creatively wicked ways he could get back at Carter's tormentors, and he devised elaborate schemes. "The only thing I ever did, despite all my daydreaming, was to go out of my way to say 'Hi!' to him every once in a while," Robert said.

Problem-solving plans become much more complex at this age. Dreamers are often catalysts for school projects in which food and clothing are collected for low-income families or recycling is encouraged. All of this action is a direct result of the increasing complexity of the child's inner life. If the ideas the child develops are encouraged in the family and peer group, he continues to openly share ideas. If the child is laughed at or told to be more realistic, he may begin to hide his inner life.

Interest in spiritual issues becomes more intense. Spiritual development is interwoven with the family value system and the parenting modeled. If you are unloving while telling your children that God loves them, your dreamer may explore different views from yours. Many dreamers have rejected the image of God as a loving father because their fathers were less than accepting and nurturing. Yet, dreamers aren't looking for an excuse to reject spirituality.

When parents are sensitive to the dreamer's spiritual needs, it can make a lasting impression. Celia recalls being plagued with questions about death and the afterlife. She composed a will, rolled it up, sealed it, and presented it to her father for safekeeping. Sometime during the years that she wrestled with these fears, her father built Celia a kneeler for praying, just like the kneelers in the church her family attended. "That made me feel special. He didn't make one for the other kids, just for me," she said.

If the parents have no religious convictions, dreamer children may explore spiritual concepts through discussions with extended family and friends and may want to visit houses of worship with friends or other family members.

Parenting the Dreamer in the Early Grades

The role of the family as shelter from the storm increases as the dreamer ventures into the world outside the home more frequently.

Fear of failure can cause a dreamer to avoid activities he would enjoy and at which he could excel. It's a balancing act to encourage your child to take more risks at this age without overprogramming him. As we discussed earlier, it's fine to require an outside activity as long as your child has some choices and knows the ground rules, such as "finish what you start." But don't allow or encourage your child to take on too many clubs, classes, and teams. A child who does too much at this age is more likely to want to quit everything by high school, feeling burned out and wanting to slow down and "find himself."

Your dreamer may not want to sign up for anything, or she may want to sign up for everything but then quit at the first embarrassing moment. Either way, saying, "You can handle it," and backing off tend to work better for the development of self-confidence than pushing or protecting. As long as you have inaction and laziness separated in your mind and remember the role fear of failure plays in dreamer thinking, you should be able to encourage and discipline the young school-age dreamer effectively.

If you have a school-age child and you skipped the chapter on infants and preschoolers, you need to go back and read the sections on active listening and conditional grounding. These are parenting tools you will need with this age child in addition to the use of the natural and logical consequences discussed earlier in the book. We don't want to repeat what we have said on gentle discipline, but we are going to deal with an issue that hasn't been fully addressed: discipline and how it relates to lying.

Telling Tall Tales

In a dramatic monologue called "The Fetcher," playwright/lecturer David C. Page says, "Lying came easily to me . . . like *breathing*."[2] And while the line is spoken by a character, Page admits it was entirely autobiographical. Since childhood, he has struggled with lying. (Fortunately, he was able to channel that "creative energy" into writing.) But as he talks to adult dreamers across the country, many of them tell him they have the same struggle.

One of the most troubling behaviors to change in dreamers, lying takes these forms: tall tales, defensive, reactive lies, and manipulative lies. Tall tales are sometimes indications of low self-esteem and a need for attention, and at other times simply efforts to entertain. Such lies are not self-protective, but self-promoting. For example, the child who said he learned to water-ski at a camp that had no lake was telling an attention-seeking tall tale. Somehow he felt that his camp experience didn't measure up, so he embellished.

Dreamers sometimes tell tall tales to express anxieties. One dreamer told her parents that her school had burned down. The details were elaborate about how scared she was on the playground during the fire and how she heroically rescued the other children and the teachers. This story expressed in part her desire that the school would burn down, and in part her need for a feeling of success in school.

But remember, dreamers can tell tall tales to be entertaining. In these cases, there is rarely any intention to deceive, and so these stories cannot be considered lies. The parents we have talked with find tall tales baffling and aren't sure whether or not discipline is called for. If your child embellishes once or twice at this age, you don't need to panic—especially if the tale takes more of a story form than an exaggeration.

When Tina was five, her kindergarten teacher was concerned about the elaborate tales she told. When the teacher described the stories to her mother, it was clear that she was engaging in story-telling and not trying to glamorize her life. One day, she went to the moon. Another day, she told about time travel to the Wild West. The teacher was beginning to think that Tina was out of touch with reality. Tina's mother calmly walked over to the bookshelf and pointed out books about rooms that turned into forests and buildings that walked. "Why do you have these books here?" asked Tina's mother.

"Those are wonderful stories," replied the teacher.

"Well, when Tina tells a story that is weirder than these, then I'll talk to a psychologist," said her mother.

Tina's mother worked with her on beginning her tales with "I want to tell you a story" or "Once upon a time." Most tall tales are like Tina's. But if the child tells realistic stories that appear true but aren't, there can be a problem. A dreamer who tries to make her life more interesting to others may have unmet emotional needs. In this case, consultation with a professional can help you know whether or not you should be concerned.

Impulsive, Defensive Lies

The more common lies for dreamers in the school years are impulsive, defensive lies that they tell to keep parents' approval or to save face. In dreamers, the impulse to present themselves in the best light comes not so much from a desire to deceive as from a desire to be loved. If you react to defensive lying with anger, the child feels a stronger need to lie. To stop this type of lying, you must create an atmosphere for honesty.

Most defensive lies occur when you have caught the dreamer violating a family rule. If you practice the use of logical consequences, it soon becomes fairly easy to select a logical consequence that makes restitution for the initial infraction. But what should you do when you catch your child red-handed at something and he lies about it? Now you have to deal with two offenses.

We have found many parents who try to get dreamers to be honest by telling them that there will be no consequence if they tell the truth. This works sometimes, but there is a problem: As much as you want your child to be honest, do you want him to believe that *anything* is okay as long as you're honest about it? Most of us would say no. Some parents get around this by telling the child that in *most* cases there will be no consequence, but most dreamers are smart enough to know when they've transgressed so severely that honesty won't get them off the hook. Remember that the real "hook" that dreamers want to avoid is parental disapproval. If she knows that the truth is so terrible that you will certainly be disappointed, she may resort to a lie or an "I don't know." If the child creates some doubt on your part with the lie, that may encourage more lies in the future.

So what should you do? Because you can't be all knowing and all seeing, there is no perfect solution. But it helps to separate the two offenses. Don't overemphasize the impulsive lie. Delaying the consequence for the initial offense while you give the child time to think sometimes brings contrition: "This is what you are telling me happened. . . . I would like you to go to your room and think about what you have said. If you would like to change any part of what you have told me, I'll be here." Try to avoid showing anger or using the term *story* or *tale*. This may add fire to an emotional situation and trigger a response like, "You never believe me!" Your goal is to get the dreamer to calm down enough to face the fear of the truth being known.

Suppose despite all your patience, your child refuses to tell the truth. If lying is a new problem and not an established habit, impose a logical consequence for the first offense, and then add a discussion with the child about lying. Not a lecture, a discussion. Don't make pronouncements as if she knows nothing about what lies do to relationships.

Ask the child gentle "feeling" questions: "Has anyone ever lied to you? How did it feel? What did you think about that person? Did you believe that person the next time?" and so forth. Tell your child that you know how hard it is to admit mistakes. The goal here is to create an atmosphere for honest communication about feelings and failures. The discussion lets him know that although you weren't fooled, you want to listen and understand his feelings.

The consequence for the original offense needs to be concretely tied to the offense. If your daughter hits her sister unprovoked, she does her sister's kitchen clean-up for that day. Lies don't get the child out of facing consequences.

The consequence for the lie is more over-arching because lying has more pervasive effects. An example of an appropriate consequence would be the loss of your trust for a day. Tell your child that you will check up on everything she does for an entire day. You will not take her word for anything. Smell her breath to be sure she brushed her teeth. Follow her to the bus stop to be sure she gets on the bus. Drop by the school to be sure she eats her lunch. For one intense day, treat her as if she cannot be trusted to do anything. Other students don't need to know what you're doing. You don't want to humiliate her. You just want her to *feel* the discomfort of mistrust. Don't threaten to do this every time she lies because it then becomes more of a punishment for you than for her. Treat it as a one-time teaching opportunity.

Habitual Lying

If your child ignores his conscience and your consequences and continues lying for months on a regular basis, it has become a habit that you'll have to address with a long-term strategy. Choose a time when your child is not in trouble and is calm to have a talk that goes something like this:

"When you see a bowl of ice cream, something inside you says, 'I want that ice cream.' We call that thought an impulse because it's a thought that tells you to do something. Now when your brother shoves you, you might have an impulse in your head like, 'Flatten him!' Sometimes people act on their impulses, and sometimes they don't. We've noticed that you have an angry look on your face sometimes when your brother is bugging you, but you usually don't do anything to hurt him. That shows us that you have good control of some of those impulses that tell you to be unkind. But we've also noticed that when you break our rules around here, you get an impulse to lie and say that you didn't. That impulse may not seem the same as shoving someone, but when you lie to us, we feel shoved. Those lies also keep us from knowing when to believe you. That hurts us because we want to always be able to believe you.

Sometimes lying is an indication that the dreamer's self-esteem is severely low or that the child is depressed.

"If you had difficulty controlling an impulse to eat ice cream, we wouldn't let you eat yourself to death. And we've decided that we can't let you lie until you have no self-respect. Therefore, we would like you to help us pick a serious consequence that we will consistently apply every time you lie. We want to help you break this habit."

You might be surprised that your child picks a more severe consequence for himself than you would have considered. Most dreamers feel controlled by their feelings, including the urge to lie, and genuinely want to gain self-control. Because the core of discipline is guidance, not punishment, there is room for discussion if there is also a logical consequence. It isn't discipline if it doesn't increase your child's self-control.

If your child insists, "But I don't lie!" leave him to think it over. Consider whether or not you need an assessment by a professional. Sometimes lying is an indication that the dreamer's self-esteem is severely low or that the child is depressed.

Manipulative Lies

Another type of lying is less well intentioned than the tall tale or the defensive lie. In this case, discussion is less important than a clear, swift consequence. These lies are creatively devised to manipulate you. For example, your child comes to you and tells you, "Sarah's parents are going out of town and she has no place to stay. Can Sarah spend the weekend with us?" But when you call Sarah's mom, you find out that Sarah's aunt, whom Sarah dislikes, is coming to keep her. You can guess that your daughter and Sarah discussed the situation, and they decided that they had a better solution. Rather than saying that Sarah doesn't want to stay with her aunt, your daughter embellished to get her own way.

This lie is not based on hidden emotion or low self-esteem. The dreamer wants what she wants and is willing to lie to get it. She may rationalize to herself that because it is for Sarah's good, it is okay to lie. This is a clear violation of family rules and should be disciplined like any other concrete offense. Try something like, "You have lied to me, so help me by folding all the laundry. In addition, you and Sarah are not allowed to play together until her parents have been back for a week."

One way to reduce your child's desire to lie is through your model of honesty. Now we don't mean bluntness that could be perceived as cruel. We are talking about your being honest about your mistakes. Admitting when you're wrong makes it easier for the dreamer to face the fear of having to admit failure. And if you are honest with your spouse, boss, and friends and don't manipulate, you are teaching vital principles about honesty in relationships.

Family Meetings and Private Moments

One way to keep the lines of communication open with all the children in the family is to have family meetings. These are regular times, perhaps once a week, in which the family sits down together and discusses family issues. We generally recommend that you start having family meetings with children at this age, so that by the time your children are teens they will be in the habit. What happens at a family meeting varies from family to family, but it should not focus on problems. Some families plan fun family activities. Others discuss family work projects.

Dreamers like family meetings because they feel like important parts of the family and their ideas are valued. Also, being able to brainstorm about plans engages their minds. And they like to see some elements of democracy in the family. Although you as parents set the agenda and limit the power of the children to make decisions, to the dreamer, the family meeting is a fair way to hear all points of view.

> **One way to keep the lines of communication open with all the children in the family is to have family meetings.**

Dreamers also need private moments with parents, especially to discuss the concerns they are mulling over. Set the pattern now for listening with an open heart to your child's inner thoughts. We say an open heart rather than an open mind because your dreamer needs more than intellectual tolerance. Tolerance may not be what your child needs at all in the sense that the word is being bandied about today. Dreamers want their parents to have intellectual and spiritual integrity, which means having a consistent worldview and showing them that parents believe what they say by the way they act. Dreamers aren't impressed by relativistic statements like, "Whatever is right for you is okay for you, but don't push it on anyone else." Dreamers are too idealistic to believe such thinking. They want to know what is true and how to build a life on that truth.

Being so interested in abstract issues, dreamers expect their parents to be open about their inner lives. If your parents thought issues like money, religion, and romance were private, almost taboo, subjects, you may have difficulty opening up and being vulnerable about the deep issues that your dreamer wants to discuss.

Dreamers in Preadolescence

Although they are idealistic, dreamers' concerns are not always spiritual or admirable as they move into preadolescence. Ten- to twelve-year-olds are caught in the pull between childhood and the glamorized teen years. Exposed to many grown-up issues and images through the popular media, by the fifth or sixth grade, many kids want to be just like the teenagers they see in magazines and on TV.

Why, it's even happening to Mattel's Barbie doll! When we were children, Barbie had elegant gowns like Audrey Hepburn wore and looked like a young adult. Today, it's Teenage Rocker Barbie, and there's nothing elegant about her. Barbie has to be cool.

Kids this age think they have to be cool, too. They may throw out phrases about sex or use foul language to appear grown up. Although compassionate dreamers may be less likely than others to direct harassing language at someone, they can deliver shocking one-liners because they crave attention. Preadolescence is a transition that dreamers don't always negotiate smoothly. Dreamers love being children and want to keep playing with toys while peers are putting aside such "foolishness." One minute your dreamer acts too old; the next he seems too young.

Although they may appear socially immature, dreamers feel much older than their classmates as they think about world events, causes, and the meaning of life. They aren't sure where they fit. This sense of displacement can lead to self-doubt. At age twelve, Joel was wondering if something was wrong with him because he didn't talk dirty about the girls in his class like his friends did; he actually liked and respected girls. How sad that he should think that he was the one with the problem!

Dreamers may have felt somewhat different earlier in life, but at this age they become fully aware of how different they are. As they try to separate from the family, dreamers can develop a tremendous sense of isolation if peers seem different and distant. Some become less communicative and more withdrawn from friends as well as from family. Dreamers may begin journaling to express their frustrations and self-doubts. Others listen to music, draw, or play sports with aggressive abandon as a means of letting out their inner turmoil.

Many preadolescent dreamers try to find a role to play that will gain attention and acceptance. Quiet Marta decided to shed her image as an introvert by becoming the class clown of the sixth grade. Her parents and teachers were baffled. Peers liked it, but inside she felt "yucky" because she wasn't being herself. In the seventh grade, her conscience got hold of her and she tried shaking the clown role. The other kids in the class made it hard for her to change. Her parents moved her to another school for eighth grade. With a clean slate, this dreamer became a class leader, running for school offices and joining many clubs. At her new school, they would never have suspected Marta's clowning and disrespectful past.

Noticing the Opposite Sex

There is tremendous variation in the amount of interest dreamers of this age show in the opposite sex. They can be very sneaky about flirting, partly because they don't want you to tease them, and partly because they don't want you to stop them.

If your child looks older than the average child in the class, there can be peer pressure to behave more like a teen and have a boyfriend or girlfriend. For most, there is no real dating at this age. But we have seen parents who push some form of dating because they think it's cute. Later, these same parents don't think it's so cute when their children expect to be able to car date at fourteen.

One unhealthy way that children of this age deal with their sexual feelings is through sexual harassment. We have seen a marked increase in some disturbing behavior among fifth and sixth graders. Unless they have been exposed at home to pornography or movies that degrade women, dreamers are more likely to be the victims of such harassment than the perpetrators.

Nancy was repeatedly victimized by sexually harassing behavior from boys in her class. They would knock the books out of her hands, and when she leaned over to pick up her books, the boys would touch her chest and then say, "Oh, sorry, it was an accident." She was frozen. Nancy wasn't confident in how she should respond. The teacher thought that she was egging the boys on somehow because she wasn't stopping it. Of course, the teacher should have stopped it. When Nancy's parents found out, they went to the school and asked the teacher how she would like it if the principal treated her that way.

Such experiences can erode the dreamer's confidence. Insecurity with peers can lead to an increase in manipulative lying in an attempt to be popular. For example, your daughter may tell you she is going to the movies with a group of girls when she is meeting a boy there. She doesn't want to admit to the boy that it is against her parents' rules, and she wants her girlfriends to think that she's allowed to date. Yet despite this desire to please the peer group, she also has a desire for family identity. Most dreamers this age haven't yet reached the point that they would "die" before being seen in public with Mom and Dad.

Parenting the Preadolescent Dreamer

As you prepare your child for adolescence, now is the time to encourage the idea that different is *good*. Forget helping him fit in. Your child will never be like the majority. If he thinks that being different is somehow to his advantage instead of a heavy burden, your child is more likely to thrive in the midst of adversity and become a leader.

Appearing disinterested in your child's popularity is important, even if the dreamer appears to be miserable. Too many well-meaning parents badger the child to have friends over or have a party only to drive the dreamer in the opposite direction. Focus on your child's character and your appropriate role as shelter from the storm. Your dreamer child can learn many social lessons only by falling flat on his face once or twice.

By being a shelter from the storm, you continue to keep the lines of communication open with your preadolescent dreamer. Try to give her as much ownership of her responsibilities as you can and then back off. Encourage academic development by spending time with your child discussing the school material, not quizzing her. Try to help her through routine tasks like homework by commiserating with her and being her cheerleader rather than lecturing her on the dangers of laziness and other vices.

With tasks around the house, continue to make things more of a game and less of a chore. Let the dreamer choose tasks that interest her rather than choosing all the tasks for her. For example, suppose your daughter likes working in the yard. Let her decide which flowers to plant and encourage her to arrange fresh flowers in the house. She may not enjoy mowing the grass nearly as much as working with the flowers but will reluctantly cut it, wanting the total presentation of the yard to encourage people to look at her flowers.

Despite the pull of the peer group, try to make being at home as enjoyable as possible. Encourage your child's interests by taking him to museums, historical sites, the symphony, or plays. Introduce him to adults in the community who would make good role models of both creativity and moral integrity. Let your child plan family outings to expose siblings to the artistic or innovative side of life. Search your local library for inspiring life stories of historical figures who shared some of your child's dreamer traits: actress Sarah Bernhardt with her dramatic flair, Jules Verne with his longing for faraway lands, Leonardo da Vinci with his love for learning, or Mark Twain with his talent for spinning tall tales. Read their biographies aloud in your home, view movies and listen to tapes about their lives, and play the music of great composers and musicians. Then use them as starting points for family discussions. These activities make family life stimulating and create shared experiences that bond the family. End your dreamer's elementary years with happy memories and the secure knowledge of your acceptance and love.

Chapter 16

The Age of Romantic Idealism: Dreamers in the Teen Years

From at least the age of six, romantic longing ...
had played an unusually central part in my expe-
rience. Such longing is in itself the very reverse of
wishful thinking: It is thoughtful wishing.

from *Narrative Poems* by C. S. Lewis

"He sleeps with his girlfriend on the phone," said the mother of a tenth grader.

"Excuse me," the counselor said. "What did you say?"

"He sleeps with his girlfriend on the phone," the mother reiterated. "They talk on the phone until they both fall asleep. They think it's very romantic, but I think it's a hassle! The phone ends up being off the hook all night. Also, don't you think that they are a little too emotionally involved for the tenth grade? I've known girls who would think this kind of thing was cute, but I'm surprised to see my son so starry-eyed."

Perhaps sleeping on the phone doesn't sound like such a big problem. After all, they aren't actually having sex. Or are they? This mother suspected that this romanticism could lead to early sexual involvement. Adolescents have many outside pressures to grow up too soon. Encouraged to think about sex by every aspect of modern media from movies to the news, dreamers are just as tempted as other teens to be promiscuous, despite their high ideals. Not that they wouldn't be thinking about sex or at least the opposite sex anyway; they would. But they wouldn't feel so much pressure to act on those impulses if they were not living in a sex-obsessed society.

Because dreamers feel so different and sometimes so alone, they can look for acceptance in romantic relationships. Being poetic and idealistic, some dreamers look to romance as a rescue from the unhappiness of home or school. They may fantasize about running away like Romeo and Juliet. In a few rare cases, they may enter into suicide pacts to become Romeo and Juliet. But if they are accepted in the family and have been nurtured in their creativity and sensitivity, they are much less likely to act rashly.

Dreamers create in their minds an ideal for the adult life they will soon enter and enjoy playing out those roles in their present relationships during the age of romantic idealism.

Not the Happiest Years of Their Lives

Life is frequently different from the ideal. Two college-age dreamers told us about their amazement when people say that the teens were the happiest years of their lives. Few dreamers would look back on those years as the happiest. Many experience depression at some time during their teens. Serious depression can be expressed in many ways from indulging in self-destructive behavior, such as drug experimentation, to losing interest in personal appearance and hygiene, to obsessing on angry and hurting song lyrics or poetry. Other teens feel misunderstood and alone. But dreamers seem to make a larger percentage of this unhappy group, partly because they are genuinely misunderstood and partly because they are naturally moodier.

Body chemistry and the rapid physiological changes happening at this age affect moods. If you are the parent of a dreamer teen, you probably aren't surprised to know that hormonal changes can cause the normally moody dreamer to be depressed, angry, or sullen. If the underlying cause is only hormonal, this negative period may pass. If another type of physiological change is occurring, such as an imbalance in the chemistry of the brain, the negativity may not go away on its own.

Teens with a family history of suicidal behavior are prone to chemical imbalance.[1] When depression keeps your teen from functioning or your teen makes veiled threats of suicide, don't try to judge the seriousness of the problem. *Get a professional opinion.* Because psychiatrists are medical doctors and can treat physiologically based emotional problems, they can be helpful in determining whether or not counseling or medication or both would be the most effective treatment.

Even when there is no physiological reason to be down, dreamers have many environmental reasons to be unhappy. There is no age at which being different is tougher to deal with than in the teen years. Sure, there are groups in every school that try to be different, but have you noticed how all the members of the group are different in exactly the same way? Dreamers don't want to be boxed in. They want to be different from peers and yet accepted by several groups. And especially in the young teen years, dreamers struggle with comparing themselves to others.

The Early Teen Years

Young teens are probably the most self-conscious people in the world. On a scale of one to ten for fear of embarrassment with ten being the most fearful, dreamers are a twelve. They think that everyone is looking at them and are embarrassed to even have parents, let alone be seen with them. Expect that nothing you do for the next two years will be right in the dreamer's eyes. But if you do your best during these years to guide your dreamer according to the principles we've discussed, at the end of that angry period you will be much better off than if you abandon all hope and take an authoritarian approach.

> **Young teens are probably the most self-conscious people in the world.**

Part of the problem is the hormones that cause even the most logical doer teen to be illogical.

Because he is already emotional, the mood swings are a sight to behold when a little hormone is added to a dreamer's life. Door slamming becomes an art, and destruction of property, a frequent event. When we mentioned this at a parenting seminar, a doer turned to her dreamer friend and said, "I can't imagine you slamming doors," to which the dreamer replied sheepishly, "I cracked a solid walnut door right down the middle."

Some dreamers in young adolescence destroy their rooms when told they can't do something. You see, to the young teen, everything is a crisis. If you tell the dreamer that he can't go to a party because the family will be out of town, he is sure to believe that he will never be able to show his face at school again, that the girl he likes will start going with some other guy, and that if he tries to go back to school, the word *geek* will be spray painted on his locker and his picture will be burned in effigy.

With all this angst, the dreamer still has a fragile soul that needs love and affection. You must never show this affection without drawing the curtains, lest he be seen by the gossip columnist from the junior high newspaper. In many ways, affection changes significantly at this age. Suddenly, you might have the privilege to punch his arm or give her a little shove when only months before he still wanted to tickle and she still wanted to sit in Daddy's lap. Don't demand that the young teen accept open affection. Your teen needs his space. Rest assured, the affection will return about the same time the anger abates, although your teen will probably always be more restrained than in the early years.

Mothers and daughters have especially inharmonious relationships at this age. A word to the wise: Mothers, hold your tongues. Anything said in anger at this point will be thrown in your face for the rest of your life. Dreamers need a shelter from the storm of school, and as much as you would like to, this is not the time to shut up the house to take a vacation from parenting.

The social environment of the young teenager is a minefield. Even those who appear confident aren't. Many dreamers can't appear confident because their insecurities exude from every pore.

With all this anxiety, grades can suffer. The boys can't think straight because they can't stop thinking about the rapidly developing girls. And the girls worry about what the boys are thinking of them and what those other angry girls are about to do. Your five-foot, one-inch dreamer daughter may come home and tell you that a very large girl named Barb is threatening to beat the stuffing out of her because Barb likes a boy who told John that he might like your daughter. Somehow John told Steve and Steve mentioned it to Barb and now your daughter can't sleep at night and has asked to be home schooled.

This atmosphere is not great for learning. Your teen continues to mature intellectually but may be too distracted to use the new thinking skills. In abstract subjects like algebra that should stimulate the dreamer, your teen may have missed key concepts during a stressful period. Although there were plenty of distractions and anxiety-causing events when we were in school, we didn't have to worry about guns and gangs, which have become a huge problem not only in the inner city but also in the suburban school. In such an environment, impulsive efforts to gain attention can become more dangerous and life changing.

Kyle wanted to look cool in this "gotta be tough" school culture. He bought a handgun at a ball game because it looked "neat." Then he took the gun to school. After all, in a teen's way of thinking, a gun is only cool if you show it to somebody. When the principal asked him about the gun, Kyle didn't want to admit his childlike fascination with the weapon, so he made up an elaborate tale about being threatened by a gang and needing the gun for protection. He was promptly expelled from school.

With all this chaos, you wouldn't think that dreamers would have time to worry about the meaning of life. But if anything, their idealistic concerns become stronger. Looking for socially acceptable outlets for their compassionate side, dreamers may do volunteer work or become involved in causes.

When Jennifer was thirteen, her community prepared to have an Ecology Day. Her older brother got her all excited about the role she could play by not riding the bus. "Buses cause terrible pollution," he told her. "If everyone walked or rode a bike to school, there'd be no more buses." Jennifer took this to heart. She organized a bus boycott, not only for Ecology Day but forever. At first, she had cooperation from other kids in the neighborhood. But little by little, the number of those walking dwindled. Her parents never belittled her efforts. When there was no one left to walk with her from the neighborhood, her parents said that she would have to start riding the bus again for safety reasons.

Along with concern over world issues, spiritual interests increase. That does not mean that dreamers want to be seen in church with you. But among their friends, dreamers are trying to decide exactly what they believe. They seek out friendships with like-minded peers and debate ideas in the corner of the cafeteria. Your teen who kicks and screams every Sunday morning as you try to get her to church may be the same person who organizes a school prayer group because no government or school official is going to tell her where she can and can't pray!

The Middle Teen Years

After the period of early adolescent hypersensitivity, the middle teen years can be something of a reprieve. Most teens have limited mobility, so you have moderate reassurance that things are in control since you know basically where your teenager is.

At school, dreamers have a more consistent school identity. Some continue to work hard to succeed academically, while others have given up and developed a negative school identity. Social influences aren't quite as academically distracting as in younger years, except when there are true crises such as the breakup of a relationship. But dreamers must try to learn in the midst of what is almost a social soap opera.

Romance becomes important to the dreamer. Even a late bloomer wants to have a boyfriend or girlfriend. Your teen is likely to develop some true friendships with the opposite sex and may be on the phone as counselor for everyone else's relationship woes. Dreamer girls tend to be popular with boys as both date and friend because they are less aggressive and blunt than driver girls. Most boys are insecure at this age and look for girls who aren't overwhelming.

Dreamer boys may experience rejection from the drivers of their own gender at this age, but they are popular with the girls because they listen well and desire meaningful relationships. Dreamers tend to be more mature in terms of their intellectual concerns, so older girls who are tired of the insensitive behavior of driver boys may pursue dreamer boys. Just because your son is intellectually mature does not make him emotionally mature enough to be in a relationship with an older girl. Older teens may seek significantly younger teens as romantic interests because they may have problems that have alienated them from their own age group.

In a dating relationship or friendship, a hurting teen may become overly attached to or obsessed with your dreamer teen. Being compassionate, a dreamer is reluctant to set limits with a friend who desires too much emotional intimacy. A friend who is hurting may feel that your dreamer teen is the only person who really accepts him. If the dreamer tries to set limits or cut off the relationship, the troubled friend may try to control the dreamer by threatening suicide in an effort to maintain the status quo. One problem for parents is that troubled peers may try to get the dreamer to swear an oath of secrecy about all of the turmoil in the relationship. Your idealistic teen may not want to betray a friend and yet may be in desperate need of your support and guidance. You can't help your dreamer handle problems you don't know about, but you can watch for signs of stress that might indicate secret burdens and express your concern. Dreamers sometimes want to spill the details of an overwhelming problem. Try saying something like, "I can tell something is terribly wrong. Please let me help you."

> **Dreamers in their mid-teens are less likely to request parental assistance because their identity is being established.**

Dreamers are less likely to request parental assistance at this age because their identity is being established and they desperately want to be able to handle their own problems. Fifteen-year-old dreamers, for example, often want to move away from the peer group identity and try to "find themselves."

Although your teen may be well liked, the doer peer group won't understand the introspection of the dreamer. For this reason, dreamers actively seek dreamer friends. These friends may be found in art, music, or psychology classes, school clubs, church, or theater groups. But dreamers may meet other dreamers in nightclubs and coffeehouses. If your teen is fairly confident and has a good relationship with you, the dreamer friends may want to gather at your house for long discussions. If your teen feels alienated from you and the cliques at school, he may seek out older friends and push for the freedom to do things like go out to concerts and clubs where alternative music is played.

Every generation has a rebellious crowd. When we were teens, there were freaks and druggies. Later, hard rockers and punks were on the social edge. Today, alternative music and clothing identify the counterculture. Before you go into complete panic, realize that not everyone who enjoys the alternative music scene uses drugs or is sexually promiscuous.

But most counterculture teens who are not using drugs or sleeping around stay straight because of their personal moral and religious convictions and not the values of the families from which they are too often alienated. Some come from abusive or alcoholic families. Others are shedding all identification with their perfectionistic and/or controlling parents.

Parents who remain calm and resist becoming openly critical of their dreamer will have an easier time successfully navigating through these transitional years. If you feel alienated from your teen, counseling could reopen the channels of communication.

The Later Teen Years

If you can make it to the late teens without a serious division developing between you and your teen, you are almost home free. Older teens are less emotionally fragile and generally more self-confident. Not so embarrassed by family involvement, your teen may ask you to go shopping with her. When talking to families, we often tell the parents and teens who are experiencing normal growing pains to just hold on—things will get better.

Even at this age dreamers will fall on their faces, and sometimes it's a long fall because all teenagers tend to think of themselves as invincible. The idealistic dreamer can be the worst for believing, "It won't happen to me," as he experiments with drugs or sex. But because dreamers aren't pure thrill seekers, those who are self-destructive usually are suffering from serious personal conflicts, depression, or addiction.

In romantic relationships, dreamers may be irresponsible because of their desire for the perfect relationship. Dreamers may think they can and should have the perfect relationship and believe they can create it.

In the midst of romantic distractions and struggles, dreamers may make a last-minute push to get into college even after years of mediocre grades. Oldest children have less difficulty than other children self-motivating in school. But the decisions that must be made about college applications and whether or not to stay at home or go away to school can be overwhelming to any dreamer who fears failure. "What if I can't get in?" he worries. "What if I flunk out and have to come home?"

Spiritual values now play an important role in the decision-making process. Your teen may seek a religious college in order to have the support of like-minded peers. Or your teen may resist religious schools because he rejects the family value system. Although dreamers have a natural spiritual bent, as teens they can make a cause or even a person their god if they reject orthodox religious beliefs.

Parenting the Adolescent Dreamer

As a teen tries to understand herself and develop her identity, she does not always feel that you are on her side. Nor does she always want you to be on her side—at least, it seems that way. But no matter how belligerent, a dreamer teen wants your love and attention. She may try to get your attention in productive ways or destructive ways, but her need for your acceptance does not diminish.

Just like the twos, the teens are a time of testing. Even though your teen may be jumping into the fire on a regular basis, he is looking to you to be rescued. If you rescue a teen too much, he will never mature into a healthy adult. But if you provide no shelter from the storm and have the attitude, "You're on your own now," your teen will feel unloved and neglected. This can be one of the hardest times in your life as a parent, not only because of your teen's issues but also because of your issues. You don't want to keep your teen from growing up, but you want him to grow up safely and happily.

As a sophomore in high school, Sharon tried to "help" a drunken senior by driving his car from the pizza parlor to a party where she hoped to find another senior to drive him home. Sharon didn't have a driver's license, and she was frightened. She rode the brakes all the way down the road—right past the police station—and was promptly pulled over.

Sharon was an honors student, quarter after quarter. She took gymnastics, ballet, and art lessons. She went to the high school fellowship group, even the weekly Bible study, sometimes. She was never the ringleader in these escapades, but she was a willing follower. What's a parent to do?

Sharon had watched while other teenagers' fathers pulled strings to get their children out of trouble with the police. So she was shocked when her mom and dad let her face the music. The day of her hearing at juvenile court, the judge came down hard. His sentence? Sharon would not be able to get the learner's permit for her driver's license until her seventeenth birthday. She was a year younger than everyone in her class. That would make it the end of her senior year before she could drive. The judge gave her only one hope: Keep your nose clean and come back next year, and maybe I'll reconsider.

From her parents, there were no lectures, no "I told you so's," and no rescues: only the natural consequences of her actions. Sharon looks back at it as a major turning point in her life.

"I remember the night it happened, crying and crying, and asking, 'Why, God? Why did You let this happen to me?' Not that I'd been talking to God that much before it happened. And then, once I stopped crying, I realized God was probably sitting up there thinking, *You're the one who drove the car without a license, kid, not Me.*

"That judge's punishment was a challenge to me; I wanted to get my license. So I looked around me and saw that the friends I had were only getting me into trouble. I stopped hanging around with them. I started going back to the fellowship regularly. I remember one girl praying, 'Lord, thank You for Sharon. I know how hard it is for her to be here.' I thought, *Am I that much of a juvenile delinquent?*

"A few years later, I realized that my former friends had become more involved in drinking and drugs, and a lot of them really messed their lives up. Today, I can see that if my parents had rescued me and hadn't forced me to face the consequences of my actions, I would have gone down the same path. My parents, my youth group leaders, my new friends, and my renewed faith in God made the difference," she said.

Like Sharon's parents, you want to do what is right, even if it means seeing your teen go through some hard learning experiences. You may be reading this in hopes that when your young child becomes a teen, he won't be depressed, angry, reckless, or unmotivated. As a parent of a dreamer teen, you must provide shelter from the storm in different ways from what you did when she was younger. Despite the fact that dreamers learn best from experience, many teenage and adult lessons are dangerous to learn through direct involvement. To develop a relationship with your teen in which he discovers that you are a fount of wisdom, you need to move to a deeper level with him. Listening and comfort continue to be important, but you must learn how to counsel your teen.

By counseling, we aren't talking about being your teen's professional therapist. Although you may do some of the same things a professional counselor does, as a parent you also are a bit like the counselor in the courtroom. Lawyers are wellsprings of information. But they don't attack a client; they help her face the world. You need to be your teen's advocate, sometimes cheering her on, sometimes setting her straight in a gentle way.

How to Take the Counselor Role with Your Dreamer

To give a dreamer wise counsel that will be heard and acted on, you must start with listening. Just as the attorney sits down with a client and gets his side of the story, so should you as a parent counselor. Going beyond active listening, you expand the depth of the questions you ask, helping your dreamer to see for himself the logical results of his immature thinking.

Here is a sample conversation:

BILL: "Don's parents are getting him a hotel room for the prom."
DAD: "What do you think about it?"
BILL: "I think it's really cool! Don is having a big party and a bunch of kids will be there."

DAD: "Why do you think that Don is having the party there instead of at his house?"

BILL: "The prom is already at the hotel. Also, I think they didn't want Don driving around late at night."

DAD: "Do his parents not think he's a good driver?"

BILL: "I don't know. I guess they just worry about drunks on the road and stuff. Anyway they must trust him a lot to let him stay in a hotel."

DAD: "So staying in a hotel to you means that they trust him. Hmm . . . I wonder if it actually means that they don't trust him."

BILL: "What do you mean?"

DAD: "What if they are afraid that Don will be drinking at the prom? Suppose the drunk they're afraid will be on the road is Don?"

BILL: "Knowing Don, that's probably true."

DAD: "When parents do things like rent hotel rooms for their kids, it makes me wonder if they really think their kids are grown up enough to handle it or if they think that their kids are immature. After all, how many adults do you know who have to get a hotel room after an evening out because they can't make it home safely?"

Other issues that could be brought in are the relationships between drinking and unplanned sex, destruction of property, and so on. Points could be made about the potential for arrest for public drunkenness and what that could do to a teen's chances for getting into a good college. The purpose of having a conversation rather than a lecture is to get Bill to think about the situation in a new light. If his dad had said from the beginning, "Well, Don may be doing that, but you're not!" he would have cut off communication with his teen and pushed Bill into an unteachable mood.

If this dreamer can be gently brought to the point of seeing the reasonableness of his dad's position without his dad directly stating his position, that would be best. You've probably heard that if you want people to do something, it's best if they think it's their own idea. For dreamer teens, it is especially true.

Since dreamers respond poorly to dominant language like "Because I said so," "No child of mine will ever . . . ," and the like, a counseling-discussion approach leads to more responsible behav-

ior than any other method. The role of counselor allows you to
provide guidance and protection without provoking your teen to
rebellion. When your child is headed down a dangerous road, however, you don't abdicate all responsibility to set and enforce limits.
The teen still desperately needs the protection and security pro
vided by limits and logical consequences.

In addition to guidance, your teen needs your help to learn to
express feelings and work through the stresses of life. As we have
seen in this chapter, the social stresses of adolescence take a great
toll on dreamers. Listening to your child, without trying to advise,
encourages her to open up.

Dreamer teens seem most comfortable talking about romantic
love with parents, at least in hypothetical terms. Most dreamers
will talk about some of the emotional upheaval they feel from
either having a romantic relationship or not having one. Why are
teens more open about this topic? Perhaps, they think parents
might actually know something about romance. The universal
quality of matters of the heart makes this an area where you can
build some bridges to your teen.

Dreamer teens want to know about your first love, how you
met your spouse, and so forth. Your openness can lead your adolescent to share her heartaches with you. Tread lightly in this area.
You may be tempted to sing the Hallelujah Chorus when your
teen breaks up with the blue-eyed, blue-haired boy from down the
street. But your teen needs to be comforted. If you criticize the
guy too much when she is still hurting over him, your daughter
may head straight back in his direction. Try to focus on the maturity of the pain, and don't simplify it. Rather than saying, "You'll get
over it," try something like, "You would be heartless if you could
walk away so easily from someone you cared about. As painful as it
is, your ability to love deeply shows what a wonderful and faithful
wife you will be one day. Someday a man will come along who
will appreciate not only your outward appearance but also your
inner beauty."

In the midst of these heart-to-heart discussions, your teen may
be interested in your specific experiences that were difficult. He
may ask personal questions about your sexual behavior and how
you coped with sexual feelings. Many parents fear that if they tell
too much about their mistakes, the teen will see it as permission

to "go you therefore and do likewise." In general, we have found that *not* talking about your failures is more likely to set the stage for the teen to repeat your mistakes.

In talking with your dreamer, be sensitive. Admit that we all struggle with sinful thoughts, but expect the best. Don't say, "I know you're going to mess up in this area." You don't *know* that, and you shouldn't label your child a failure.

Helping a teen through romantic and sexual stresses may be easier than dealing with family problems. If your dreamer has questions about Dad losing a job or Mom and Dad getting a divorce, it's fine to answer those questions in more detail than you would have at earlier ages, but you should not use your teen as your confidant. Because dreamers like to listen to problems and they like the counselor role, you can be pulled into an unhealthy pattern of confiding in your teen. You can be the child's counselor, but it should never be the other way around.

What Are You Modeling for Your Idealistic Teen?

You should make every effort to notice and encourage character development and spiritual maturity in your dreamer. You create an environment that stimulates development in these areas by listening to the child's thoughts and questions and by being a person your dreamer wants to emulate. Do you care more about people than about things? Have you made an effort to live a life of integrity by trying to do what you say you will do?

Although you may never be able to fully meet the standards expected by your idealistic teen, you don't change those ideals by trying to make the teen more realistic. As one dreamer friend said, "If a dreamer is an incurable romantic, what's a cured romantic? A cynic?"

If your teen has rejected your moral and spiritual values because he perceives hypocrisy, don't expect to be able to force him back in the right direction. Encourage an adult such as a youth leader to take an interest in your teen. In front of your dreamer, appear indifferent about his relationship with others in the youth group. Pray a lot, maneuver a little, and keep your mouth shut. If your teen doesn't know what you believe and why by this age, you aren't going to be the best teacher of spiritual values now. When you talk to your teen about spiritual things, forget dogma and concentrate on feeling concepts such as love and mercy. Leave the theology to great writers and teachers. Work on being who you need to be, and admit your failings openly while noticing your teen's strengths.

Express confidence in her ability to be a responsible adult: "Soon you will be on your own. You won't always need me, and I have to get used to that. There may be times that you want to come back to the nest. As an adult, there have been plenty of times that I wished my daddy was still paying the bills. But if he was, I would never have grown up. With the freedom to make all your own decisions comes responsibility. I see great things ahead for you because I know that you are going to be an adult of integrity and character in work and in the family you will have of your own. What a wonderful parent you will be with all your sensitivity and compassion!" Take the time to give her a blessing.

Chapter 17

Delighting in Dreamers: Some Closing Thoughts

We are the music makers
And we are the dreamers of dreams ...

From "Ode" by Arthur O'Shaughnessy

"And so the secret garden became an almost magical place for the children."

Do you have a secret garden at your house? Is there a place within your walls where a dreamer child can blossom? Dreamers tell us that the story *The Secret Garden* is among their favorites. When the garden is first described, it is winter. Mary, who has discovered the key that opens the door to this hidden treasure, is unsure whether anything can grow there. Everything appears to be dead. But then, she spies some bulbs just poking through the frozen soil. Life![1]

Helping dreamers to grow involves loving labor and the willingness to listen and understand. Gardener H. Fred Ale said, "My green thumb came only as the result of the mistakes I made while learning to see things from the plant's point of view." No gardener is perfect from day one. But with time and a willingness to learn, the gardener can find the right ingredients to develop a fertile environment for dreamers.

The idea of the garden as described in *The Secret Garden* represents themes that are common in the lives of dreamers: the heart of the garden where a little loving care brings beauty and the walls that hide its beauty from unappreciative eyes. It is the ideal that only a few are privileged to enjoy. Have you found the key to the secret garden within your child's heart?

A Dreamer's Approach to Parenting

David C. Page, a poet and playwright, and his artist wife, Terry, have developed some special family rituals to encourage their children to dream. They try not to let the ages of their children limit them from a broad range of experiences. As a rite of passage, each child has taken a major trip with Mom or Dad at ages four and fourteen. Usually, they backpack through Europe, seeing people, sights, and museums and experiencing the adventure. When practical friends have suggested that taking a preschooler to Europe is useless, "since he won't remember any of it,'" the Pages reply, "You're missing the point." They take the children to expose them to the vastness of the world, the joy of aesthetic experience, and endless possibilities. But more than that, they take them to be together. For the Pages, it is inconsequential whether or not their children remember a specific painting or castle. The focus is on being. They are teaching a lifestyle—a lifestyle in which every member of the family can dream.

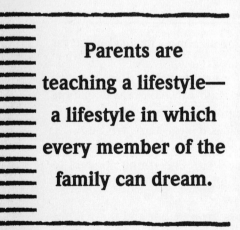

Parents are teaching a lifestyle— a lifestyle in which every member of the family can dream.

David Page was thirteen when he and his fifteen-year-old sister stayed home alone for the first time, while his parents and younger sister took a weeklong trip to Massachusetts. Once the parents were gone, he promptly bought some paints, went into the living room, and commenced work on a painting. "I painted a pond, with flamingos, all sorts of wild birds and trees. It was huge—I'm talking mural. And I got so into it that I came down around the corner of the room, painted some dangling vines, then I worked my way up the stairwell, and painted a huge apple tree with a girl sitting in it and apples," he said. "I never thought for a moment that my parents would not want me to do this.

"My older sister who watched me was not so confident. 'Look what you've done!' she said."

When the day arrived for his parents to return, the young artist had no fear. "I can remember standing in the living room, and I'm all proud of this, and they walked in . . . and they *loved* it." Pretty magnanimous of them, we thought, to go in for all that redecorating without their consent.

"As a kid, it's a wonderful feeling to have acceptance of that size. What if they had walked in and said, 'What did you *do*?' But that was not their way.

"They didn't understand why I had to do the things I did, but they allowed me to do them and praised me." David went on to become an art major in college. "That mural was on the wall for years, by the way," he said. And it will remain in his heart for many years to come.

David's parents weren't dreamers in terms of cognitive style, but they respected his dreams, and he learned to respect theirs. David explains, "My father drove a bus, and my mother was a housewife. They dreamed of getting away to the mountains to go camping. I have learned that their dreams were just as important as mine."

If You Are a Dreamer

Perhaps you are a dreamer trying to make sense of your own childhood. Perhaps, unlike David Page, you were discouraged from dreaming. We have a special word to say to you. If after reading this book, you have decided that your parents are guilty of intentionally stifling you, please reconsider that view. Your parents probably did the best they could with the information they had. When we began looking for resources on dreamers, we found almost nothing—and we knew what to look for. What tools did your parents have to help them understand your inner workings?

Now is the time to embrace your future. If you allow your childhood to control your adulthood, you have become your own worst enemy. From this day forward, the choices that you make are your choices. Are you choosing to nurture bitterness? Why not decide to move forward? This is your day. Don't let bitterness be your master.

Not all dreamer adults are angry about the past. Many have made a decision to bless their parents. Perhaps you thought that you were among them, but reading this book has uncovered some old wounds. Don't spend your emotional energy mulling over what might have been. Find a positive outlet for what you have learned. Become a crusader in your family and community for the dreamers who are children now and those who will follow.

A Parting Word to Parents

We hope that you have learned some things about how to keep from exasperating your dreamer. If your child is young, you may want to keep this book close by in the coming years so that you can review your progress toward understanding your enigmatic dreamer. But remember, there are no perfect parents. No matter how much you know, you'll mess up from time to time. Step back and take a breath. Regroup. Plan your strategy for guiding your child through the next stage of development.

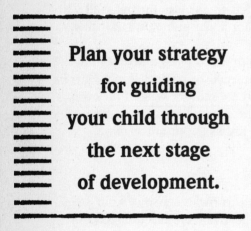

Plan your strategy for guiding your child through the next stage of development.

Dreamers are glorious children, teens, and adults, but we all must take the time to listen to their song. We close with part of a poem by Kevin Zier, a college-age dreamer:

I couldn't tell you if I fell asleep
Eyes open or closed would be the same
You've never listened close enough
To hear the music of the rain
You think I live my life asleep
But it's easier for me to smile
I cannot hear your ridicule
For I am the dreamer child.

Notes

All quotes not specifically cited are from the following:

Barlett, John. *Barlett's Familiar Quotations.* 14th ed. Boston: Little, Brown, 1968.

Peter, Lawrence. *Quotations for Our Time.* London: Methuen, 1980.

Chapter 1

1. Louisa May Alcott, *Little Women* (London: Octopus Books, 1978), p. 184.
2. Ken Voges and Ron Braund, *Understanding How Others Misunderstand You* (Chicago: Moody, 1990).
3. Gary Smalley and John Trent, *The Two Sides of Love* (Colorado Springs: Focus on the Family, 1990).
4. James Dobson, *The Strong-Willed Child* (Wheaton, Ill.: Tyndale House, 1978).
5. Ibid., p. 18.
6. Gary Smalley and John Trent, *The Blessing* (Nashville: Thomas Nelson Publishers, 1986), p. 18.

Chapter 2

1. Ken Voges and Ron Braund, *Understanding How Others Misunderstand You* (Chicago: Moody, 1990).

Chapter 3

1. Saying, paraphrase of Horace in *Satires,* and William Shakespeare, *Hamlet,* act 2.
2. John Boe, "Messiness Is Next to Goddessness: Why It's Hard to Be Creative and Neat," *Psychological Perspectives,* vol. 27, 1992.

Chapter 4

1. Rudolf Driekers, *Children: The Challenge* (New York: Hawthorn Books, 1964).
2. William S. Gilbert, *The Mikado,* act 2.

3. Elizabeth Ehrlich, *Nellie Bly: Journalist* (New York: Chelsea House, 1989).

4. D. P. Gushee, "Why They Helped the Jews," *Christianity Today,* vol. 38, pp. 32–35.

Chapter 5

1. Mary Hoffman, *Amazing Grace* (New York: Dial, 1991).

2. Anne Tyler, *Tumble Tower* (New York: Orchard, 1993).

3. Harry Chapin, "Flowers Are Red," on *Living Room Suite,* Electra Records, 1978.

4. E. B. White, *Charlotte's Web* (New York: Harper and Row, 1952).

5. Peter Spier, *Bored, Nothing to Do!* (New York: Doubleday, 1978).

6. Richard Ferber, *Solve Your Child's Sleep Problems* (New York: Simon and Schuster, 1985), p. 164.

7. Ibid.

8. Ibid., p. 169.

9. Lucy Maud Montgomery, *Anne of Green Gables* (New York: Crown, 1985), p. 31.

Chapter 6

1. American Psychiatric Association, *Diagnostic and Statistical Manual of Mental Disorders,* 4th ed. (Washington, D.C.: American Psychiatric Association, 1994).

2. Mark Twain, *The Adventures of Tom Sawyer* (New York: Grosset and Dunlap, 1946), pp. 28–29.

3. Gustav Mahler, from program notes on his Fifth Symphony, Atlanta Symphony Orchestra, February 9–11, 1995.

Chapter 7

1. Brian Lanker, *I Dream a World: Portraits of Black Women Who Changed America* (New York: Stewart, Tobori and Chang, 1989), p. 48.

Chapter 8

1. Betty Edwards, *Drawing on the Right Side of the Brain: A Course in Enhancing Creativity and Artistic Confidence* (Los Angeles: J. P. Tarcher, 1979).

2. Barbara Meister Vitale, *Unicorns Are Real: A Right-Brained Approach to Learning* (New York: Warner, 1982).
3. Elizabeth Murphy, *The Developing Child* (Palo Alto, Calif.: Consulting Psychologists Press, 1992), and Cynthia Ulrich Tobias, *The Way They Learn* (Colorado Springs: Focus on the Family, 1994)
4. Tobias, *The Way They Learn.*
5. Cheri Fuller, *Unlocking Your Child's Learning Potential* (Colorado Springs: Piñon Press, 1994).

Chapter 9

1. Milton Dank, *Albert Einstein* (New York: Franklin Watts, 1983), pp. 7, 9, 11, 12.
2. Daniel J. Boorstin, *The Creators: A History of Heroes of the Imagination* (New York: Vintage, 1992).
3. Philipp Frank, *Einstein: His Life and Times* (New York: Knopf, 1947), pp. 11–12.
4. Robert Andrews, *The Concise Columbia Dictionary of Quotations* (New York: Columbia University Press, 1987), p. 295.
5. Susan Schaeffer Macaulay, *For the Children's Sake: Foundations of Education for Home and School* (Westchester, Ill.: Crossway, 1984).
6. Henry David Thoreau, *Walden* (New York: Peter Pauper Press, 1900).

Chapter 10

1. Brian Lanker, *I Dream a World: Portraits of Black Women Who Changed America* (New York: Stewart, Tobori and Chang, 1989), p. 125.
2. Isabell Myers, *Manual: The Myers-Briggs Type Indicator* (Palo Alto, Calif.: Consulting Psychologists Press, 1962).
3. Nolan Bushnell, foreword to *A Whack on the Side of the Head: How to Unlock Your Mind for Innovation,* by Roger von Oech (New York: Warner, 1983).
4. N. H. Kleinbaum, *Dead Poets Society,* a novel based on the motion picture by Tom Schulman (New York: Bantam, 1989), pp. 40–42.

Chapter 11

1. Grant Martin, *The Hyperactive Child* (Wheaton, Ill.: Victor, 1992).

2. Thom Hartman, *Attention Deficit Disorder: A Different Perception* (Novato, Calif.: Underwood-Miller, 1993).

3. Ibid., p. 55.

4. American Psychiatric Association, *Diagnostic and Statistical Manual of Mental Disorders,* 4th ed. (Washington, D.C.: American Psychiatric Association, 1994).

5. Carl Schurtz, address, Faneuil Hall, Boston, April 18, 1859.

Chapter 13

1. Robert Conot, *A Streak of Luck: The Life & Legend of Thomas Alva Edison* (New York: Seaview, 1979).

2. Eudora Welty, *One Writer's Beginnings* (New York: Warner, 1984), pp. 24–25.

3. Ibid., pp. 22–24.

Chapter 14

1. Else H. Minarik, *Little Bear* (New York: Scholastic, 1957).

2. Christine Allison, *I'll Tell You a Story, I'll Sing You a Song: A Parent's Guide to Fairy Tales, Fables, Songs, and Rhymes of Childhood* (New York: Delacorte, 1987).

3. Hans Augusto Rey, *Curious George* (Boston: Houghton Mifflin, 1941).

4. Ludwig Bemelmans, *Madeline* (New York: Viking, 1939).

5. Katherine Holabird, *Angelina Ballerina* (New York: C. N. Potter, 1983).

6. Ruth Krauss, *Open House for Butterflies* (New York: Harper and Row, 1960).

7. Kevin Henkes, *Chrysanthemum* (New York: Greenwillow, 1991).

8. Don Dinkmeyer and Gary McKay, *Systematic Training for Effective Parenting: Leader's Manual* (Circle Pines, Minn.: American Guidance Service, 1976).

9. Michael Popkin, *Active Parenting Handbook* (Atlanta: Active Parenting, 1983).

Chapter 15

1. Robert Conot, *A Streak of Luck: The Life & Legend of Thomas Alva Edison* (New York: Seaview, 1979).

2. David Page, "The Fetcher" on a cassette entitled *Heart Etchings* (Telford, Penn.: Fame Foundation, 1989).

Chapter 16

1. American Psychiatric Association, *Diagnostic and Statistical Manual of Mental Disorders,* 4th ed. (Washington, D.C.: American Psychiatric Association, 1994).

Chapter 17

1. Frances Hodgson Burnett, *The Secret Garden* (Philadelphia: Lippincott, 1962).

Selected Bibliography

Books for Parents

Allison, Christine. *Teach Your Children Well: A Parent's Guide to the Stories, Poems, Fables, and Tales That Instill Traditional Values.* New York: Delacorte, 1993.

———. *I'll Tell You a Story, I'll Sing You a Song: A Parent's Guide to the Fairy Tales, Fables, Songs, and Rhymes of Childhood.* New York: Delacorte, 1987.

Backus, William, and Marie Chapian. *Why Do I Do What I Don't Want to Do?* Minneapolis: Bethany House, 1984.

Downs, Hugh. *Fifty to Forever.* Nashville: Thomas Nelson Publishers, 1994.

Ferber, Richard. *Solve Your Child's Sleep Problems.* New York: Simon and Schuster, 1985.

Fuller, Cheri. *Unlocking Your Child's Learning Potential.* Colorado Springs: Piñon Press, 1994.

Keirsey, David, and Marilyn Bates. *Please Understand Me.* Del Mar, Calif.: Prometheus Nemesis, 1984.

Lawrence, Gordon. *People Types & Tiger Stripes.* Gainesville: Center for Applications of Psychological Type, 1979.

Leman, Kevin. *The Birth Order Book.* New York: Dell, 1985.

Macaulay, Susan Schaeffer. *For the Children's Sake: Foundations of Education for Home and School.* Westchester, Ill.: Crossway, 1984.

Meisgeier, Charles, Elizabeth Murphy, and Constance Meisgeier. *A Teacher's Guide to Type: A New Perspective on Individual Differences in the Classroom.* Palo Alto: Consulting Psychologists Press, 1989.

Murphy, Elizabeth. *The Developing Child.* Palo Alto: Consulting Psychologists Press, 1992.

Narramore, Bruce. *Adolescence Is Not an Illness.* Old Tappan, N.J.: Revell, 1980.

————. *Why Children Misbehave.* Grand Rapids: Zondervan, 1980.

Smalley, Gary, and John Trent. *The Two Sides of Love.* Colorado Springs: Focus on the Family, 1990.

Tobias, Cynthia Ulrich. *The Way They Learn.* Colorado Springs: Focus on the Family, 1994.

Voges, Ken, and Ron Braund. *Understanding How Others Misunderstand You.* Chicago: Moody, 1990.

Wilson, Elizabeth. *Books Children Love: A Guide to the Best Children's Literature.* Westchester: Crossway, 1987.

Books for Adults About Dreamers

Boorstin, Daniel J. *The Creators: A History of Heroes of the Imagination.* New York: Vintage, 1992.

Carpenter, Humphrey. *The Inklings: J. R. R. Tolkien, C. S. Lewis, Charles Williams, and Their Friends.* New York: Ballantine, 1978.

Gaebelein, Frank E. *The Christian, the Arts, and Truth: Regaining the Vision of Greatness.* Portland, Oreg.: Multnomah, 1985.

Lanker, Brian. *I Dream a World: Portraits of Black Women Who Changed America.* New York: Stewart, Tobori and Chang, 1989.

L'Engle, Madeleine. *Walking on Water: Reflections on Faith and Art.* Wheaton, Ill.: Harold Shaw, 1980.

Lewis, C. S. *Surprised by Joy.* New York: Harcourt Brace Jovanovich, 1955.

Veith, Gene. *The Gift of Art.* Downers Grove, Ill.: Inter-Varsity, 1983.

Children's Books for Dreamers

Baum, L. Frank. *The Wizard of Oz.* New York: Grosset & Dunlap, 1956, and *The Land of Oz.* New York: Morrow, 1985.

Bjork, Christina. *Linnea in Monet's Garden.* Stockholm: R & S Books, 1985.

Bunyan, John. *Pilgrim's Progress.* New York: Lippincott, 1939.

Burnett, Frances Hodgson. *The Secret Garden.* Philadelphia: Lippincott, 1962.

Carroll, Lewis. *Alice's Adventures in Wonderland* and *Through the Looking Glass and What Alice Found There.* London: Oxford University Press, 1971.

de Regniers, Beatrice Schenk, ed. *Sing a Song of Popcorn: Every Child's Book of Poems.* New York: Scholastic, 1988.

Eliot, T. S. *Old Possum's Book of Practical Cats.* New York: Harcourt Brace Jovanovich, 1939.

Fleming, Ian. *Chitty Chitty Bang Bang: The Magical Car.* London: Gilgrose Productions, 1964.

Grahame, Kenneth. *The Wind in the Willows.* New York: Macmillan, 1908.

Haskins, Jim. *Outward Dreams: Black Inventors and Their Inventions.* New York: Walker and Co., 1991.

Henkes, Kevin. *Chrysanthemum.* New York: Greenwillow, 1991.

Hoberman, Mary Ann, ed. *My Song Is Beautiful: Poems and Pictures in Many Voices.* New York: Little, Brown, 1994.

Hoffman, Mary. *Amazing Grace.* New York: Dial, 1991.

Houston, Gloria. *My Great-Aunt Arizona.* New York: Harper Collins, 1992.

Hughes, Langston. *The Dream Keeper and Other Poems.* New York: Knopf, 1932.

Jansson, Tove. *Finn Family Moomintroll.* London: Ernest Benn, 1950.

Joosse, Barbara M. *Mama, Do You Love Me?* San Francisco: Chronicle Books, 1991.

Joslin, Sesyle. *What Do You Say, Dear? A Book of Manners for All Occasions.* New York: Addison-Wesley, 1958.

————. *What Do You Do, Dear? Proper Conduct for All Occasions.* New York: Addison-Wesley, 1961.

Joyce, William. *George Schrinks.* New York: Harper Collins, 1985.

Kipling, Rudyard. *The Just So Stories.* New York: Viking Kestrel, 1987.

Krauss, Ruth. *Open House for Butterflies.* New York: Harper and Row, 1960.

Larrick, Nancy, ed. *Piper, Pipe that Song Again: Poems for Boys and Girls.* New York: Random House, 1969.

L'Engle, Madeleine. *A Wrinkle in Time.* New York: Farrar, Straus & Giroux, 1962.

Lewis, C. S. *The Lion, the Witch, and the Wardrobe.* New York: Macmillan, 1950.

MacDonald, George. *The Light Princess and Other Fantasy Stories.* Grand Rapids: Eerdmans, 1980.

Milne, A.A. *When We Were Very Young.* London: E. P. Dutton, 1924.

Minarik, Else H. *Little Bear.* New York: Scholastic, 1957.

Montgomery, Lucy Maud. *Anne of Green Gables.* New York: Crown, 1985.

Moon, Nicola. *Lucy's Picture.* New York: Dial, 1995.

Spier, Peter. *Bored, Nothing to Do!* New York: Doubleday, 1978.

Strickland, Dorothy, ed. *Listen Children: An Anthology of Black Literature.* New York: Bantam Skylark, 1982.

Swift, Jonathan. *Gulliver's Travels.* New York: Grosset and Dunlap, 1947.

Tolkien, J. R. R. *The Hobbit or There and Back Again.* Boston: Houghton Mifflin, 1938.

Tyler, Anne. *Tumble Tower.* New York: Orchard, 1993.

White, E. B. *Charlotte's Web.* New York: Harper and Row, 1952.

About the Authors

Dr. Dana Scott Spears holds a Ph.D. in child and family development from the University of Georgia and is a licensed professional counselor. A former assistant professor of child development at Lamar University in Texas, Dr. Spears joined AlphaCare Therapy Services in Atlanta as a human development specialist in 1987. Since she and her husband, Phillip, became parents in 1993, Dana has shifted her professional focus with AlphaCare to speaking and writing so that she can work at home while raising her daughter, Anna Kate.

Dr. Ron L. Braund is the founder and president of AlphaCare Therapy Services in Atlanta, Georgia, and is a licensed marriage and family therapist. He serves as the executive director of the International Coalition on Christian Counseling, is the host of the daily radio program *Marriage & Family Today,* and is the author of the *Instep Student Bible* and coauthor of *Understanding How Others Misunderstand You.*

To contact Dr. Spears and Dr. Braund, or to request information about AlphaCare seminars, radio broadcasts, out-patient therapy, or hospital treatment programs, write:

> AlphaCare Therapy Services
> 1827 Powers Ferry Road, Building 15
> Atlanta, Georgia 30339

Or call the Life Line:

> 1-800-95ALPHA (1-800-952-5742) outside the Atlanta area
> (770) 916-9020 in the Atlanta area